The Regulation of Banks in the Member States of the EEC

SECOND EDITION

Edited by
Jane Welch, B.A. (Mod.) LL.M.
For the
British Bankers Association

1981

MARTINUS NIJHOFF PUBLISHERS
THE HAGUE/BOSTON/LONDON

GRAHAM & TROTMAN LTD.
LONDON

Distributors:

for the United States and Canada

Kluwer Boston, Inc.
190 Old Derby Street
Hingham, MA 02043
USA

for continental EEC

Kluwer Academic Publishers Group
Distribution Center
P.O. Box 322
3300 AH Dordrecht
The Netherlands

for the U.K. and Republic of Ireland

Graham & Trotman, Ltd.
Bond Street House, 14 Clifford St.
London W1X 1RD
U.K.

for all other countries

Kluwer Accademic Publishers Group
or
Graham & Trotman Ltd.

ISBN 90 247 2573 9

CONTENTS

FOREWORD

It is, of course, a truism to say that in today's world money touches on almost every aspect of human activity. Against this background it is not surprising that the subject of finance, and especially its provision and management, has assumed such importance in the affairs of man, nor that an extensive and highly-skilled industry has grown up around it.

Banks have been with us now for many centuries, and although they have undergone their fair share of evolution during that time, their essential function is the same now as it always has been - namely, to accept the surplus funds of one section of the community and to lend those same funds to other sections of the community. In this way their banks have provided an invaluable lubricant to the economic machine and have done so to the ultimate profit of all parties.

It is not difficult to make the connection between the role of the banking industry as I have just described it and the task which the member countries of the European Community have set themselves, of creating one single common market from the present ten separate national ones. If that task is to be successfully completed, as it must be, the lubrication provided by the banking industry will be needed as never before, both to assist in the construction, and to ensure the subsequent smooth running, of an economic machine of immense proportions.

It follows from this that any obstacle which prevents banks from operating freely within the geographical confines of the Community (or, to pursue the mechanical analogy, hinders the free circulation of the banking lubricant) is frustrating the aims of the Community. A proliferation of different banking regulations presents a potential obstacle of this sort and it is for this reason that the Commission, in its efforts to create a common market, has identified the coordination of banking legislation as an area of legitimate concern.

This is not to say, of course, that there is no place for the regulation of banks. Patently, any industry which occupies such an important and influential position in the economic scheme of things, and in particular is responsible for the funds of so many private individuals, must expect to undergo a degree of public scrutiny. At the same time, however, it should not, in my view, be expected to undergo such scrutiny ten times, and in ten different ways, within the one economic environment of the Community - hence our efforts to establish a common European approach to the prudential supervision of banks.

It has to be admitted that those efforts are still in their early stages: the banking edifice, for all its deep foundations and solid appearance, is also a delicately balanced structure, and it would be wrong to make precipitate changes in its construction. Moreover, it is an edifice which has a different form in different member countries, and a thorough knowledge of those forms is a prerequisite to any attempt at change. It is here that this book can play such a vital part: a reference work such as this, which highlights at once areas of similarity and contrast, both provides a useful focus of attention for future coordination work and affords that deeper appreciation of the other man's point of view which is so essential to working out a joint way forward. The CLCB Research Group (formerly part of the Inter-Bank Research Organisation) which was responsible for compiling the original study and for editing this second edition, the British Bankers' Association (which commissioned the original study) and the banking supervisory authorities of the Member States (which provided the necessary amendments for this present updating) are all to be congratulated on the contribution they have made to the production of the edition now before us which will, I hope, be the first in a regular series of updatings.

Christopher Tugendhat
EEC Commissioner for Financial Institutions

PREFACE

The first published edition of this work appeared in 1978. Since that time several major changes have taken place in the regulation of banks in a number of Member States: Denmark, Luxembourg, the Netherlands and the United Kingdom have all introduced a system of prior authorisation in accordance with the first EEC Banking Directive of 1977. Other Member States have had to amend their banking legislation where it was inconsistent with the Directive. A new chapter dealing with Greek banking regulation has been added in the light of the accession of Greece to the European Community in January, 1981. Finally in view of the importance of the two EEC banking directives in determining the content of national banking legislation, a separate chapter setting out existing EEC requirements has been included.

As in the first edition, each chapter follows the same format, so that the regulatory requirements in different Member States can be easily compared:

Section 1 : lists the institutions covered.

Section 2 : gives details of the basic legislation governing the regulation and supervision of banks.

Section 3 : describes the functions of the supervisory authority, and outlines the operation of the supervisory system. Details of the returns required by the supervisory authority, inspection procedures and any special auditing requirements are also given.

Section 4 : sets out the criteria for authorisation, covering in particular legal form, minimum capital, management qualifications and management plans.

Section 5 : deals with any restrictions on domestic or foreign branching.

Section 6 : covers any restrictions on the type of business that may be carried on by banks, on loans to directors, on equity participations and on mergers.

Section 7 : describes the regulations governing the use of banking names and descriptions.

Section 8 : deals with any special rules covering the form and content of banks' advertisements.

Section 9 : gives details of the solvency and liquidity ratios applied to banks.

Section 10 : describes any monetary and credit controls in operation.

Section 11 : sets out the controls applied to foreign exchange business.

Section 12   : deals with any provisions for a credit information exchange.

Section 13   : describes any deposit insurance system in operation.

Section 14   : lists the sanctions which can be imposed on banks and the rights of appeal.

Section 15   : covers any special rules applicable to branches of foreign banks: in particular, establishment, nationality of management and restrictions on business.

Section 16   : considers any regulations applicable only to subsidiaries of foreign banks: in particular, local ownership, nationality of directors and guarantees from the parent bank.

Section 17   : describes the nature and function of the banking associations.

Section 18   : provides a list of further reading material.

The previous edition was produced by the Inter-Bank Association. This edition, which has been extensively revised and expanded, has been prepared by the staff of the recently-formed Research Group of the Committee of London Clearing Bankers (formerly part of IBRO) with the assistance of the supervisory authorities of the EEC Member States. The chapter on Greece was compiled by Dimitri Vittas, the chapter on the EEC by Jane Welch, while Roger Brown was responsible for the new sections dealing with monetary and credit controls. The assistance of Peter Conoboy, then on secondment from the Bank of England, in covering solvency and liquidity ratios is also gratefully acknowledged.

We are particularly indebted to the following supervisory authorities of the Member States for their help and guidance in revising the earlier edition: the Belgian Commission Bancaire, the Danish Tilsynet med Banker og Sparekasser, the French Commission de Contrôle des Banques; the German Bundesaufsichtsamt für das Kreditwesen; the Greek Currency Committee (Nomismatiki Epitropi); the Central Bank of Ireland; the Banca d'Italia; the Luxembourg Commissariat au Contrôle des Banques; the Nederlandsche Bank; and the Bank of England. Our thanks are also due to the EEC Commission for their overall assistance and for their comments on the EEC chapter.

Finally, special thanks are due to Dorothy Saunders, who typed innumerable drafts of the manuscript and coped with impossible demands from authors and printers; and to Chameleon Press, who managed to produce the publication in record time.

CHAPTER 1

BELGIUM

1.1 INSTITUTIONS COVERED

All Belgian and foreign institutions which regularly receive sight deposits or time deposits for periods of up to two years with the aim of employing these deposits for banking, credit or investment operations on their own account are subject to the Belgian Banking Law, and are supervised by the Commission Bancaire (Art.1 of the 1935 Banking Law).[1]

Institutions specifically excluded from this Law (because they are established and controlled under individual laws and decrees - they are known as public law financial institutions) are the Banque Nationale de Belgique (National Bank of Belgium), the Institut de Réescompte et de Garantie (Institute of Rediscount and Guarantee - IRG), the Caisse Générale d'Epargne et de Retraite (General Savings and Pensions Fund), the Société Nationale de Crédit à l'Industrie (National Industrial Credit Company), the Crédit Communal de Belgique (Belgian Municipal Credit Institution), the Caisse Nationale de Crédit Professionel (National Fund for Credit to Trade and Industry), the Office Central de Crédit Hypothécaire (Central Office for Mortgage Credit), and the Institut National de Crédit Agricole (National Institute for Agricultural Credit (Art. 1).

Holding companies which manage the liquid assets of their subsidiaries are also specifically excluded from this law as are the Société Nationale d'Investissement (National Investment Corporation) and the Regional Investment Corporations in respect of the liquid assets which they receive from their subsidiaries. The exception does not apply if any of the exempted bodies carries out banking or credit operations outside their group. (Art. 1(2), as amended by the Law of August 4, 1978).

Neither the private savings institutions, which are also supervised by the Commission Bancaire, nor the undertakings subject to Chapter I of the Law of June 10, 1964[2] on the raising of capital from the public are subject to the Banking Law. Other private sector financial institutions (mortgage companies, hire-purchase companies, investment companies, etc.) are controlled under specific laws and decrees.

Until 1976 the private savings institutions were supervised by the Office

Central de la Petite Epargne, under the Law of June 23, 1967 on the control of private savings associations. In the Law of June 30, 1975 on the regulation of banks, private savings institutions and of certain other financial intermediaries, provision was made for the Office Central de la Petite Epargne to be wound up, and for control of the private savings institutions to be transferred to the Commission Bancaire. This was done by the Decree of January 23, 1976 effective on April 30, 1976.

The scope of this chapter is limited to those institutions which are at the present time subject to the Banking Law.

1.2 BASIC LAWS

The basic laws, as amended, are as follows:

(i) The main law governing the activities of banks is Decree No. 185 of July 9, 1935, on the control of banks and regulation of the issuing of securities (the Banking Law), as amended by Decree No. 262 of March 26, 1936, Decree of October 22, 1937, Decree No. 67 of November 30, 1939, Laws of October 6, 1944, December 23, 1946, June 16, 1947, March 11, 1948, March 14, 1962, April 2, 1962, and May 3, 1967, Decree No. 43 of October 9, 1967, and the Laws of June 30, 1975, August 4, 1978, and August 8, 1980;

(ii) Decree of November 24, 1937, on information to be provided by banks to the Banque Nationale de Belgique and to the Commission Bancaire;

(iii) Law of June 10, 1964, on the control of deposit-taking institutions which are not banks, and of take-over bids, etc.;

(iv) Commission Bancaire Regulation on own funds, June 13, 1972;

(v) Chapter I of the Law of December 28, 1973, on the 1973/74 Budget proposals;

(vi) Law of June 30, 1975 (la Loi Mammouth) on the regulation of banks, private savings institutions and certain other financial intermediaries, amending Decree No. 185 of July 9, 1935, as well as certain other Laws and Decrees;

(vii) Law of August 8, 1980, on the 1979/80 Budget proposals, amending Decree No. 185 and bringing banking into public sector credit.

1.3 SUPERVISORY SYSTEM

1.3.1 Supervisory Authority

The Commission Bancaire (Banking Commission) was established under the 1935 Banking Law (Arts. 35-41) and is the main body controlling the day-to-day activities of the Belgian banking system; all banks operating in Belgium come under its control and supervision.

The Commission is a public institution set up as an autonomous body (organisme autonome). It consists of a full-time chairman and six members who meet regularly. The chairman and members are appointed and may be dismissed by Royal Decree, countersigned by the Finance Minister, the Minister for Economic Affairs and the Minister for Justice. Two of the six members are appointed from a list drawn up jointly by the Belgian Bankers' Association (Association Belge des Banques) and the Association of Private Savings Banks (Association des Caisses d' Epargne Privées) in accordance with the procedure laid down by the Royal Decree of March 29, 1976. Two other members are appointed from a list drawn up by the Banque Nationale de Belgique and the IRG. One of these members is usually a member of the Management Committee of the Banque Nationale de Belgique. The chairman and the two other members are chosen by the King (Art. 37(1)-(3)).

The chairman and members of the Commission Bancaire may not hold any office in an undertaking subject to the permanent control of the Commission (Art. 37(4)). The members nominated by the banks and savings banks do not therefore represent these institutions.

The members of the Commission, its staff and approved auditors are bound by professional secrecy (Art. 40). The Commission is required to publish an annual report on its activities (Art. 41).

The Commission Bancaire covers its operating costs from its own resources. These consist of a contribution from the Banque Nationale de Belgique and contributions or dues levied on the companies under its supervision (Art. 36 and Royal Decree of May 17, 1979).

The duties of the Commission Bancaire are:

(i) the supervision of the banking system, as defined in 1.1 above (Art. 35). This includes the elimination of tax evasion devices set up by banks, private savings institutions or deposit-taking non-banks with the aim or effect of facilitating fiscal fraud by third parties. This is an exception to the general rule that the Commission has no role in taxation questions (Art. 39, as amended by the Law of August 8, 1980), (see 1.14.3 below);

(ii) the control of investment trusts and unit trusts (Law of March 27, 1957 and Decrees of April 18 and 22, 1958);

(iii) the control of companies subject to the Law of June 10, 1964 on the raising of capital from the public;

(iv) the control of public issues of shares and bonds and of offers for sale of shares and other securities, including the control of take-over bids (Art. 26 as applied by the Law of June 10, 1964);

(v) the control of holding companies (Decree No. 64 of November 10, 1967);

(vi) the control of investment contracts (Art. 1 of the Law of July 10, 1969);

(vii) the control of private savings institutions (see 1.1 above);

(viii) the control of the savings bank of the Caisse Générale d'Epargne et de Retraite after its conversion into a public bank (Law of August 8, 1980).

1.3.2 Outline of System

Institutions subject to banking law are required to register with the Commission Bancaire before they may undertake any operations. The Commission is required to publish annually in the *Moniteur Belge* a list of the banks so registered (Art. 2).

The registration is only effected when the Commission is satisfied that the applicant has met all the necessary criteria for authorisation (see 1.4 below). These criteria are sufficiently subjective to leave the Commission Bancaire with a limited degree of discretion in accepting or rejecting an application for registration, despite the provision for a right of appeal against rejection to the Minister for Finance.

Since the Commission has power to revoke a bank's registration under Article 25 (see 1.14.1 below), it will obviously take account of the grounds for revocation set out in that Article, when assessing applications (see 1.4.2 and 1.4.3 below).

The Commission Bancaire has power to impose sanctions on any bank ranging from the imposition of conditions to the appointment of a special Commissioner and the revocation of authorisation (see 1.14 below).

These sanctions provide the backing for the Commission's approach in interpreting and applying the banking laws. Thus, any bank considering the introduction of a new type of banking service will seek the approval of the Commission at an early stage, particularly if it involves the establishment of a subsidiary company (see 1.16 below).

Under Article 18 of the Law of August 4, 1978, the King may appoint, on the recommendation of the Minister for Finance, a Government representative to the four largest banks (in terms of total assets in Belgian francs) incorporated under Belgian law.

The representative attends all meetings of the board of directors and receives all the documents submitted to the board. His task is to remind the board of any public interest considerations arising out of the Government's economic and financial policy and he submits a report on this subject to the Minister for Finance. The attendance fees for government representatives are borne by the State.

The strong international character of the Belgian banking industry is recognised by amendments to the 1935 Banking Law effected by the Law of June 30, 1975. This entitles the Commission Bancaire to pass on to the relevant authorities in another country information which it has received from any branches or subsidiaries in Belgium of banks or financial intermediaries based in that other country. This information can relate to banking business, or to operations in the area of investment trusts or securities - cf. 1.3.1 above; the initiative for the exchange of information can come from the Commission Bancaire or the foreign authority (Art. 40).

Similar provisions have been introduced to enable the Banque Nationale de Belgique and the Commission Bancaire to pass on to central risks offices in other countries information provided by credit institutions in Belgium to the Central Risks Service of the Banque Nationale de Belgique (Art. 12) (see 1.12 below).

In the provisions of the Banking Law dealing with offers for sale of securities etc., it is expressly forbidden to mention or refer to the Commission Bancaire in any way whatever in the publicity or the documents relating to any issue or offer for sale (Art. 30). The intention is presumably to exclude any suggestion that, by authorising securities to be sold to the public, the Commission Bancaire assumes any legal or moral responsibility for the strength of the issuing company, or for any statements or forecasts made in the offer. No similar provision is found in the provisions of the Banking Law dealing with the registration of banks. The point was, however, made in the Commission Bancaire Annual Report for 1936 that inscription on the register of banks is of itself no guarantee of security for depositors.

1.3.3 Returns to Supervisory Authority

The accounting requirements for banks are laid down by the Law of July 17, 1975 on companies' annual accounts, several provisions of which apply to financial institutions. In addition, the banks must comply with the legal requirements governing the drawing up and publication of banks' annual accounts (Art. 12 of the royal decree No. 185) and with the rules implementing Article 73 of the Law of June 30, 1975.

Article 73 of the Law of June 30, 1975 gave the King power to lay down rules on how credit institutions should keep their accounts, value their assets and liabilities, and draw up their balance sheets and profit and loss accounts. The royal decree could require the drawing up and publication of consolidated accounts and lay down the necessary rules. Up to now, no decree has been made under Article 73.

Under Article 12 of the royal decree, every bank has to submit to the Banque Nationale de Belgique and to the Commission Bancaire an annual balance sheet and profit and loss account, and a monthly balance sheet.

Pending the amendments to be introduced under Article 73 of the Law of June 30, 1975, the annual balance sheet and profit and loss account, together with the monthly balance sheets, must be in the form prescribed by the royal decree of November 24, 1937, which implemented Article 12 of the Banking Law.

The returns to be made to the Banque Nationale de Belgique and the Commission Bancaire, and those filed at the Tribunal de Commerce by branches of foreign banks must show the results of all their places of business in Belgium (Art. 12). The full balance sheet and profit and loss account must be filed once a year.

All the banks must file a copy of their balance sheet and profit and loss account at the registry of the Tribunal de Commerce (Commercial Court) of the district in which they are established. The accounts are then published by the Centrale des Bilans.

Banks are also required to provide the Commission Bancaire with any other statistical information requested (Art. 12).

Each bank has to notify the Commission Bancaire of all approved applications for credit in excess of one million francs. At the request of the Commission Bancaire, banks have to report the drawing on these credits. Reports of credits granted are made each week by the largest banks, twice per month by the other banks and once per month by some public credit institutions and the private savings banks. Reports of credits drawn are made at the end of each quarter (Art. 12). This applies equally to branches in Belgium of foreign banks.

As part of their monthly reports to the Commission Bancaire, banks have to report all credits granted which individually exceed 20% of their own funds (see below 1.9.1). The beneficiary of each credit has to be identified. The total of credits drawn is only shown if it exceeds the total of credits granted, ie., if a customer has exceeded his limit. Credits to separate but connected borrowers (cf. 1.9.1) are added up for the purpose of this return.

The Law of June 30, 1975 extended the duty to declare credits and drawings to the private savings banks and other private financial institutions which raise funds from the public. The same law provides (Art. 71) that a similar duty may, by royal decree, be imposed on agents, brokers and others involved in banking operations, as well as on other institutions. So far, no such decree has been issued. Some public credit institutions also declare such credits in excess of one million Belgian francs to the Central Risks Service on a voluntary basis.

1.3.4 Auditing requirements

The system of control of auditors was altered initially by the Law of June 30, 1975 and again by the Law of August 8, 1980. Henceforth, the

Commission Bancaire will appoint one or more approved auditors for each bank. The auditors are appointed for a three-year period, which can be renewed; they can also be removed from office at any time by the Commission Bancaire. Their salaries are decided and paid by the Commission Bancaire (Art. 19 bis (1)).

The responsibilities of the auditors are clearly set out in the law. They must in particular verify: 1) the annual accounts and returns sent to the Commission Bancaire by means of on-the-spot checks; 2) the bank's compliance with regulatory requirements; 3) the adequacy and efficient operation of the administrative and auditing organisation and internal control system. Apart from these specific requirements they are obliged to monitor the solvency, liquidity and profitability of the bank (Art. 19 bis (2)).

The Law of August 8, 1980 separated the functions of approved auditor and "commissaire" which were previously carried out by the same auditor. However, if the Commission Bancaire considers it necessary, it can authorise exceptions to the rules and allow the auditor to carry out the duties of the "commissaire." In this case, the commissaire's salary must be approved by the Commission Bancaire (Art. 19 bis (3)).

The banks established under Belgian Law must also appoint one or more "commissaires" under Belgian company law. In applying this provision to banks, two changes have been made: the first is that the commissaires must be members of the Institut des Reviseurs d'Entreprises. Secondly the obligation to appoint commissaires also extends to banks set up in the form of partnerships although this is not the case for non-banking partnerships (Art. 20).

Under the Law of August 8, 1980, the Commission Bancaire is obliged to inform the Minister of Finance if it believes that a bank has been involved in setting up any arrangements which are either designed to infringe the tax laws or which have that effect in practice, and which involve collusion between the institution and its customer in a tax fraud. It was made clear in the course of the preliminary consultations before the Law was passed that the duty to inform the Minister would not apply when the information had been obtained by the Commission Bancaire from foreign supervisory authorities so that international cooperation between national supervisory authorities would not be prejudiced.

1.3.5 Inspection

Every bank (including a branch of a foreign bank) is subject to inspection by the Commission Bancaire. The latter can obtain all the information it requires about the organisation, functioning, statements and transactions of every bank. It can inspect a bank and all its documents, both to verify the bank's compliance with the banking laws and regulations and the accuracy of the reports and returns sent to it by the bank. An inspection may also be made if the Commission believes that there are grave irregularities in the running of the bank, or that imprudent or dangerous business is being undertaken which is liable to endanger the bank's liquidity, solvency or profitability, or that the auditors are failing in their duties (Art. 19).

The Commission Bancaire is entitled to ask the Banque Nationale de Belgique to undertake any inspections on its behalf. The Commission can only enquire into a bank's relationship with an individual client to the extent necessary for the supervision of the bank (Art. 19).

The powers set out above were added to the Banking Law by the Law of June 30, 1975. The inspection department of the Commission Bancaire operates in parallel with the on-the-spot checks carried out by the approved auditors. Its inspections are, however, specific and irregular, whereas the on-the-spot checks carried out by the approved auditors are comprehensive and regular. The approved auditors therefore carry the main burden of the on-the-spot inspections.

1.4 CRITERIA FOR AUTHORISATION

1.4.1 Legal Form

A bank must take the form of a *société commerciale* (a commercial company with legal personality) (Art. 5). Under the Belgian Commercial Companies Code a *société commerciale* encompasses the following legal forms: public and private limited companies, partnerships and co-operative companies. The effect is to prohibit a bank from taking the form of a one-man firm. This prohibition was introduced by the Law of June 30, 1975; until then the only prohibited form was that of a co-operative company, which is now permitted again.

1.4.2 Minimum Capital

A minimum paid-up capital requirement of at least 50 million francs is imposed on banks which take the form of a *société anonyme* (a public limited company), a *société en commandite par actions* (a limited partnership with shares whose directors are personally liable for the company's debts) or a *société de personnes à responsabilité limitée* (a private limited liability company). The same requirement applies to the statutory minimum 'social fund' of a bank that is organised in the form of a *société co-operative* (a co-operative company).

A bank set up as a *société en nom collectif* (a general partnership) or a *société en commandite simple* (a limited partnership) must have fully paid-up own capital of at least 50 million francs. The Commission Bancaire is empowered to determine what constitutes own capital for this purpose (Art. 9). These banks are not subject to the prohibitions on equity participations (see 1.6.3 below) or on the exercise of management functions in *sociétés commerciales* (see 1.4.3 below), nor are they subject to the ban on loans to directors and managers (see 1.6.2 below). They are also exempt from the provision requiring the investment of the legal reserve in public bonds (see 1.4.5 below).

In practice, all banks in Belgium (except for branches of foreign banks) are constituted as either a *société anonyme* or a *société en commandite simple.* Thus the major effect of the Law of June 30, 1975 (1.2) above) will be to permit co-operative savings banks in due course. Up to now, however, no bank in this form has been registered.

The minimum capital requirements set out above were raised by the Law of June 30, 1975, from 10 million and two million francs respectively. For the banks which were already registered when the Law came into force, the Commission Bancaire could permit a delay (of up to five years) in meeting the new minimum requirement (which applies whatever the balance-sheet size of the bank, and therefore irrespective of the own funds required under the solvency ratio - see 1.9.1 below).

When the Law of June 30, 1975 came into force, there were 22 listed banks with a capital of less than 50 million francs. The Commission invited these banks to submit plans for increasing their capital to the required minimum.

The Commission Bancaire had in practice for some time applied the 50 million Belgian francs minimum capital requirement to all banks seeking registration, without waiting for the law to come into force.

1.4.3 Management Qualifications

Any new bank seeking registration has to satisfy the Commission Bancaire that its management is reputable and capable of running its affairs smoothly. In accordance with the 1977 EEC Banking Directive this requirement will have to be laid down by legislation. At present the Law provides that persons who have been declared bankrupt, or who have been sentenced to three months or more in prison for one of a number of specified offences (forgery, theft, etc.) may not take any part in the management of a bank (Art. 7).

This applies equally to foreign nationals and also to the controlling personnel of branches in Belgium of foreign banks.

Administrators and managers of a bank set up as a public or private company, a limited partnership with shares, or a co-operative company, and any other persons engaged in the management of such a bank may not take part in the management of a commercial enterprise other than a bank, an insurance company or a mortgage institution, although certain exceptions to this rule are listed. The provision is the result of the prohibition on universal banks *(banques mixtes)* and is therefore linked with the rules on participations in companies other than credit institutions (see 1.6.3 below). It reflects the concern to prevent interdependence between the banking and commercial or industrial sectors through personal links or shareholdings.

Although foreign banks are not subject to the prohibition on universal banks, the staff of their Belgian establishments who are involved in day-to-day management are subject to the rules on other managerial positions laid down in Article 16 (Art. 6(3)).

One of the Commission Bancaire's concerns is to ensure the independence of the management of banks forming part of an industrial or commercial group. To this end the Commission Bancaire signed a protocol on February 1, 1974 with each of the three largest banks in Belgium on the 'Autonomy of the Banking Function'. Since mid-1975 the Banking Commission has entered into negotiations with most of the other banks with a view to concluding similar protocols, adapted, where necessary, to the characteristic features of the banks concerned. A protocol has been concluded with some 30 banks, all set up in the form of a public company. The purpose of the protocol is to ensure that all decisions as to the management or conduct of the banks are taken without being subject to pressure from large shareholders in the banks. Such decisions must be taken on prudent banking grounds only. To achieve this end, the protocol requires action on two fronts.

The overall management of any bank is (under Belgian company law) entrusted to the Board of Directors (Conseil d'Administration), which itself may appoint and guide a Management Committee (Comité de Direction). Under the 1974 Protocol, the Management Committee is the body solely responsible for the management of a bank's affairs. Accordingly the Board transfers to it all decision-making powers and authority to represent the bank (the Commission Bancaire is consulted on the precise powers delegated to the Management Committee). The role of the board of directors is therefore restricted to exercising the powers reserved for it by the laws applicable to *sociétés commerciales* or by the bank's articles of association, to determining the bank's general policy and to supervising management.

The regulations governing the appointment, dismissal and remuneration of the members of the Management Committee are designed to ensure its independence and accountability. Any change in the composition of the Management Committee must be notified to the Commission Bancaire, who must also be consulted before the chairman of the Committee is appointed.

1.4.4 Management Plans

There is no legal requirement for an applicant for registration to disclose its plans. In practice, however, the Commission asks for informal forecasts of the bank's profit and loss account and balance sheet for at least six months ahead. This information is needed so that the Commission can be sure that the bank's structure and management are adequate (see also 1.3.4 and 1.4.3 above).

1.4.5 Other Requirements

Banks established as a public or private company, a limited partnership or a cooperative company are required to maintain a legal reserve, which must be invested in bonds issued or guaranteed by the State or local authorities. These bonds must be shown separately in the balance sheet; they may be shown at book cost, provided that such cost is lower than maturity value.

This legal reserve (which is required of all joint stock companies under Belgian company law) is intended to form a guarantee for depositors and shareholders. It is created by transferring 5% of the company's annual net profits, until the legal reserve attains a maximum of 10% of the capital.

If a bank wishes to buy or sell public sector securities or foreign currencies for its customers, it has to pay into the Caisse des Dépôts et Consignations a surety bond *(cautionnement)*, amounting to at least 300,000 Belgian francs. This sum, which may be in cash or in approved securities, is only reimbursed six months after the bank has ceased to undertake these operations. There are separate funds for security and foreign currency business (Arts. 75, 78 of Chapter V, Book I of the Code of Commerce, and Ministerial Decree of December 18, 1975).

Each bank has to provide the Commission Bancaire with the complete text of its articles of association and of any amendments.

1.5 BRANCHES

1.5.1 Restrictions on Branching in Belgium

There are no legal restrictions on the opening of branches in Belgium by Belgian banks. For the rules governing foreign bank branches, see 1.15 below.

1.5.2 Branching and Operations in Other Countries

Although there are no legal restrictions on the opening of branches
abroad, there are practical constraints on both branches and subsidiaries:

(i) The balance sheets of a Belgian bank's branches in any other country
are included in the bank's global figures for solvency ratio purposes (see
1.9.1 below). This is irrespective of any local solvency controls applied to
those branches.

(ii) Under the solvency ratio requirement (see below) all the
participations held by a bank in companies in the same group - i.e., including
its subsidiaries abroad - must (with certain other assets) be covered
completely by own funds; and the volume of own funds used to cover these
assets is not available to meet the 'risk assets' solvency ratio.

The setting up of branches or subsidiaries outside Belgium is, of course,
subject to any exchange control or similar restrictions on the outflow of
capital.

1.6 RESTRICTIONS ON BUSINESS

1.6.1 Restrictions on Types of Business

The only statutory restrictions on the types of business which can be
undertaken by the banks in Belgium are those defining the types of
participation they may hold (see 1.6.3 below).

1.6.2 Loans to Directors

Banks set up in the form of a *société anonyme,* a *société en commandite
par actions,* a *société de personnes à responsabilité limitée* or a *société co-
operative* are not in general allowed to grant loans to any of their directors or
managers. The Commission Bancaire may, in special cases, permit a bank
to make such a loan, but the loan must be repaid and the liability redeemed
within six months (Art. 17). This applies equally to the branches of foreign
banks in Belgium (Art. 6).

In its Annual Report for 1976/77 the Commission Bancaire stated that,
where there existed a general neutral scheme for making loans to all staff
members, it did not object to such loans being made to managers. It also
ruled that the facilities available through a cheque guarantee card, being
impersonal and limited, were not covered by Article 17.

Banks set up as a general partnership or as a limited partnership under
Article 9 (see 1.4.2 above) are not subject to any restriction on loans made
to their partners, managers, etc.

1.6.3 Equity Participations

There are no restrictions on the participations which may be held by any bank established under Article 9 (i.e., in the form of a general partnership or a limited partnership) or by the Belgian branches of foreign banks, except for the reserve powers laid down in the Law of June 30, 1975 (see below).

However, a bank set up as a public or private company, a limited partnership with shares or a co-operative company (Art. 8) is normally prohibited from holding shares and participations in *sociétés commerciales* except in accordance with Article 14:

(i) The bank may, for a period not exceeding one year, hold Belgian and foreign shares if it is responsible as an issuing house or underwriter for offering them to the public. (This period may be extended to a maximum of three years). These shares may not in any circumstances have been acquired on a stock exchange;

(ii) It may become the temporary owner of securities to cover doubtful or frozen credits, but is obliged to dispose of them within two years. (This period may be extended to a maximum of four years).

In special cases, the Commission Bancaire may, by way of derogation, extend the periods referred to in (i) and (ii).

Further exceptions have been introduced by the Law of June 30, 1975 allowing a bank formed under Article 8 to hold shares in non-credit institutions provided that their book value and their voting power do not exceed limits fixed by royal decree made on the advice of the Commission Bancaire. No decree has been issued as yet setting out the new limits.

The 1975 Law also gave the Commission Bancaire power to authorise in special cases derogations from the general rule that banks shall not hold shares and participations. The Commission makes use of this power in particular to allow participations in firms or companies whose activities are linked with banking business (leasing or factoring companies, data processing centres etc).

The prohibition is supplemented by the rules preventing individuals holding administrative or managerial posts in both banks and *sociétés commerciales* (see 1.4.3 above).

The Law of June 30, 1975 has also given the Commission Bancaire powers to discover and to limit the risks run by banks in relation to their portfolios. The Commission may, with the approval of the Ministers for Finance and Economic Affairs, issue regulations setting out the amount of information which banks must provide on the composition of, and movements in, their portfolios of shares and participations; and on the information banks must obtain on the situation and operations of individual companies before they can acquire direct or indirect participations in those companies. Finally, the Commission can by regulation impose a limit on the liability and the risks run by a bank by virtue of any affiliation links, whether to its subsidiaries and sub-subsidiaries or to any other company. No such regulations have yet been issued. They will apply to banks in any legal form (cf. 1.4.1 above).

The decree and regulations under the Law of June 30, 1975 may only be issued after consultation with the banking industry, acting through its professional organisation (see below 1.17).

Different rules apply to participations in credit institutions: a bank may, without any direct limit, hold shares or participations in banks, in savings banks and in credit institutions established by or in accordance with a special law (i.e., those excluded from the terms of the banking law (see 1.1 above) (Art. 14).

Under the rules in force before the Law of June 30, 1975, the Commission Bancaire interpreted the term "bank" broadly to allow shares or participations to be held in firms or companies whose activities were limited to banking business. Since the 1975 Law gave the Commission Bancaire the power to authorise derogations from the prohibition on banks holding shares and participations, the Commission can no longer apply the same broad interpretation to the term "bank". However, the Commission can achieve the same end by use of its power of derogation (see above).

Regulations on disclosure of shares and participations under the Law of June 30, 1975 (see above) will apply to participations in banks, as well as in non-credit institutions.

1.6.4 Mergers

All bank mergers require, on pain of cancellation, the prior approval of the Commission Bancaire (Art. 4). This applies equally to foreign banks (including their branches in Belgium). "Merger" is interpreted to include the acquisition or disposal of large shareholdings in a bank, together with agreements affecting the transfer of part of a bank's business - whether a type of banking operation or a regional division.

Under the 1974 Protocol on the Autonomy of the Banking Function, the major shareholders in the three largest banks agreed to report any significant change in the size of their shareholding to the Commission Bancaire and to the bank itself (see further 1.4.3 above).

1.7 BANKING NAMES AND DESCRIPTIONS

Only duly registered banks are authorised to use the term "bank" or "banker" as part of the title of their firm, in reference to the purpose of the firm, or in their publicity (Art. 3). This applies equally to branches in Belgium of foreign banks.

1.8 ADVERTISING

Banks are invited to submit to the Banking Commission two examples of every item of printed matter (circulars, prospectuses, etc.) they publish which gives details of their operating conditions and in particular the rates of interest paid on all forms of deposits.

Banks may not use their resources so as to exert, directly or indirectly, influence on public opinion to further their interests. This prohibition does not apply to overt commercial publicity. Banks must record separately all expenses for publicity and must submit a statement of those expenses to the Banque Nationale de Belgique (Art. 15). This applies equally to branches in Belgium of foreign banks.

All financial institutions have agreed not to carry out advertising campaigns involving lotteries and tombolas.

1.9 SOLVENCY AND LIQUIDITY

The Commission Bancaire has powers (set out in Article 11) to regulate banks with a view to controlling their solvency and liquidity (these are quite distinct from the powers to regulate banks for the purposes of monetary policy - see 1.10 below). Solvency and liquidity regulations may only be issued by the Commission Bancaire after consulting the Banque Nationale de Belgique and obtaining the approval of the Ministers for Finance and Economic Affairs. These regulations may fix, for all banks or for categories of banks, the proportions to be observed between:

(i) certain of their assets and claims and all or part of their liabilities and guarantees;

(ii) their own funds and all or part of either their liabilities and guarantees or their assets and claims;

(iii) their own funds and their assets or claims on one borrower (see 1.9.3 below);

(iv) their assets and their liabilities in foreign currencies (see 1.11.2 below).

The regulations may also establish absolute limits on any of the elements mentioned in (i-iv) above. The regulations may be based on absolute figures, on changes in a reference period, or on both criteria. They may also be based on the consolidated position of the bank and its subsidiaries and sub-subsidiaries.

The regulations may only be made after consulting the banking industry, through its professional association. The Commission Bancaire may authorise derogations from the regulations.

The regulations will apply to branches in Belgium of foreign banks.

The detailed powers set out above were contained in the Law of June 30, 1975. They replaced earlier powers which enabled the Commission Bancaire to impose ratios of liquid assets to sight and short term liabilities, and of capital and reserves to either total deposits or sight and short term liabilities. Under these powers a capital/deposit ratio was applied in different forms and at different levels from 1946 to 1972.

1.9.1 Solvency Ratios

In June 1972, (Commission Bancaire Regulation of June 13, 1972, confirmed by Ministerial Decree of August 7, 1972), anticipating the introduction of the powers set out above, the capital/deposit ratio was replaced by a capital/risk assets ratio. This is calculated according to a complex formula designed, among other aims, to require a relatively higher capital cover from a small bank than from a large bank, and to require a greater capital cover for relatively risky assets and high concentrations of risks on a small number of borrowers. At the same time, the Commission Bancaire introduced a rule stipulating that a bank's holdings of fixed assets (property, investments etc) should not exceed its capital and reserves (own funds). The details of the two solvency ratio requirements applied to banks at present - the risk assets ratio and the fixed assets ratio - are set out in the Appendix.

1.9.2 Liquidity Ratios

The powers of the Commission Bancaire to issue regulations controlling banks for solvency and liquidity purposes (as distinct from monetary policy purposes) are described in 1.9 above. No liquidity ratio is at present in force for prudential purposes. For these purposes the Commission Bancaire monitors banks by means of their normal monthly returns and by a general survey every six months to ensure that all banks are sufficiently liquid. It also requires bank auditors (see 1.3.4 above) to pay particular attention to the liquidity policy and practice of every bank. It has not, however, laid down a precise definition of the phrase 'sufficiently liquid': this is judged in the light of each bank's individual circumstances and mix of customers.

1.9.3 Loan Limits

The Commission Bancaire may make regulations (after consulting the

Banque Nationale de Belgique and obtaining the approval of the Ministers for Finance and Economic Affairs) to fix, for all banks or for one or more categories of banks, the proportions to be observed between, among other balance sheet items, their own funds and the total of their assets and claims and contingent claims on one specified enterprise or on a group of affiliated enterprises which, in practice, form one single risk. This power was introduced by the Law of June 30, 1975.

The regulations may only establish absolute limits on any of the elements mentioned above. The regulations may be based on absolute figures or on changes in a reference period, or on both criteria. They may also be based on the consolidated position of the bank and its subsidiaries.

The regulations may only be made after consulting the banking industry, through its professional association. The Commission Bancaire may authorise derogations from the regulations.

In its Annual Report for 1975/76, the Commission Bancaire states that, at this stage, it prefers not to limit credit risks by regulation, but that it will gradually step up its individual controls where it finds that the spread of credit risks is inadequate. Under the rules in force prior to the Law of June 30, 1975, the Commission Bancaire had already recommended various banks to reduce loans amounting to half of their own funds and granted to a single borrower or group of borrowers constituting a single economic risk. Subsequently, it extended and defined this recommendation. The restriction to half of the bank's own funds applies whatever the activity or rating of the borrower and irrespective of the guarantees by which the loan is backed; however, an exception is made for the portion of the risk backed by the guarantee of another bank, a savings bank or a public credit institution or by the unconditional guarantee of the Office National du Ducroire (National Del Credere Office).

In the calculation of the capital/assets ratio, the extent of capital cover required is specifically increased to take account of risks assets relating to a particular customer (or to several customers who can be considered connected so far as risk is concerned, irrespective of their legal status) when the total of such assets exceeds 20% of the bank's own funds (see Appendix, paragraph (i) and (ii)).

1.10 MONETARY AND CREDIT CONTROLS

The Banque Nationale de Belgique (the Central Bank) is the principal organ for the execution of monetary policy. Whilst it must support the overall economic policies of the Government, the Banque Nationale plays a leading role in the formulation of monetary control techniques. Important responsibilities in the monetary field are also discharged by the Fonds des

Rentes (the Bond Fund) and the IRG (the Rediscount and Guarantee Institute). The Fonds des Rentes undertakes open market operations while the IRG, together with the Banque Nationale, exercises control of the money markets.

Following the Law of December 28, 1973, the Banque Nationale de Belgique is empowered to make recommendations, for monetary reasons, to banks and other financial intermediaries. These recommendations may concern:

(i) The establishment of prescribed relations between various elements of their balance sheets and the observation of prescribed limits on certain of these elements.

(ii) The placing of deposits at the Banque Nationale in francs or foreign currency as the central bank requests.

(iii) The observation of prescribed maxima on the interest rates they may offer on various liabilities.

At the demand of the Banque Nationale, legal force may be given to these recommendations by means of regulations made by the appropriate authorities (in the case of the commercial and savings banks, this is the Commission Bancaire). Though this power has been invoked on several occasions, even when the Banque Nationale's recommendations do not have the legal force of a regulation they are, in practice, equally binding.

1.10.1 Direct Credit Controls

Though not currently in force, credit ceilings have been imposed on a number of occasions (1964-65, 1966-67, 1969-71, 1974-75 and 1978). In 1978 ceilings applied only to short-term lending to companies established in Belgium and Luxembourg. Controls may be imposed in terms either of credit extended or credit commitments.

1.10.2 Selective Credit Controls

The credit ceilings referred to above have generally been applied with considerable selectivity, with credit categories deemed to be of particular economic importance either exempt from controls or afforded relatively favourable treatment. The obligation to invest in public sector securities mentioned below may also be considered as a selective instrument. Official loan guarantees and interest rate subsidies have been provided by the authorities for certain credit categories, with the primary purpose of stimulating investment.

1.10.3 Regulation of Interest Rates

Interest rates on deposits of less than 5 million francs are collectively agreed by the banks under the control of the Banque Nationale de Belgique.

1.10.4 Central Bank Accommodation

The primary channel of accommodation is the rediscounting of commercial paper. Each bank's ability to rediscount paper is subject to a ceiling. The rediscount ceilings are limits which are formally imposed on each bank with regard to its recourse to the Banque Nationale in the form of rediscounting of trade bills. This recourse can occur directly by presenting the bills at the Banque Nationale de Belgique or indirectly through the IRG. The rediscount ceilings are calculated on the basis of:

(i) the deposits of clients in Belgian francs for less than one year;

(ii) the undrawn short-term credit commitments to companies and private individuals;

(iii) short-term credits to companies and private individuals.

Particular percentages are applied to these three categories. The individual ceilings are, in principle, recalculated four times a year, on the basis of the average of the relevant aggregates over a 12 month period. The Banque Nationale de Belgique may always modify the percentages and even revoke an institution's rediscount facility for reasons of monetary policy or banking security.

Banks can also obtain advances on current account from the Banque Nationale de Belgique on the security of government bonds. Since 1974 ceilings on this form of refinancing have been formally imposed.

1.10.5 Reserve Requirements

There are currently no monetary reserve requirements in Belgium though this instrument has been employed on both deposits and credits in past periods. In addition, since 1972 the banks have been periodically obliged to observe minimum ratios between their holdings of public sector debt and their deposit liabilities. This requirement is not currently in operation.

1.11 FOREIGN EXCHANGE

1.11.1 Authority to Deal in Foreign Exchange

Only banks authorised by the Institut Belgo-Luxembourgeois du Change

(IBLC) are authorised to operate in the official market, where most current transactions are settled.

1.11.2 Limits on Positions

The powers of the Commission Bancaire to issue regulations for solvency and liquidity purposes (as distinct from monetary policy purposes) are described in 1.9 above. These powers (which were added to Article 11 of the Banking Law by the Law of June 30, 1975) enable the Commission, after consulting the Banque Nationale de Belgique, and obtaining the approval of the Ministers for Finance and Economic Affairs, to issue regulations fixing, for all banks or for categories of banks, the proportions to be observed between their spot and forward foreign currency assets and claims, and their spot and forward foreign current liabilities; if desired, the required proportions may be expressed in terms of an individual foreign currency, or between certain of these assets and liabilities.

The regulations may also establish absolute limits on any of the figures or on changes in a reference period, or on both criteria. They may also be based on the consolidated position of the bank and its subsidiaries.

The regulations may only be made after consulting the banking industry, through its professional association. The Commission Bancaire may authorise derogation from the regulations.

The regulations will apply equally to the branches in Belgium of foreign banks.

The Commission Bancaire stated in its Annual Report for 1975/76 that it had, however, decided not to fix statutory limits on exchange transactions for the time being.

The only ratio control on foreign exchange positions at present in force is included in the Commission Bancaire's solvency ratio of June 13, 1972. Each bank has to maintain an amount in own funds equal to 0.2% of the total of claims in Belgian and foreign currency arising from forward foreign exchange transactions on both the official and the free markets[3] (see Appendix, paragraph 1 (iv)).

The controls described in the following paragraph which, as stated, relate solely to banks' operations on the official market, are imposed and operated by the IBLC, under the provision of the Decree-Law of October 6, 1944, on the control of foreign exchange. More extensive powers to control foreign transactions by banks and other financial intermediaries were given to the IBLC by the Law of December 20, 1974 on the Budget for 1974-75: this amended the Decree-Law of October 6, 1944 to take account of the increasing despecialisation of financial intermediaries.

With effect from June 18, 1976, a ceiling of 20 million francs has been applied to the long and short spot positions on the official market of each recognised bank in Belgium (and in Luxembourg). For large banks, the relevant ceilings are set in relation to the volume of each bank's transactions, and are therefore higher. A temporary excess of 10% over the ceiling is tolerated so as not to disturb the normal operation of current transactions. At the same time, banks were also instructed that their overall foreign currency position relating to the official market (spot and forward combined) should normally be close to balance and should not register a substantial debtor or creditor position. (These instructions replaced similar control measures imposed on January 25, 1974, and September 18, 1973).

Under the Decree of November 24, 1937 on reports to be made by banks to the Banque Nationale de Belgique (see 1.3.3 above), banks are required to make a monthly return of their claims and liabilities to non-residents, in foreign currencies and in Belgian francs. These reporting requirements have recently been strengthened, to require daily information on certain points, as well as more detailed monthly information, which break down foreign currency liabilities and claims by currency and by maturity date, for both the official and the free market. Banks also have to report to the Commission Bancaire monthly all advances in foreign currency, and all forward foreign exchange transactions which exceed 10% of their own funds.

The IBLC are empowered to send inspectors into banks to verify the statements and returns covering their exchange transactions. Inspectors regularly make such visits to banks.

The Commission Bancaire relies to a large extent on bank auditors to ensure that each bank's internal controls on its foreign exchange dealers and their confirmation systems, etc., are fully adequate. It was thus through the auditors that the Commission sought, in August 1974, details from every bank of the limits it placed on every name in the foreign exchange market, and details of how those limits were calculated.

1.12 CREDIT INFORMATION EXCHANGE

The Credit Information Exchange or Central Risks Service of the Banque Nationale de Belgique was set up in 1965 and its powers were extended by a Decree of October 9, 1967.

Registered banks are required to notify the Service Centrale des Risques of the Banque Nationale de Belgique and the Commission Bancaire of all applications for credit in excess of one million francs that have been approved. At the request of the Banque Nationale de Belgique or the Commission Bancaire, banks have to report the drawing on these credits. Reports of credits granted are made each week by the largest banks, twice per month by the other banks and once per month by some public credit institutions and the private savings banks. Reports of credits drawn are made at the end of each quarter (Art. 12). This applies equally to branches in Belgium of foreign banks.

The Law of June 30, 1975 has extended this reporting requirement to the private savings banks and other private financial institutions which raise funds from the public. The same law provides (Art. 71) that a similar duty may be imposed, by royal decree, on agents, brokers and others involved in banking operations, as well as on other institutions. Up to now, no such decree has been issued. Some public credit institutions also notify credits in excess of one million francs to the Central Risks Service on a voluntary basis.

The Central Risks Service collates the information provided under 1.9.3 above with any information derived from the Banque Nationale de Belgique's own operations, or available from other central risks bureaux in Belgium or abroad; it may transmit part or all of the information gathered to the banks and other financial institutions which supplied the information, and also to the Commission Bancaire; it may set any conditions for the supply of this information. In practice information is given on request to any bank which says it is considering lending to the company in question (Art. 12).

The Banque Nationale de Belgique is entitled to pass on to the central risks bureaux of other countries the information supplied to its own Central Risks Service; and the Commission Bancaire is entitled to pass such information on to the authorities supervising banks or other financial intermediaries in foreign countries (Art. 12). These powers were brought in by the Law of June 30, 1975 (cf. 1.3.2 above).

1.13 DEPOSIT INSURANCE

There are no requirements in the Banking Law or elsewhere for a deposit insurance scheme of any sort.

Safeguards do exist, however, in the activities of the Rediscount and Guarantee Institute (Institut de Réescompte et de Garantie (IRG)). The IRG not only comes promptly to the assistance of banks facing a temporary liquidity squeeze, but also supports banks that are up against more fundamental liquidity and solvency problems, in order to maintain confidence in the commercial banking system. The decision to supply funds is at the discretion of the IRG, which is jointly controlled by the commercial banks and the Government. In 1974 it was feared that the IRG would not have sufficient resources in the event of substantial losses by a bank. Accordingly, in 1975, through an agreement with the Institute, the banks incorporated under Belgian law and the private savings associations created a supplementary special intervention reserve on which the IRG may draw at its discretion. For the same purpose its capital will be gradually increased. The special intervention reserve is subscribed by the banks and the private savings associations to the amount of 3,000 million francs. Under the terms of the agreement, any funds drawn on by the IRG are fully reimbursed except where the final loss incurred through the rescue operation amounts to more than 500 million francs, in which case the excess is borne by the reserve. The agreement with the IRG expired at the end of 1979, but has been tacitly renewed for a further period of five years. In contrast to the subsidiaries of foreign banks, which have signed the agreement, branches of foreign banks in Belgium do not participate in this scheme.

1.14 SANCTIONS

1.14.1 Revocation of Authorisation

The Commission Bancaire has explicit powers to revoke a bank's registration (Art.25). If the Commission becomes aware that a bank is not functioning in accordance with the laws and regulations, if its management or its financial situation does not offer sufficient guarantees that it will be able to meet its liabilities, or that there are grave faults in its administrative or accounting organisation or in its internal control system, the Commission may stipulate a period within which these faults are to be put right. If this is not done, the Commission may in the last resort, revoke the bank's authorisation.

1.14.2 Imposition of Conditions

As an alternative to outright revocation of an institution's registration, the Commission Bancaire may:
    (i) Nominate a *commissaire spécial*, whose written authorisation is required for all (or a specified part of) management and administration acts and decisions;
    (ii) Suspend all or a selected part of the bank's activities for not more than a month (though this period is renewable).

1.14.3 Other Sanctions

As noted in 1.3.1 above, the Commission Bancaire is responsible for the control of tax evasion devices set up by banks and certain other institutions for the benefit of third parties. If a bank fails to follow the Commission's instructions that such a device should be done away with, the Commission may suspend all or part of the bank's activities for a renewable period of one month. The Commission Bancaire has issued two documents (the latest dated January 25, 1977), enlarging on the nature of the tax evasion devices to be regulated by Article 39 of Decree No. 185.

1.14.4 Penalties

Bankers, administrators, directors, etc., who contravene any of the mandatory provisions of the Banking Law or the regulations of the Commission Bancaire are subject to penal sanctions, including imprisonment. The penalty for ignoring the solvency and liquidity ratio regulations is from eight days to three months in prison and/or a fine of from 50 to 100,000 francs (Arts. 42-46). The Commission Bancaire must report any criminal offence of which it has knowledge to the Public Prosecutor (Procureur du Roi).

1.14.5 Appeals

Any penal sanctions are subject to the normal Belgian appeals procedure. The Commission Bancaire's own powers of sanction are subject to appeal to the Minister for Finance. In addition, since the Commission Bancaire is an administrative body, its decisions are subject to review by the Conseil d'Etat.

An appeal against a decision of the Commission Bancaire to refuse authorisation can be made to the Minister for Finance. The appeal must be lodged within 15 days of the notification of the decision (Art. 2). An appeal against the decision of the Minister for Finance may be made to the Conseil d'Etat.

Appeals against any decision of the Commission to impose sanctions under 1.14.1 and 1.14.2 above may be made to the Minister for Finance, but must be lodged within three days of their notification. An appeal will normally suspend the decision, but where this would seriously endanger the interests of creditors, the Commission Bancaire can override this suspension.

1.15 FOREIGN BANK BRANCHES

1.15.1 Establishment

There are no restrictions on the activities in Belgium of branches of foreign banks; they must be registered with the Commission Bancaire, and they are subject to the same operations controls and regulations as Belgian-based banks, except for the controls on the acquisition of participations and some of the controls on personnel (see 1.15.3 and 1.15.4 below) (Art. 6). Before establishing a branch, the Commission Bancaire requires a certified copy of the decision of the bank's board of directors (or equivalent body) giving authority to one or more officials to bind the bank in respect of its future operations in Belgium. These officials must work at the branch and be resident in Belgium.

Foreign banks which maintain one or more branch offices (*sièges d'opérations*) in Belgium are required to maintain (at the principal branch, if there is more than one) a separate balance sheet of their operations in Belgium (Art. 6).

Under an amendment to Article 40 of the Banking Law effected by the Law of June 30, 1975, the Commission Bancaire is entitled to pass on to the relevant authorities in another country information which it has received from any branches (or subsidiaries) in Belgium of banks or financial intermediaries based in that other country. This information can be related to banking business or to operations in the area of investment trusts or securities. The initiative for the exchange of information can come from the Commission Bancaire or the foreign authority.

In general, any foreigner, other than a national of the Netherlands or Luxembourg, who wishes to carry on an independent activity in Belgium must obtain a *carte professionelle* (professional card) from the Ministry of the Middle Classes. The card is valid for a maximum of five years, but may be renewed (Law of February 19, 1965).

Exemptions from this requirement may be made by royal decree, because of the nature of the work involved, or in order to comply with international obligations. A Royal Decree of December 5, 1974 has implemented EEC Directive 73/183 on Freedom of Establishment for Banks; it has removed the need for anyone to whom this Directive applies to obtain a professional card.

1.15.2 Earmarked Capital

The minimum own capital required of foreign banks who operate branches in Belgium and keep a separate balance sheet of their operations in Belgium (see 1.15.1 above) is 50 million francs. The Commission Bancaire is empowered to determine what is regarded as own capital for this purpose (Art. 10).

In accordance with these powers, the Commission Bancaire has defined the "own capital" (own funds) of a branch of a foreign bank (or, if there is more than one branch, of all its branches in Belgium) as the endowment of the branch plus any additions to it, to the extent that the total of these two corresponds to a net surplus of assets over liabilities in the Belgian balance sheet of the branch. These terms are defined below:

(i) The endowment of the branch is that portion of the capital funds of the bank as a whole, which has been permanently allocated to the branch for its activities in Belgium; this endowment must not be used to undertake operations outside Belgium - it must not, for instance, be used to acquire assets in a currency other than Belgian francs. The Commission Bancaire requires proof that this endowment in no way corresponds to liabilities of the parent bank to third parties, and that its allocation has been effected with the knowledge of the competent supervisory authorities in the bank's country of origin;

(ii) Additions to that endowment are free reserves and accumulated profits of previous years which have been retained by the branch. General provisions are included, provided that the Commission Bancaire has approved the bank's system of accumulating and dealing with provisions, but not those against losses which have already occurred;

(iii) The Belgian balance sheet of the bank includes all the liabilities, assets, guarantees and contingent liabilities written in Belgian francs;

(iv) A net surplus of assets over liabilities is the difference between, on the one hand, total assets, less any losses incurred and less any amounts to be written off, and on the other hand total liabilities, plus accumulated but allocated profits;

(v) Amounts to be written off include initial expenses of establishing the branch, goodwill and any probable or certain losses against which no provisions have been made;

(vi) In the definition of own funds to be used in calculating the capital/assets ratio (Regulation of June 13, 1972 - see 1.10.1) amounts to be written off are not deducted from total assets.

The definition in (iii) above of the Belgian balance sheet is applied solely in the context of the calculation of own funds needed to establish the branch of a foreign bank. It is not the same as the definition used in the ongoing capital adequacy tests applied to all banks (see 1.10.1 above).

1.15.3 Nationality and Competence of Personnel

There are no separate provisions in the Banking Law concerning the nationality of those responsible for controlling the operations in Belgium of branches of foreign banks. The Commission Bancaire would, however, expect to see some Belgians involved, if only for their knowledge of local laws and regulations and of market practices and methods. Those in charge of the branches are subject to the same provisions as Belgian bankers, so far as their reputation is concerned. Managers of Belgian branches of foreign banks who take part in the day-to-day management of their branch are also subject to the prohibition on exercising managerial functions in other companies (Art. 6(3)) (see 1.4.3 above).

As mentioned above in 1.15.1, a foreign bank branch must have one or more officials authorised to bind the bank, so far as its operations in Belgium are concerned.

1.15.4 Restrictions on Business

Foreign banks with branches in Belgium are required to ensure that all Belgian business is put through those branches, except where there is a legitimate case for using a branch outside Belgium. There are no limitations on the business a branch can undertake.

The restrictions on the participations which banks can hold in commercial companies do not apply to foreign bank branches but the latter are subject to the controls which can be imposed by the Law of June 30, 1975 (see 1.6.2 above).

1.15.5 Representative Offices

The Commission Bancaire will permit foreign banks to open representative offices in Belgium subject to strict limitations on their activities. The Commission's intention is that such offices must be information centres, and must in no way solicit business to be channelled through a branch outside Belgium. They are permitted to use the word "bank" or "banker" in their title, or advertisement etc, despite the fact that they are not listed banks (cf. 1.7 above), provided that the description "bureau de renseignements" or "bureau d'informations" is used, and not "bureau de représentation", which is thought to be misleading.

1.15.6 Other Provisions

Branches of foreign banks in Belgium do not participate in the special intervention reserve operated by the banks and the Institut de Réescompte et de Garantie (see 1.13 above).

The returns filed by foreign bank branches at the Tribunal de Commerce must show the results of all their places of business in Belgium (see 1.3.3 above).

1.16 FOREIGN BANK SUBSIDIARIES

1.16.1 Local Ownership

There is no requirement for any of the shareholders of a *société anonyme* (the usual form a foreign bank's subsidiary will take -see 1.4.1 above) to be Belgian nationals.

There are no separate banking regulations applying to foreign-owned banks in Belgium. They are treated exactly as a Belgian-owned institution, and are subject to the same rules and regulations.

1.16.2 Nationality of Directors

There are no provisions in the Banking Law concerning the nationality of the directors of Belgian subsidiaries of foreign banks, since these subsidiaries are regarded in law as Belgian banks. Nevertheless, the Commission Bancaire would expect to see some Belgians involved at a senior level, for their knowledge of local laws and regulations and of market practices and methods.

1.16.3 Guarantees from Parent Institution

There is no requirement for such a guarantee, but banks which do enjoy such guarantees from their parent body may benefit from a concession that the regular capital/assets ratio calculations may in certain circumstances be based on their domestic (i.e., Belgian) business, and may exclude their international business. (The details are set out in 1.9.1 above).

1.16.4 Other Provisions

Under an amendment to Article 40 of the Banking Law effected by the Law of June 30, 1975, the Commission Bancaire is entitled to pass on to the relevant authorities in another country information which it has received from any subsidiaries (or branches) in Belgium of banks or financial intermediaries based in that other country. This information can relate to banking business or to operations in the area of investment trusts or securities. The initiative for the exchange of information can come from the Commission Bancaire or the foreign authority.

1.17 BANKING ASSOCIATIONS

1.17.1 Membership

The Association Belge des Banques (Belgian Bankers' Association) contains five subgroupings for different categories of banks - large banks (three), private banks (11), medium-sized banks (21), Belgian subsidiaries of foreign banks (21), and Belgian branches of foreign banks (24). There is some overlapping between categories; total membership of the Association Belge des Banques was 80 in September 1980 against 86 listed banks. Any bank applying for membership is normally expected first to sign various interbank agreements, although some members have not signed all the agreements. The agreements cover 29 different subjects, including maximum rates of interest on various categories of deposits, and minimum commissions and fees for sundry operations. Membership is not compulsory.

1.17.2 Relations with Supervisory Authorities

The Association Belge des Banques does not play any direct part in the supervision of banks for prudential purposes. It does, however, maintain close relations with the Banque Nationale de Belgique and the Commission Bancaire, and expects to be consulted at an early stage in the formulation of any banking laws or proposals. This consultation is expressly provided for in the banking laws: for instance, under Article 1 of the Budget Law of December 28, 1973 (see 1.10 above), the Banque Nationale de Belgique can only formulate recommendations on banking ratios etc., after consultation with interested financial intermediaries or with their representative agents. Similar provisions apply under the Banking Law (as amended by the Law of June 30, 1975) to regulations made by the Commission Bancaire on participations held by banks (see 1.6.2); on solvency and liquidity ratios (see 1.9.1 and 1.9.2); on controls on large risk assets (see 1.9.1); and on the publication of balance sheets (see 1.9.2).

The Association Belge des Banques, together with the Association des Caisses d'Epargne Privées (Association of Private Savings Banks), is responsible for the banking industry's nominations for membership of the Commission Bancaire. Two of the six part-time members are chosen from a list presented jointly by these bodies (cf. 1.3 above) (Decree of March 29, 1976).

1.18 BACKGROUND SOURCES

1. Abraham, J.P. and Simal, M.: Dépôts et Crédits en Belgique, (Centre d'Etudes Bancaires et Financières, Brussels), (Cahier No. 255), (March, 1974).
2. Association Belge des Banques: Annual Reports.
3. Aufricht, H.: Central Banking Legislation, Vol. II: Europe, (International Monetary Fund, Washington, D.C.), (1967).
4. Banque Nationale de Belgique: Monthly Bulletins and Annual Reports.
5. Bruyneel, A.: 'La Commission bancaire belge', Banque, (1972), no. 303, p. 1, no. 304, p. 125, and no. 305, p. 247.
6. Bruyneel, A.: 'La loi du 30 juin 1975: Mammouth, souris ou pot-pourri?' Journal des Tribunaux, (1975), p. 649.
7. Bruyneel, A.: 'Les prêts subordonnés', Revue de la Banque, (1976), p. 530.
8. Commission Bancaire: Annual Reports.
9. Commission Bancaire: Lois et Arrêtés Organiques, Règlements et Mesures d'Exécution.
10. Elstob, M., (ed.) Banking structures and Sources of Finance in the European Community (Banker Research Unit, London) (1979).
11. European Community's Monetary Committee: Monetary Policy in the Countries of the European Economic Community, Institutions and Instruments, (Brussels), (1972).
12. Grosfils, M.: Les Contraintes de Gestion du Système Bancaire Belge, (Centre d'Etudes Bancaires et Financières, Brussels), (Cahier No. 163), (May, 1970).
13. Hodgman, D.R.: National Monetary Policies and International Monetary Co-operation, (first ed.), (Little, Brown and Company, Boston), (1974).
14. IBRO: Banking Ratios in the EEC (A study commissioned by Directorate-General XV of the EEC Commission from the Inter-Bank Research Organisation, 1979).
15. International Monetary Fund: Annual Report on Exchange Arrangements and Exchange Restrictions, (Washington, D.C.), (1979).
16. Jura Europae, Droit Bancaire et Boursier/Bank und Borsenrecht, (Editions Techniques Juris-Classeurs, Paris), (C.H. Beck, Munich), (1974).
17. Le Brun, J.: La protection de l'épargne publique et la Commission bancaire, (Bruylant, Brussels) 1979.
18. Le Brun, J.: 'Le régime légal des portefeuilles-titres des banques', Revue de la Banque, (1966), p. 709.

19. Le Brun, J.: 'Nature et modalités juridiques du contrôle revisoral des banques, Reflets et perspectives de la vue économique', (1971), p. 31.
20. Lempereur, C.: 'Le renforcement du statut légal des banques en Belgique', Banque, (September, 1976).
21. Lempereur, Cl.: 'L'implantation en Belgique des banques étrangères', Droit et pratique du commerce international, (1975), p. 395.
22. Smets, F.A.: 'L'autonomie et la stabilité des banques', Revue de la Banque, (1976), p. 415.
23. Wijckaert, O.: Structure du Système Bancaire Belge, (Association Belge des Banques, Brussels), (September, 1972).

APPENDIX

SOLVENCY RATIO REQUIREMENTS
APPLIED TO BANKS IN BELGIUM

Risk Quotient

1. The first step in calculating the capital required is to establish the risk quotient. This is calculated once a month (or once every three months, on the authorisation of the Commission Bancaire, provided that it is sufficiently representative) and consists of the total of:

(i) 5% of the following assets (but excluding any assets also listed in (5) below:

commercial bills held in portfolio, rediscounted or for collection (other than those accepted by the bank or bearing the signature of another bank, of a private savings bank, or of a public credit institution and except those received for collection without immediate credit to the remitter);

customers' liabilities on acceptances (but acceptances given by order and in the name of other banks are charged at 1%);

current or term advances (except those mentioned in (iii) below);

securities other than Belgian Government debt instruments or foreign Government bonds held as an investment or loan certificates of another bank or of a private savings bank held as an investment;

participations other than those in public credit institutions;

guarantees issued on behalf of third parties as well as assets of any kind pledged as collateral for account of third parties (avoiding duplication);

documentary credits not 100% covered by deposits, opened by order of and for the account of customers;

(ii) An additional 2.5% of the risks mentioned in (i) above whenever the total of all types and forms of these risks relating to a particular customer (or to several customers who can in any way be considered connected as far as risk is concerned, notwithstanding their status and legal form) exceeds 20% of the bank's own funds;

(iii) 1% of:

loans granted on the 'non-guaranteed call money market';

'own accounts' with banks, head office, branches and subsidiaries as well as advances granted to such;

short-term funds receivable other than commercial bills taken out of portfolio for collection, or taken for collection against immediate credit;

commercial bills held in portfolio, rediscounted or taken for collection, bearing the signature of another bank, private savings bank or public credit institution, except those taken for collection without immediate credit to the remitter;

loan certificates of another bank or private savings bank held as an investment;

confirmed irrevocable documentary credits not fully covered by deposits opened by order of banks;

(iv) 0.2% of the total of claims in Belgian and foreign currency, arising from forward foreign exchange transactions.

2. The total of items (i-iv) is then increased by 10 million francs against the first 10 million francs tranche of that total; a further sum of five million francs is added against the second 10 million francs tranche. (No further increments are applied against a risk quotient total higher than 20 million francs: this formula reflects the Banking Commission's belief in the safety of size).

3. The total thus achieved, of risk quotients plus increments, is averaged over a 12 month 'observation period' ending in the ante- penultimate month of the bank's financial year - i.e., it is on a fixed 12 month basis, rather than on a moving average basis, and so is recalculated but once a year.

4. In its Annual Reports for 1977/78 and 1978/79, the Banking Commission stated that the following changes had been made in applying the regulation on own funds:

the weighting of 1% is - instead of 5% - extended to all credit risks, whatever their form, that are backed by a guarantee from another bank, savings bank or public credit institution;

the rules exempting Belgian public funds from any own-funds requirement is extended to loans to Belgian provinces and communes and to loans guaranteed by the Belgian State, a Belgian province or Belgian commune;

loans to Member States of the EEC and loans guaranteed by a Member States and granted to a public institution carrying out the function of exchequer in the State concerned be disregarded in calculating the own funds requirement. This also applies to loans granted to the EEC, the ECSC and Euratom.

Loans granted to a foreign State and loans guaranteed by a foreign State may be disregarded in calculating the own funds requirement provided that such loans promote Belgian exports and provided that they involve a principal credit backed by the guarantee of the Office Nationale du Ducroire (National Del Credere Office).

Paper acquired by way of investment and negotiated by the IRG or representing export credits accepted by the Credit export pool is no longer included in calculating the own funds requirement.

Fixed Assets and Investments

5. A separate calculation is made of assets which have to be covered entirely by own funds; these are accordingly excluded from the assets used

in calculating the risk quotients. These consist of the total of:

(i) Amounts to be written off: These comprise the legal and other fees involved in setting up or establishing the bank and its branches; goodwill; premiums and other costs involved in leasing property; other expenses or charges to be amortised and, if they exist, any loss or deficit against which special provision has not be made;

(ii) Participations: These comprise all holdings in a bank or in a company carrying out a related activity where such holdings are 10% or more of the capital or of the voting rights; and, if the bank concerned is in a group, all holdings in any company within the group. 'Group' is widely defined, to include: (1) companies of which the bank is a direct or indirect subsidiary, as well as other direct or indirect subsidiaries of those companies; (2) all shareholders in the bank who hold 5% or more of its capital and/or sit or are represented (directly or indirectly) on its Board of Directors; (3) institutions directed or dominated by those in (2) above; and (4) the direct and indirect subsidiaries of the bank.

One company is considered to be unquestionably a subsidiary of another when the first holds, directly or indirectly, at least 50% of the capital or the voting rights. It is presumed to be a subsidiary when the first holds at least 50% of the votes present or represented at the last annual general meeting. It is presumed (in the absence of proof to the contrary) to be a subsidiary if the first company dominates it by any mechanism whatever.

(iii) Investments and claims (remplois et recours). These consist of investments, other than participations, in the group (as defined in (ii) above) to which the bank belongs, and potential claims on the group arising out of transactions undertaken by the bank for account of the group (to the extent that these investments and claims cannot be taken over, on the same conditions, by other banks carrying out similar operations). A good example would be an advance to a subsidiary at a concessionary rate of interest.

6. A third calculation is made of the total of fixed and assimilated investments (remplois permanents et assimilés). This consists of those listed in 5(i), (iii) above, property, shares in and claims on property-holding subsidiaries, furniture and equipment, investments forming the legal reserve (see 1.4.5 above), and participations. For this calculation, participations consist of paid-up shares or holdings in companies, institutions and other organisations whose continuing ownership by the bank is necessary or useful for the activities of the bank (leaving aside the income from these participations); it also includes advances to such companies etc. when these advances are of a permanent nature.

Solvency Tests

7. Having performed these calculations, there are two separate tests of capital adequacy. The first is that own funds must always exceed fixed and assimilated investments ((6) above).

8. The second test is that own funds must exceed the total of the risk quotients plus increments added to the list of assets to be covered entirely. This calculation ensures that the bank's own funds are sufficiently large to cover the realisation risks on both the whole range of its marketable assets (1) and the total of its assets arising in the group, and therefore of possibly doubtful marketability (5). The bank is given a grace period of nine months from the end of the 'observation period' (see (2) above) in order (if necessary) to bring its capital up to the amount required on this second test.

The Definition of 'Own Funds'

9. 'Own funds' are defined (Commission Bancaire Regulation of June 13, 1972) as the sum of capital, reserves (including the legal reserve, see 1.4.5 above), profits carried forward, less incurred losses, and provisions (published and hidden) for non-specific risks which had not yet occurred (provided that the Commission Bancaire has approved the rules for accumulating and dealing with these provisions).[4]

10. In its Annual Report for 1975/76 the Commission set down further guidelines on its treatment of provisions. The internal guarantee fund (hidden provisions) may be assimilated into the bank's own funds only if it is included in the balance sheet as a long term liability or if it is mentioned in the report on the balance sheet. Banks which consider the internal guarantee fund as own funds may not extend this fund any further and any newly constituted provisions must be included in the long-term liabilities. Loan risks provisions are considered as own funds provided they are stated on the liabilities side of the balance sheet. Write-offs on government bonds as well as commissions for underwriting and placement of government bonds kept in a bank's own portfolio may be assimilated into the bank's own funds on condition that such commissions are not recorded as profit. Furthermore the bank in its annual report must state the difference between book value and stock market value of the listed securities and of the amount of the commissions.

Loan Capital

11. The treatment of loan capital is not mentioned in the Regulation. The Commission Bancaire is, however, prepared to see subordinated loans and subordinated lines of credit included in own funds to a limited extent, on

certain conditions and subject to detailed consideration of each case.

12. The Commission Bancaire regards subordinated loans merely as a temporary means of meeting the own funds requirement. A bank must therefore show that it is able to replace a loan on maturity by its own funds. For the purposes of calculation of the statutory requirement, subordinated loans may be included only up to a limit of 50% of own funds. Subordinated loans must meet the following conditions:

(i) The grantor of the loan (creditor) must, without any question, rank behind all other creditors of the bank. If the creditor resides outside Belgium, he must prove that this requirement is in accordance with his own national law, and that there will be no legal or regulatory obstacles, particularly in respect to foreign exchange;

(ii) The loan must be for a period of at least three years, and at least two years' notice of withdrawal must be given to the bank and to the Commission. The latter may suspend the period of notice, if the withdrawal would have serious effects on the bank's own funds. Special rules apply to convertible subordinated loan stock (see below).

(iii) The loan should be in Belgian francs; if it is in a foreign currency it can only be included in the bank's own funds pro rata to that fraction of own funds required by claims on a non-resident denominated in foreign currency.

13. Subordinated lines of credit must meet the following conditions in order to be allowed as part of a bank's own funds:

(i) As in (i)-(iii) above;

(ii) Drawings on the line of credit must be made solely on the initiative of the beneficiary bank;

(iii) The line of credit is only available to cover the fractions of own funds required by the concentration of risks (see (i) (ii)), and by its international business - all assets, liabilities, guarantees and claims in foreign currencies on non-residents (cf.(15) below).

14. Convertible subordinated loan stock may be included, provided that the conversion rights expire at least two years before the maturity of the loan stock (so that the bank knows well in advance by how much its own funds will be reduced).

Foreign Banks

15. Foreign banks' branches in Belgium, and their subsidiaries enjoying a parent bank guarantee on their business, may be granted a concession whereby these capital adequacy tests are applied to their domestic (i.e. Belgian) business and not to their international business. For this purpose, the Belgian balance sheet of such a branch or subsidiary is taken as the total of its liabilities, assets, guarantees and claims expressed in Belgian francs,

whether in relation to residents or non-residents, as well as such liabilities, assets, etc. expressed in foreign currency in relation to residents of Belgium. This effectively excludes from the tests their foreign currency non-resident business. This concession is granted only if the Commission Bancaire is fully satisfied that the balance sheet structure of the entire foreign bank is sound, or is adequately controlled by the supervisory authorities in its country of origin, and if the branch or subsidiary files separate returns of its domestic and international business.

Belgian Bank Subsidiaries

16. A similar concession may be applied to a subsidiary of a Belgian bank, provided again that the parent bank provides an adequate guarantee (which may take the form of the extension on a permanent basis of a subordinated line of credit) and satisfies the Commission Bancaire of its soundness.

NOTES

1. Unless otherwise specified, references hereafter are to Articles of the 1935 Banking Law, as amended.
2. These are, for the most part, finance companies which raise their funds from the public.
3. The official market is used mainly for current transactions, as distinct from the free market, on which mainly capital transactions are settled. The markets have been fully separate since May 1971.
4. See 1.15.2 for the definition of own funds required for the establishment of branches of foreign banks.

CHAPTER 2

DENMARK

2.1 INSTITUTIONS COVERED

The Danish banking system is basically divided into two sectors: the commercial banks and the savings banks. The Commercial Banks and Savings Banks Act 1974[1] allows commercial banks and savings banks to carry on the same types of business - by which is meant "the performance of functions relating to transactions of money, instruments of credit and securities and the associated services" (ss. 1(2) and 1(3)). The major distinction between the sectors is that, under the Act, commercial banks are joint stock companies, while savings banks are independent (mutual) institutions.

References in this chapter are to both commercial banks and savings banks, unless otherwise specified. Mortgage credit institutions, which are not part of the banking system, are subject to separate comprehensive legislation and are not within the scope of this chapter.

Only the commercial banks, the savings banks and the State are entitled to canvass for deposits from the public (s. 1(5)).

2.2 BASIC LAWS

The basic laws (as amended) are as follows:

(i) Commercial Banks and Savings Banks Act No. 199 of April 2, 1974, which came into operation on January 1, 1975, and was amended by Act No. 260 of June 8, 1977, Act No. 299 of June 8, 1977, Act No. 177 of May 14, 1980, and Act No. 268 of June 16, 1980;

(ii) the Danmarks Nationalbank Act No. 116 of April 7, 1936;

(iii) the Credit Regulation Act No. 543 of October 17, 1973;

(iv) the Companies Act No. 370 of June 13, 1973 (in relation to commercial banks, which must be set up as limited liability companies);

(v) Act No. 59 of February 15, 1974, on prices and profits, amended by Act No. 415 of August 20, 1976, and Act No. 51 of March 9, 1979, Act No. 87 of August 14, 1979, and Act No. 530 of December 28, 1979;

(vi) Act No. 252 of June 8 1977, on the marking and display of prices, amended by Act No. 53 of March 9, 1979, Act No. 89 of March 14, 1979, and the Order of July 2, 1979;

(vii) Act No. 102 of March 31, 1955, on monopolies and restrictive practices, amended by Act No. 115 of April 2, 1971, and Act No. 52 of March 9, 1979.

2.3 SUPERVISORY SYSTEM

2.3.1 Supervisory Authority

The Tilsynet med Banker og Sparekasser (the Inspectorate of Commercial Banks and Savings Banks) is responsible for enforcing the Act and for controlling the activities of banks.

The Tilsynet is a public directorate subject to the Minister for Industry and staffed by permanent civil servants. It was established in 1880 to supervise the savings banks, and in 1920 it took on (in a separate office) responsibility for the commercial banks: the offices were amalgamated in 1963. The basic functions of the Tilsynet are to ensure that the Act and instructions issued under the Act are observed and to submit an annual report to the Minister for Industry on the activities of the commercial and savings banks (s. 49).

Activities of the employees of the Tilsynet are restricted -e.g., they must not be members of the board of directors of a bank, and must not, except with the permission of the Minister for Industry, be actively involved in business (s. 51).

The expenses of running the Tilsynet are met by the banks, in proportion to their total debts and guarantees, but with a minimum annual contribution of 500 kroner per bank (s. 52).

2.3.2 Outline of System

A formal licensing system for commercial and savings banks was set up by Act No. 177 of May 14, 1980. An institution wishing to set up as a commercial or savings bank must now obtain the prior authorisation of the Tilsynet. Reasons must be given if authorisation is refused and the decision can be appealed to the courts.

In addition, a commercial bank must be entered in the Register of Companies: the Registrar examines whether the normal legal requirements for setting up a company have been met. The bank's articles of association must also be approved by the Tilsynet which examines them to ensure they comply with current legislation.

A savings bank, being a mutual institution, is not entered in the Register of Companies but in the local Trade Register. It is therefore the duty of the Tilsynet to ensure that the legal requirements have been met, and to confirm the savings bank's by-laws, before it can commence business.

The task of the Tilsynet is to ensure that all banks comply with the Act, particularly the requirements relating to the competence of management and the protection of depositors' funds.

2.3.3 Returns to Supervisory Body

Each bank must submit to the Tilsynet a copy of its annual audited accounts together with a copy of the auditor's records within 10 days of the general meeting (commercial banks) or the meeting of the board of representatives (savings banks) at which they are adopted, and not later than four months after the end of the account year (s. 37(1)). Annual accounts, which must be drawn up to December 31, consist of the balance sheet, profit and loss account, and annual report. They must be in a form prescribed by the Tilsynet, who may also lay down rules relating to the preparation of consolidated accounts and to particulars which may be included in notes to the accounts (s. 30(3)).

At the end of the accounting year, banks must provide the Tilsynet with any information which the Minister for Industry regards as being necessary for statistical purposes.

Banks are also obliged to give to the Tilsynet such information as is necessary for its activities, including any details of the affairs of individual customers. In practice this information is provided in the form of monthly returns (in balance sheet form); these can be amplified if necessary. Loans exceeding 35% of a bank's net capital must be reported to the Tilsynet (see 2.9.3 below).

Monthly balance sheets (as at the end of each month) must also be submitted to the Tilsynet, for all banks except those savings banks with working capital (deposits plus accountable capital deposits plus net capital) of less than 10 million kroner, who must submit balances quarterly.

The annual report must contain information about the number of management and other staff and total amount of their salaries.

2.3.4 Auditing requirements

The Act itself gives some guidance as to the form of accounts and annual reports, particularly regarding the valuation of its assets (see also 2.9 below). The detailed regulations are contained in the Announcement on the Presentation of Accounts etc. of Commercial Banks and Savings Banks, issued by the Tilsynet on December 13, 1974; and in the Announcement of the Presentation of Accounts etc. of Branches of Foreign Commercial Banks and Savings Banks, issued by the Tilsynet on December 17, 1974. The accounts must be signed by the board of directors and the management, and any objections to the accounts by members of these bodies must be included in the annual report (s. 29 (2)).

The annual balance sheet and profit and loss account and quarterly balances must be published by each bank's registered office; the annual balance sheet and profit and loss account also have to be published in the localities where branches of the banks are situated (s. 37(2)).

2.3.5 Inspection

The Tilsynet is required to make regular inspections of all banks, and banks are required to give to the Tilsynet such information as is necessary for its activities (s. 50). In practice, the Tilsynet relies to a large extent on an examination of each bank's monthly statistical returns and annual accounts (see 2.9.1 below); it can inspect banks to verify or amplify these returns if appropriate.

The Tilsynet can also direct a bank's auditors to give it unlimited information about the bank, and about the affairs of any particular customer of a bank (s. 36).

As part of the regular examinations of all banks, all lending is normally scrutinised every three years; in examining the loan portfolio, the quality of the loans is of more concern than the size (subject of course to the controls on large loans set out in 2.9.3 below). Banks may be examined in other respects at varying intervals.

2.4 CRITERIA FOR AUTHORISATION

2.4.1 Legal Form

Commercial banks must be set up as limited liability companies. Savings banks must be independent (i.e., mutual) institutions (s. 1). It is thus not possible to have a bank in the form of a partnership or of a one-man firm, unless it is a branch of a bank with its head office in another EEC Member State (see 2.15.1 below).

2.4.2. Minimum Capital

The minimum share capital for a commercial bank is five million kroner. The shares must always be fully paid up and must not be divided into classes with different voting rights. There must be at least 10 original subscribers (founders), each subscribing a minimum of 1,000 kroner (s. 3).

Savings banks must have a paid-up guarantee capital of not less than five million kroner. There must be at least 50 guarantors, each paying in a minimum of 1,000 Kroner (s. 4). These requirements do not apply, however, to savings banks established before the Act came into force (s. 56 (5)).

2.4.3 Management Qualifications

Notification of election, appointment and retirement of general managers, auditors, members of the board of directors, and members of the shareholders' committee (commercial banks only) must be submitted to the Tilsynet within one month (s. 17(2)).

Under s.6(3) of the 1980 Act, the Minister for Industry can, following a recommendation from the Tilsynet, refuse or withdraw authorisation from a bank, if a member of the board of directors or the board of managers has 1) inadequate experience to carry out his duties; 2) been convicted of an offence which is incompatible with the proper discharge of his functions; 3) been guilty of conduct which indicates that he will not carry out his duties properly.

The 1974 Act contains detailed provisions dealing with the management and board structure of savings banks (ss. 7, 10-15). These mirror the provisions of the Danish Companies Act, No. 370 of June 13, 1973 (as amended), which applies to all limited companies and therefore to the commercial banks. Savings banks must have a board of representatives, a board of directors and a board of management (s.10), whereas the commercial banks must have a board of directors, a separate management and an optional shareholders committee. Members of the board of directors and general managers must not be minors, and must be resident in Denmark unless exempted by the Minister for Industry (s. 16). By Order No. 567 of November 29, 1974, the Minister has exempted members of the board of directors from this requirement in accordance with EEC Directive 73/183 of June 28, 1973, and managers in accordance with EEC Regulation 1612/68 of October 15, 1968.

A member of the board of directors or a member of the shareholders' committee cannot also be a general manager, except temporarily in the absence of a general manager, when he would not have voting powers (s. 17).

The general managers and the staff of a commercial or savings bank must not engage in speculative transactions (s. 19(4)), and general managers, deputy managers, assistant managers, and branch managers must not be actively involved in business other than running the bank, except with the permission of the Minister for Industry (s. 19(5)).

Authority to sign for a bank must be exercised by not less than two persons (the 'Four Eyes' Principle). Every branch requires two managers (s. 20).

2.4.4 Management Plans

An application for authorisation must contain a detailed statement of the proposed business and management structure of the bank (s.6(1) of the 1980 Act).

2.4.5 Other Requirements

As mentioned above, the articles of association of a commercial bank and the by-laws of a savings bank must be approved by the Tilsynet, which ensures that they are in conformity with existing legislation and regulations (s. 6(2)).

2.5 BRANCHES

2.5.1 Restrictions on Branching in Denmark

There are no legal or other restrictions on the opening of branches in Denmark by Danish banks. Banks are not required to notify the Tilsynet when opening or closing branches.

2.5.2 Branching and Operations in Other Countries

There are no prudential restrictions on opening branches or conducting business abroad. These activities are, of course, subject to any exchange control or similar restrictions on the outflow of capital which may be in force.

A bank must submit separate monthly and annual balance sheets for each branch outside Denmark, even though such a branch's figures are also included in its global reports.

2.6 RESTRICTIONS ON BUSINESS

2.6.1 Restrictions on Types of Business

Banks must not engage in business other than banking business. The only exception is that they may temporarily engage in non-banking business with the purpose of settling previous engagements, and in such circumstances they must submit a report to the Tilsynet (s. 1(4)).

Banking business is defined as "the performance of functions relating to transactions of money, instruments of credit and securities and the associated services" (s. 1(3)).

The Act and associated regulations do not define "associated services", it is rather a question for the Tilsynet to decide. The basic approach of the Tilsynet is to permit only 'traditional' banking activities, and those fields where the financing of operations in one way or another is the object of the exercise. Thus activities such as factoring, leasing or the financing of hire-purchase transactions are permitted, but such operations as an insurance agency (let alone a principal) or a travel agency would not be permitted.

2.6.2 Loans to Directors

Without the approval of the board of directors, a bank cannot grant loans to, give guarantees for, or take security from, members of the board of directors or the shareholders' committee (commercial banks only), general managers, deputy managers, assistant managers, and branch managers. The same rule applies to their relations and to any company in which they or their relations are general managers or members of the board of directors (s. 19).

The permission of the Tilsynet is necessary for a bank to grant loans to, or give guarantees for, persons or enterprises who, through ownership of shares or otherwise, can exercise directly or indirectly a decisive influence over the bank, or who are dominated by persons or enterprises having such influence (s. 27). Where the bank maintains that permission is unnecessary, it must prove that there is no such influence.

This is one of the points which is examined particularly carefully by the Tilsynet in its regular inspection of a bank's loan portfolio (see 2.3.5 above).

2.6.3 Equity Participations

A bank must not own, or grant loans on shares or guarantee certificates in any single limited company, cooperative society or institution, either banking or non-banking, to the extent of more than 15% of the bank's net capital (s. 24). (This interest must also be taken into account in calculating the total liability of a customer to a bank - see 2.9.3 below).

A bank must not invest more than 20% of its net capital in real property or in shares in real estate companies (at book value), except where that property will be used for carrying on banking activities (s. 25) (cf. 2.6.1 above). The total value of shares and guarantee certificates acquired by a bank in other companies, whether banking or non-banking, must not exceed 50% of its own net capital (s. 24). The Tilsynet may allow exemptions from these provisions (s. 26). In practice such an exemption is very rarely granted.

There is nothing in theory to prevent a bank from holding a participation up to the permitted limits in a non-banking service or similar company. Since commercial banks and savings banks are not allowed to carry on non-banking business, the Tilsynet will only allow a bank to hold over 50% of the shares of a company (or under 50% but still with effective control) if the company is engaged in a 'traditional' or otherwise acceptable banking activity, or is engaged in property or real estate transactions inside the permitted limits.

As far as participations in credit institutions are concerned, a bank must not acquire shares in excess of 30% of the share capital of a commercial bank or the guarantee capital of a savings bank; nor may it, by granting loans on the security of such shares or guarantee certificates, acquire the right to exercise voting rights in excess of 30% of the share capital (s. 24).

It would thus be possible for a bank unexpectedly to acquire a holding of over 30% in another bank as a result of taking a parcel of shares as security for loans, in addition to a beneficial holding of its own. But since the control mentioned above is based on voting rights, the bank would not be prevented from taking the shares as security.

When submitting its annual report, each bank must also submit to the Tilsynet a statement of the shares in commercial banks and guarantee certificates in savings banks which it owns and those which it has received as security for loans (s. 24(2))

2.6.4 Mergers

A commercial or savings bank must not acquire or merge with a commercial bank, a savings bank, or a branch of such banks without the permission of the Minister for Industry. In the case of a savings bank merger, the Minister for Industry may grant exemptions from the requirement for guarantors and the amount of guarantee capital required for the new savings bank (s. 48) (see 2.4.2 above).

The Minister uses this power to take account both of the interests of the banks and the banking system and of the wider national interest. Permission has so far never been refused for a merger.

2.7 BANKING NAMES AND DESCRIPTIONS

Only commercial banks and savings banks are allowed (they, indeed, are obliged) to use the names 'bank' and 'savings bank' (s. 2). Other enterprises, apart from "banks founded under Special Acts", must not use these or other names which may give the impression that they are banks. A commercial bank must not give the impression that it is the central bank, and if any bank operates under a name other than its principal one, the principal name must be added to the subsidiary name.

2.8 ADVERTISING

There are no restrictions on types of advertisements, but only banks coming within the Act and 'the State' are allowed to solicit deposits from the general public (s. 1(5)). In practice, the Tilsynet would warn a bank if it considered that the bank's advertising contravened acceptable banking practice.

2.9 SOLVENCY AND LIQUIDITY

The main solvency and liquidity ratio requirements applied to banks in Denmark are laid down specifically in the 1974 Act.

2.9.1 Solvency Ratios

The net capital (see below) of a bank must be at least 8% of its total liabilities and guarantees (s. 21). In calculating this ratio, the statement of liabilities and guarantees may leave out:

(i) loans obtained from the Nationalbank, but not exceeding the amount deposited by the bank on current account with the Nationalbank;

(ii) guarantees which are secured by specific deposits with the bank;

(iii) accountable capital deposits (see below).

In addition, the Minister for Industry may permit liabilities of a quite extraordinary character to be excluded. This power has been used by the Minister in a Decree of May 21, 1976, permitting the exclusion of guarantees by way of guarantee capital supporting certain Danish mortgage institutes, the Ship Credit Fund of Denmark and the Danish Export

Finance Corporation. Similarly, certain export guarantees supported by the Danish Export Credit Council have been granted exemption.

'Net capital' is defined to include paid-up share capital plus reserves (the statutory reserve fund, the securities fluctuation fund (if any) and the revaluation fund). Provisions for specific risks are not included in net capital but are deducted from the appropriate asset item in the balance sheet.

Neither loan capital nor convertible loan capital (until the conversion rights have been exercised) can be included in net capital. There is, however, an alternative type of debt known as 'ansvarlig indskudskapital' (subordinated debt or 'accountable capital deposits') which, under certain conditions, can be considered as net capital for the purpose of calculating the solvency ratio. In order to rank equally with net capital, the subordinated debt must not be repayable on notice of less than five years. Once notice of repayment has been given, only debt due in more than one year is allowed. Even then, this subordinated debt is allowed to be included in the solvency ratio calculation only up to an amount not exceeding 40% of net capital. The other conditions attached to the issue of this type of debt are set out in detail in section 22 of the Act.

Since 1976 the Nationalbank has allowed banks to issue subordinated debt abroad within a limit of 40% of their net capital.

If the monthly or annual statement shows that this solvency ratio requirement is not being complied with, a bank has six months to regularise the position, though this time limit may be shortened or lengthened by the Tilsynet according to the circumstances of each particular case.

The figure of 8% is very much a floor. The Act provides (ss. 38,39) that if the net capital (excluding subordinated debt) of a commercial bank or a savings bank falls below 15% of the bank's total debts and guarantees (as defined above), at least 15% of the profits available each year (after meeting deficits from previous years) must be transferred to the statutory reserve, which forms part of the net capital. Only if net capital is above the target level of 15% of debts and guarantees, are profits freely at the disposal of the bank (subject to the normal requirements of company law).

The statutory reserve fund referred to above is a requirement imposed on all companies. In the case of commercial banks, at least 10% of the profits not used to cover previous years' deficits must be transferred to the statutory reserve fund until this fund amounts to 10% of the share capital. Then at least 5% must be appropriated until the fund amounts to the maximum level of 25% of the share capital. There is, in addition, a requirement that a further portion of profits should be transferred to the fund when a bank's solvency ratio falls below 15%, as described above.

2.9.2 Liquidity Ratios

Section 28 of the Act imposes three separate liquidity requirements on banks:

(i) a bank must hold 'cash in hand that is adequate considering its circumstances'. This includes absolutely secure and liquid current accounts with Danish and foreign banks and Post Office cheque accounts, as well as notes and coins and balances with the central bank. No specific figure is laid down for what is considered adequate. The Tilsynet assesses each bank's returns to decide what is adequate for that bank in the light of its particular circumstances;

(ii) cash in hand (as defined above) plus secure, easily marketable, unpledged securities and "instruments of credit" must equal at least 15% of a bank's liabilities which are repayable on demand or at up to one month's notice; and

(iii) cash in hand must also equal at least 10% of a bank's total liabilities and guarantees.

If these requirements are not met and the position is not rectified within a week, the matter must be reported to the Tilsynet, which will then stipulate a time limit for the requirements to be fulfilled.

2.9.3 Loan Limits

A bank must not lend money to (or give guarantees on behalf of) one customer in excess of 35% of its own net capital (excluding subordinated debt) (s. 23). The same applies to enterprises which are so connected as to form one single risk. The limit can be increased to 50% in any one case on the unanimous recommendation of the management supported by at least two thirds of the members of the board of directors. In such cases notification must be given to the Tilsynet.

The Minister for Industry can lay down rules to the effect that 'particularly secure' claims may be omitted from this calculation (s. 23(2)) and the Tilsynet may allow exemptions from this provision (s. 26).

In making this calculation, the bank must include in its claims on any one enterprise the amount of any shares in that enterprise owned by the bank, or taken as security for a loan or guarantee by the bank.

The Industry Ministry rules on 'particularly secure claims' are set out in Order No. 586 of November 29, 1974. This provides that, in calculating the total of claims on one customer, the bank can exclude claims secured by equivalent deposits with itself, or by pledged deposits with other banks in Denmark; claims guaranteed by the State, a Danish municipality or the Nationalbank; claims guaranteed by another bank in Denmark, provided that they do not exceed 20% of the net capital of the guarantor; claims secured by a mortgage within half of the latest assessed value of the property; claims secured by bonds issued by the Danish public sector, mortgage credit associations or similar institutions, within 75% of the Stock Exchange buying price at any time; and claims on a mortgage credit association consisting of the bank's own holding of its bonds, within 75% of the Stock Exchange buying price at any time.

A bank must not grant or acquire loans on its own shares to a total amount exceeding 10% of the share capital (not the net capital), and such a loan must not exceed 75% of the market value of the shares. All such transactions must be reported to the Tilsynet each month (s. 24(3)).

2.10 MONETARY AND CREDIT CONTROLS

Under the Credit Regulation Act No. 543 of 1973, the Minister for Economic Affairs has power to make regulations applying credit ceilings, special deposit arrangements and selective credit policies, after consulting the Danmarks Nationalbank (Central Bank). These regulations would normally apply only to commercial banks, savings banks, co-operative banks and the Post Office Giro, but they could be extended to cover other credit giving institutions. These are reserve powers which would only be implemented if the Nationalbank was unable to reach a satisfactory voluntary agreement with the financial institutions concerned. Thus far there has been no need to invoke these powers.

2.10.1 Direct Credit Controls

Direct credit controls, which have been in force continuously since 1970, are the primary method of credit control in Denmark. The credit ceilings, which are fixed for each bank (except for those savings and cooperative banks with a working capital - deposits plus net capital - of less than 10 million kroner) are framed in terms of credit commitments rather than credit actually extended. In recent years the permitted annual increases in commitments have been of the order of 10%. Excess lending is normally penalised by a requirement on the banks concerned to place non-interest-bearing deposits with the Nationalbank equivalent to the excess amount for one month.

2.10.2 Selective Credit Controls

Credit ceilings have not generally been employed in a selective manner; intermediary credits to non-profit-making mortgage credit institutions is the only lending category exempt from controls. On a number of occasions the Nationalbank has issued qualitative lending guidance, with the banks being asked to accord lending to industry (in particular, those firms involved in exports) the highest priority. In early 1980 an agreement between the Nationalbank and the banks was reactivated which limited the availability of consumer loans to those customers having previously saved on a regular basis for at least one year.

2.10.3 Regulation of Interest Rates

For an extended period the interest rates of Danish banks have been subject to various controls. Currently the average lending rates of the commercial banks and the savings banks are fixed by agreement with the Nationalbank on an individual bank basis and can only be changed in accordance with changes in the discount rate. In addition the seven largest banks, under the auspices of the monetary authorities, have since February 1978 observed a maximum on the rate of interest payable on special deposits (large demand deposits from local authorities and the corporate sector) of the Nationalbank's discount rate plus 4%.

2.10.4 Central Bank Accommodation

The Nationalbank does not engage in rediscounting but rather lends directly to the banks. Banks may borrow from the Nationalbank without specific security within borrowing limits fixed quarterly as a percentage of each bank's net capital (plus accountable capital deposits considered equivalent to net capital). The borrowing limits apply to the maximum average borrowing per day over the quarter. Since their introduction in May 1975, the borrowing limits have varied between 5% and 40% of banks' net capital. The borrowing limits are normally divided into a (varying) number of tranches with interest charges on an ascending scale (rates in lower tranches being linked to the official discount rate and the rate in the highest tranche to the average yield on mortgage credit bonds).

2.10.5 Reserve Requirements

Currently there are no monetary reserve requirements in force on banks in Denmark. A requirement on banks to hold a proportion of their deposits (or increase in deposits) in balances with the Nationalbank could, however, be applied under the Credit Regulation Act. As a separate measure the Nationalbank, after negotiations with the Government and the banks, introduced a system of special deposits in October 1975 in order to limit the liquidity creation resulting from government deficits. These were repaid to the banks in 1977 and this instrument has not been reintroduced.

2.11 FOREIGN EXCHANGE

2.11.1 Authority to deal in Foreign Exchange

The Nationalbank controls the operation of foreign exchange transactions. By an Executive Order of the Minister for Industry, dated March 12, 1973, the Bank has the power to authorise foreign exchange dealers (most banks, Post Office Giro, Stock Exchange brokers) and kroner depositories for non-residents (Post Office Giro, banks, Stock Exchange brokers, Public Trustee, etc). Authorised kroner depositories who are not authorised foreign exchange dealers and others to whom the Nationalbank has issued a special licence may deal in foreign exchange in the form of cheques, bank notes and coins within specified limits.

2.11.2 Limits on Positions

The net 'commercial' spot foreign position of authorised foreign exchange dealers is subject to limits. Under the rules in force from the spring of 1978 the net foreign 'commercial balances' of banks must in principle not be negative[2] and net commercial claims must not exceed 15% of the bank's equity capital, including accountable capital deposits considered equivalent to net capital, or 2 million kroner, whichever is the larger amount. 'Commercial balances' comprise all foreign currency balances together with the kroner deposits of foreign correspondents, shipowners and insurance companies. Kroner deposits of other non-residents are not included.

The Nationalbank has from time to time allowed banks to exceed the maximum limit stipulated for commercial balances in order to cover forward contracts with customers for delivery of foreign exchange. Under such exemptions foreign currency assets have been allowed to represent up to 60% of a bank's equity capital.

There are no separate controls on the net spot position in individual currencies, though the Tilsynet would be able to warn a bank if it thought, on the basis of that bank's monthly returns, that a position in one currency was imprudently large.

Banks have to give a considerable amount of detailed information to the authorities on their foreign exchange positions and transactions. In the monthly returns, which are on a balance sheet basis, details are required of the spot position and uncovered forward position, separately by currency, above the line; the covered forward position is shown below the line. Banks also have to provide details of all transactions in the past month effected for customers above a limit of 5,000 kroner.

The Tilsynet sent a letter to all authorised banks on June 19, 1975, setting out rules and guidelines for management control of forcign exchange dealings. It is in effect a code of prudent management.

2.12 CREDIT INFORMATION EXCHANGE

There is no credit information exchange or central risks bureau, but if the Tilsynet discovers (for instance, through notification from banks under the provisions described in 2.9.3 above), that a debtor or guarantor has incurred considerable obligations to several financial institutions, the Act gives it power to advise those institutions accordingly (s. 50(5)).

This provision is not often applied. It is not, for instance, usual practice for a bank to make enquiries of the Tilsynet before extending a large credit to a new customer. It would more often be the case that the bank would talk to the customer's other banks.

2.13 DEPOSIT INSURANCE

There is no legal requirement for deposit insurance in Denmark.

2.14 SANCTIONS

2.14.1 Revocation of Authorisation

A bank's licence may be revoked by the Minister for Industry if:

1) the bank no longers meets the conditions on which it was originally granted a licence;

2) the bank is guilty of a major violation of the 1980 Act or of a number of repeated offences;

3) the bank has not undertaken any banking business within 12 months of the date when it was granted a licence;

4) the bank has stopped carrying on any banking business for more than six months;

5) the bank's management do not meet the criteria laid down in section 6(3) of the 1980 Act (see 2.4.3 above).

In addition, under sections 43-44 of the Act, a commercial bank's licence may be revoked if it has lost more than 25% of its share capital (though the Minister for Industry may allow a bank a period of time in which to regularise its affairs). Similarly, if a savings bank's net capital falls below the 8% required by the solvency ratio (see 2.9.1 above) and the position is not rectified within a time limit fixed by the Tilsynet, the Minister for Industry will revoke the savings bank's licence.

If an institution's licence is revoked, its banking business must be wound up immediately. The Tilsynet may report that a bank is unable to meet its obligations, if the Tilsynet believes that disclosure would be in the interest of depositors.

2.14.2 Imposition of Conditions

The Tilsynet may impose any conditions on banks which it feels are necessary to ensure the protection of depositors' funds.

2.14.3 Other Sanctions

Under s.47(d) of the Act, the Tilsynet may file a petition in bankruptcy if a commercial or savings bank becomes insolvent.

2.14.4 Penalties

If the board of directors, management, shareholders' committee (commercial banks only), or auditors fail in their obligations to the Tilsynet under the Act, the Minister for Industry may penalise them by daily or weekly fines (s. 53).

Unless the Penal Code provides for a more severe penalty, a fine or imprisonment is the penalty for infringing any of the reporting or control requirements laid down in the Act and regulations. Fines are imposed by the Minister for Industry.

If directors, general managers, members of the shareholders' committee (commercial banks), auditors, etc. disclose without authorisation information acquired in the course of their duties, they can be fined, provided that the Penal Code does not lay down more severe penalties (s. 54(2)).

If persons connected with a bank give any incorrect or misleading information to the Tilsynet or other public authorities about matters concerning the bank, they are liable to a fine or to imprisonment, provided the Penal Code does not lay down more severe penalties (s. 54(3)). They will be subject to the same penalties if deliberately, or by gross negligence, they give incorrect or misleading information to the general public or the bank's depositors, if they inflict a loss or if they are obviously putting the bank at risk (s. 54(4)).

2.14.5 Appeals

The sanctions are subject to the normal appeals procedure of the Danish legal system.

2.15 FOREIGN BANK BRANCHES

2.15.1 Establishment

Branches of foreign banks are subject to the same registration and authorisation requirements as domestic banks, with the exception that a branch of a commercial or savings bank with its head office in another EEC Member State may obtain authorisation, even though the bank has not been set up in the form of a limited company or an independent mutual institution. Branches of foreign banks are also subject to rules laid down by the Minister for Industry regarding earmarked capital, audit arrangements and any other matters necessary to ensure equality of competition and control with domestic banks.

2.15.2 Earmarked Capital

(i) The registered paid-up capital of a branch must be at least five million kroner (Order No. 571);

(ii) The net capital (paid-up capital, plus reserves, minus any deficit) is reduced by the amount of claims by the branch on its head office and on other companies or enterprises in the same group;

(iii) The net capital must not be reduced to less than the registered branch capital;

(iv) In calculating the liquidity of a branch (see 2.9.2 above), claims on its head office and other companies or enterprises in the same group shall not be considered (notwithstanding stipulated terms of notice) as liquid assets;

(v) In drawing up the statement of debts of a branch (see 2.9.2 above), liabilities to its head office and other companies or enterprises in the same group shall be considered (notwithstanding stipulated terms of notice) as debts due on demand.

2.15.3 Nationality and Competence of Personnel

Foreign bank branches are subject to the same management requirements as domestic banks. (See 2.4.3 above).

An order from the bank's management indicating the power of the local branch managers to grant loans without referring back to the management must be available and must be approved by the Tilsynet.

2.15.4 Restrictions on Business

Branches are not allowed to engage in any business other than banking business (see 2.6.1 above). A branch may conduct business through more than one office, but these are subordinate to the main branch in Denmark.

2.15.5 Representative Offices

There are no legal or other restrictions on the setting up and operation of representative offices. Since these do not carry out banking business, they are not controlled by the Tilsynet under the Act.

2.16 FOREIGN BANK SUBSIDIARIES

2.16.1 Local ownership

There are no requirements regarding the nationality of shareholders of Danish subsidiaries of foreign banks. Foreign-owned banks are treated in exactly the same way as Danish banks and are subject to the same rules and regulations, including the minimum capital requirements.

2.16.2 Nationality of Directors

Since subsidiaries of foreign banks are treated in exactly the same way as Danish banks, they are subject to the same residence (see 2.4.3 above) provisions.

2.16.3 Guarantees from Parent Institution

There is no requirement, in the Act or in practice, for such a guarantee.

2.17 BANKING ASSOCIATIONS

2.17.1 Membership

Almost all the commercial banks are members of the Danske Bankforening (Danish Bankers Association). Membership is open to all commercial banks (of which there were 78 in June 1980), including branches of foreign banks (of which there were 4 in 1980), but it is not compulsory. All four branches are in fact members. Most of the 169 savings banks are members of the Danmarks Sparekasseforening (Danish Savings Banks Association).

2.17.2 Relations with Supervisory Authorities

Both the organisations act as representative bodies for the banking industry as a whole in discussions with the Nationalbank, the Tilsynet and the Minister of Industry, and in any other matters of common interest.

Agreements on monetary policy are usually reached between the Nationalbank and the Associations, acting on behalf of all their members (cf. 2.10 above). The Associations do not play any part in the supervisory process.

2.18 BACKGROUND SOURCES

1. Aufricht, H.: Central Banking Legislation, Vol. II: Europe, (International Monetary Fund, Washington, D.C.), (1967).
2. Banking Federation of the European Community: Monetary Policy and the Banking System in the Countries of the European Community (Brussels) (1980).
3. Danish Bankers Association: The Danish Banking System 1979.
4. Danmarks Nationalbank: Annual Reports and Monetary Reviews.
5. Danmarks Nationalbank: Instruments of Monetary and Foreign Exchange Policy in Denmark (1979).
6. Elstob, M. (Ed): Banking Structures and Sources of Finance in the European Community, (Banker Research Unit, London) (1979).
7. IBRO: Banking Ratios in the EEC (a study commissioned by the EEC Commission from the Inter-Bank Research Organisation, 1979).
8 International Monetary Fund: Annual Report on Exchange Arrangements and Exchange Restrictions, (Washington, D.C.), (1979).

NOTES

1   Unless otherwise specified, all references to sections relate to sections of this Act, which will be referred to henceforth as 'the Act'.
2   A bank which has granted loans to residents in foreign exchange to finance Danish foreign trade may, however, owe a net foreign debt of up to 5% of its equity capital or 3 million kroner, whichever is the larger amount.

CHAPTER 3

FRANCE

3.1 INSTITUTIONS COVERED

Banks are defined as 'those enterprises or institutions whose customary business (profession habituelle) is to receive from the public, in the form of deposits or otherwise, funds which they employ for their own account, in discount, credit or financial transactions'.[1] 'Funds received from the public' are funds received in any form whatever by an enterprise or a person from or for the account of a third party, and subject to repayment, with the exception of funds raised to form or increase the capital of an enterprise, whatever the form of the securities issued (including the issue of convertible bonds); funds received from associated persons or partners; funds received by the sale *en pension* to, or the discount of assets with, a banker; and deposits from employees amounting to not more than 10% of the capital. Funds raised by the issue of non-convertible bonds or loans are considered as funds received from the public.[2]

Any institution other than a bank or a savings bank is prohibited from accepting from the public sight deposits or time deposits due in not more than two years.

Banks are divided into three categories according to criteria set out in Article 5 of the Nationalisation Law of 1945, as amended.[3] There are restrictions, mentioned in 3.6 below, on the business the different categories may undertake.

(i) deposit banks (*banques de dépôt*) - 'those whose principal activity consists of effecting credit transactions and of receiving from the public sight and term deposits;'

(ii) *banques d'affaires* - 'those whose principal activity is, in addition to the extension of credits, the holding and the management of participations in companies which are in existence or being formed;'

(iii) long and medium-term credit banks - 'those whose principal activity consists of opening credits for a term of at least two years.'

These types of bank are known as 'registered banks.' Any institution whose customary business is to carry out discount, credit or financial transactions, but does not receive funds from the public, is defined as a financial institution (*établissement financier*) and is subject partly to banking laws and partly to separate laws. They are not dealt with in this study.

The nationalised banks (Crédit Lyonnais, Banque Nationale de Paris, Société Générale) are generally subject to the same constraints on management, ratios, etc., as deposit banks in the private sector, though they are directly controlled by a different decree.[4]

Banks or institutions with a special legal status (banques populaires, Caisses de Crédit Agricole, Caisse Centrale de Crédit Cooperatif, Caisses de Crédit Mutuel) are in principle not subject to the basic banking laws and are not covered here, even though they may meet the definition of a bank set out above. Thus the provisions of Decree No. 46-1247 of May 28, 1946, on the basic rules on the functioning of private sector banks, may, by order of the Minister for Finance and of other relevant departments, be extended to those banks or institutions with a special legal status (other than the nationalised banks) (Art.1).

The public or semi-public credit institutions (e.g., Crédit National, Crédit Foncier de France) are not subject to the banking laws either. Finally, the savings institutions (Caisses d'Epargne) are also excluded: they are governed by separate laws and have in any case up until recently not been covered by the definition of a bank set out above (because they did not have any credit business for their own account).

3.2 BASIC LAWS

The basic laws and amendments are as follows:-

(i) Law No. 2532 of June 13, 1941, on the regulation and organisation of the banking profession;

(ii) Law No. 45-015 of December 2, 1945, on the nationalisation of the Banque de France and the large banks and on the organisation of credit;

(iii) Law No. 46-1071 of May 17, 1946, on the organisation of credit in France;

(iv) Decree No. 46-1246 of May 28, 1946, on the basic rules on the functioning of the nationalised deposit banks;

(v) Decree No. 46-1247 of May 28, 1946, on the basic rules on the functioning of the private sector banks;

(vi) Decree No. 66-81 of January 25, 1966, changing certain points on the regulation of banks;

(vii) Law No. 66-455 of July 2, 1966, on undertakings carrying out leasing operations;

(viii) Decree No. 72-103 of February 4, 1972, amending Law No. 2532 of June 13, 1941;

(ix) Law No. 73-7 of January 3, 1973, on the Banque de France;

(x) Law No. 75-601 of July 10, 1975, modifying the nationality requirements for the banking profession.

(xi) Decree of November 13, 1978, on the minimum capital of banks;

(xii) Decree No. 79-561 of July 5, 1979, introducing rules for covering and spreading risks.

3.3 SUPERVISORY SYSTEM

3.3.1 Supervisory Authority

The Commission de Contrôle des Banques (Banking Control Commission) is responsible for overseeing the application of the regulations and controls on the banking profession in France and in French overseas territories and departments. It was set up in 1941[5] and has five members - the Governor of the Banque de France (Chairman), the Chairman of the Finance Section of the Conseil d'Etat, the Director of the Treasury in the Finance Ministry, a representative of the banks nominated by the Association Française des Banques (AFB) and appointed by a decree of the Minister for Finance, and a representative of bank staff nominated by the most representative workers' organisation and appointed by a decree of the Minister for Finance. The secretariat and staff of the Commission are seconded from the Banque de France. In legal terms the Commission is an office of the State (un service de l'Etat) and not an office of the Banque de France.

The Commission de Contrôle des Banques is responsible for overseeing the application of the regulations and controls on the banking industry. Its powers are divided into three separate categories - regulation, administration and jurisdiction. They are summarised below, and set out in more detail elsewhere in this study.

(i) It can make regulations setting out the rules of good management to be followed, particularly with regard to balance sheet ratios designed to protect depositors; and it can set out the rules for applying any decisions on credit policy taken by the monetary authorities. These regulations and rules apply to specified categories of banks, rather than to individual banks.

(ii) It can oversee the application of these regulations and rules by examining regular reports and statistical returns which banks are required to make, and then, if necessary, by arranging for on the spot inspections of banks.

(iii) If these examinations and inspections disclose serious irregularities, the Commission can impose sanctions on the offending bank.

Banks are prohibited from making any mention in their correspondence or in their publicity of the powers exercised over them by the Commission and the Conseil National du Crédit (CNC): the intention is to avoid any public suggestion, even implicit, that a bank's liabilities are in any way guaranteed by either body.[6]

The costs of the Commission are met partly by a levy on the banking industry; the balance is paid by the Banque de France.

The business of the *banques d'affaires* is supervised by a Commissaire du Gouvernement. He is appointed by the Minister for Finance, on the recommendation of the CNC, to every *banque d'affaires* constituted in the form of a *société par actions* (see 3.4.1 below) and whose balance sheet total plus contingent liabilities is at least 20 million francs. The Commissaire has a power of veto on any decisions of the bank which seem to him to be contrary to the national interest, though this power is very rarely, if every exercised. The post is of more value as providing an informal channel of communication between the Minister for Finance and the *banques d'affaires*.[7]

3.3.2 Outline of system

The system of banking authorisation operates as follows:

Any bank must, before it can carry on operations in accordance with the banking laws, be registered on a list of banks maintained by the Conseil National du Crédit. This list is published in the *Journal Officiel*. This requirement applies equally to all foreign banks.

Every bank applying for registration must specify the category of bank (see 3.1 above) under which it seeks registration. If a bank wishes to change from one category to another, it must make a fresh application.

Applications for registration have to be forwarded by the Association Française des Banques (see 3.17 below), which must give its own opinion of the application. The applicant will be registered if it meets the definition of a bank (see 3.1 above), if it is established in the correct legal form (see 3.4.1 below), if its management is reputable and not otherwise disqualified (see 3.4.3 below), if it has adequate capital (see 3.4.2 below) and if the CNC considers that the request for registration is justified by general and local economic needs (see 3.4.5 below).[8] This last requirement, being relatively subjective in nature, gives the CNC a considerable degree of discretion in deciding whether to register an applicant.

The prior authorisation of the Conseil National du Crédit must be obtained before a registered bank can change its legal form (see 3.4.1 below); its name or description (see 3.7. below); the area in which its registered office is located; the nature of the transactions it carries out (where these are limited by the bank's registration in one particular category - see 3.1 above and 3.6 below); the ownership of substantial shareholdings (see 3.6.2 below); and its directors or partners, (see 3.4.3 below).

Authorisation is implicitly given if no objection has been received within three months of the date when the application is lodged with the CNC.

Certain other changes effected by a bank must be notified to the CNC (through the AFB) within one month. These include any change in the bank's capital, the address of its registered office or administrative head office, the names of its senior management, directors, etc. and any changes in its articles or statutes (CNC General Decision 68-01). This information also has to be given to the Commission de Contrôle des Banques.

An appeal against a decision of the Conseil National du Crédit concerning the registration or striking off of banks, the opening or closing of branches (see 3.5.1 below), etc., may be made to the Commission de Contrôle des Banques within eight days of notification of the decision. Action on the decision is suspended until the Commission has issued its ruling, which must be done within 30 days. Appeals against decisions of the Commission may be made to a Tribunal Administratif only on the grounds of abuse of power (excès de pouvoir). Appeals from the decisions of the Tribunal may be made to the Conseil d'Etat.

3.3.3 Returns to Supervisory Body

Every listed bank must send regular documentary evidence of its assets and liabilities to the Secretariat of the Commission de Contrôle des Banques, with other information needed to ensure that the rules are respected, or as required by the monetary authorities.

They must also send:

(i) interim accounts at the end of every six-month period;

(ii) balance sheets, profit and loss accounts and ancillary statements at the end of every accounting year.

As a general rule banks must submit returns every quarter to the Commission de Contrôle des Banques, but the the larger banks are required to submit some returns every month.

3.3.4 Auditing requirements

The accounting rules of the Commission de Contrôle des Banques which came into force on January 1, 1978 include an 'accounting plan' and layouts for the periodic statements and accounts to be drawn up by the banks.

Each bank is required to appoint one or more auditors from a special list. These auditors are required to countersign the annual accounts of the bank before its submission to the Commission de Contrôle des Banques.[9] The duties of the auditors are set out in the Company Law 66-537 of July 24, 1966, Articles 218-235.

3.3.5 Inspection

The Commission de Contrôle des Banques is entitled to arrange for inspectors, assisted by other officials of the Banque de France, to make on-the-spot inspections of banks.[10] Inspection must come after, and be based on the regular returns made by banks to the Commission (see 3.3.3 above). In practice, the Banque de France places a number of inspectors and other officials permanently at the disposal of the Commission.

The Commission also verifies, on behalf of the Banque de France, the monetary policy returns made by banks: it is concerned to ensure that all credits are correctly recorded, and that the appropriate non-interest-earning deposits have been made at the Banque de France.

There are no rules requiring regular on-the-spot inspections but in practice the Commission inspects about 60 banks each year, which means that each bank is inspected about once every five or six years. Inspection can of course be very much more frequent if required.

3.4 CRITERIA FOR AUTHORISATION

3.4.1 Legal Form

A body which intends to carry on banking business must be set up as:

(i) A *société en nom collectif* (a general partnership);

(ii) A *société en commandite simple* (a limited partnership);

(iii) A *société en commandite par actions* (a limited partnership with shares whose directors are personally liable for the company's debts); or

(iv) A *société anonyme à capital fixe* (a public limited company with fixed capital).[11]

Sole proprietorships (affaires personnelles) are no longer allowed, following the implementation of EEC Directive 77/780 of December 12, 1977.[12]

If a registered bank wishes to change its legal form, it has to obtain the prior authorisation of the Conseil National du Crédit. The application is submitted through the Association Française des Banques, which has itself to give an opinion on the application (see also 3.1 above) (CNC General Decision 68-01).

3.4.2 Minimum Capital

Every bank must possess an amount of capital which is at least equal to a sum fixed by a Decree made by the Minister of Finance.

The minimum capital may be fixed at a different amount depending on whether banks are formed as *sociétés par actions* (cf. 3.4.1 above) or in a different form, whether they are classified as *banques d'affaires* or as other banks (cf. 3.1 above), and whether the number of their permanent branches is more than two. Account may also be taken in fixing the minimum capital of the total of the balance sheet, as shown at the end of the last two financial years.

The minimum capital must be fully paid up, within a time limit set by the Commission de Contrôle des Banques. The Commission has the right to require every bank to prove that its assets exceed by an amount equal to its minimum capital its liabilities to third parties.[13]

The minimum capital currently required is set out in Table A. The figures represent an increase of 50% over the minimum capital figures in force before January 1, 1980, and apply to new establishments or to establishments whose legal status, management or classification have changed. Those approved before January 1, 1980, have until December 31, 1982, to comply with the new figures.

When the total of the balance sheet of a bank exceeds 600 million francs for the second consecutive year, the bank has 18 months from the second balance sheet date to raise its capital to the minimum shown.

Every bank taking the form of a *société par actions* (see 3.4.1 above) is required under company law (in common with all non-banking *sociétés par actions*) to maintain a statutory reserve (réserve légale). This is created by transferring a minimum of 5% of the net profits after tax each year, until the reserve attains the maximum level of 10% of the company's capital.

3.4.3 Management Qualifications

There are no explicit requirements as to the professional qualifications of the management of an applicant bank, but when an application for registration as a bank is received from a *société en nom collectif* or *société en commandite* (see 3.4.1 above), the reputation and the personal standing of each of the partners or directors is scrutinised before the CNC will effect the registration. If a bank set up in one of these forms wishes to change a partner or director, it has to seek the prior authorisation of the CNC. The application is forwarded through the Association Française des Banques (see below 3.17), which has to give its opinion on it (see also 3.3.2 above). When a bank in any other legal form changes its directors or senior managers, it has to inform the CNC within one month of the event (CNC General Decision 68-01).

No one may regularly take part in the management of a bank, nor sign for a bank, if he has been convicted of certain criminal offences (including theft, etc.); if he is an undischarged bankrupt; if he is not a French national or a national of another EEC Member State (though the Minister of Finance

TABLE A

MINIMUM CAPITAL REQUIREMENT FOR A BANK*

Number of Permanent Places of Business		Deposit Bank, and Long and Medium-Term Credit Bank		Banque d'Affaires	
		1	2	1	2
Less than Three	A	F7,500,000	F3,000,000	F30,000,000	F15,000,000
	B	F15,000,000	F6,000,000	F60,000,000	F30,000,000
Three or more	A	F15,000,000	F6,000,000	F60,000,000	F30,000,000
	B	F30,000,000	F12,000,000	F120,000,000	F60,000,000

KEY

1. In the form of a company or partnership with share capital (société par actions).
2. In any other legal form.
A With a balance sheet total of not more than 600 million francs.
B With a balance sheet total of more than 600 million francs at the end of each of the last two financial years.

* Decree of November 13, 1978

may authorise individual derogations from this requirement); or if he was, as a manager or as an administrator, responsible for the failure of a company.[14]

No one may without the express approval of the Conseil National du Crédit simultaneously hold a managerial post both in a bank and in an enterprise in which the bank holds a capital participation.[15] (It is understood, however, that in practice this rule is not enforced).

There are strict rules prohibiting bank staff and management from obtaining any employment outside the bank, though exceptions can be made.[16]

3.4.4 Management Plans

There is no explicit legal requirement for an applicant for banking registration to disclose its plans. These are, however, required in order to satisfy the Conseil National du Crédit that there is a general and local economic need for the bank - see 3.4.5 below. No set form of plan is specified: the CNC merely needs to know the bank's targets, and the means of financing those targets.

3.4.5 Other Requirements

A bank can only be registered on the list of banks if the Conseil National du Crédit considers that the application is justified by general and local economic needs.[17] This requirement, being relatively subjective in nature, gives the CNC a considerable degree of discretion in deciding whether to register an applicant. This can, for instance, be taken as far as an assessment of the professional qualifications of the management: if they are not properly qualified, they will not be able to benefit the economy. In practice, however, this is rarely used as a reason for refusing an application.

An application for registration must be accompanied by the opinion of the Association Française des Banques when the application is forwarded by the latter to the CNC.[18]

3.5 BRANCHES

3.5.1 Restrictions on Branching in France

A bank must give prior notice to the Conseil National du Crédit (through the Banque de France) of its intention to open, close, assign, transfer or change any branch. The bank must specify whether the new branch is open permanently (at least five days a week all the year round) or not, whether the hours of business have been reduced and, in the case of branches which are not permanently open, details of the days and times when they are open for business.

Every year each bank has to provide the Commission de Contrôle des Banques with a full list of all its branches, both inside and outside France.

When a bank has duly notified the CNC of its intentions and has received an acknowledgement from the Banque de France, it may go ahead with its decision. If no acknowledgement has been received from the Banque de France within one month of the notification, the bank may implement its decision provided that it already has at least one permanent branch in the geographical area in question. By 'geographical area' is meant Metropolitan France, the Principality of Monaco, the overseas territories as a whole and each overseas department taken separately.

The prior authorisation of the CNC is required before a bank can open a branch in a geographical area where it does not yet have a permanent place of business. Applications from banks established in the overseas departments or territories are submitted through the appropriate issuing authority.

3.5.2 Branching and Operations in Other Countries

An approved bank with its head office in France does not require the prior authorisation of the CNC before it can establish a branch abroad. These branches will, however, be subject to any exchange control restrictions, under which authorisation is required for investments abroad by French residents.

3.6 RESTRICTIONS ON BUSINESS

3.6.1 Restrictions on types of business

Banks are prohibited from taking part on a regular basis (habituellement) in an industry or a trade which has no connection with banking business. Specific derogations may, however, be granted by the Commission de Contrôle des Banques.

Activities which can be regarded as a legitimate part of banking business are those involved in the receipt from the public, in the form of deposits or otherwise, of funds which the banks employ for their own account, in discount, credit or financial transactions.[19]

This prohibition applies to those activities undertaken directly by a bank, rather than through a subsidiary. There are, however, separate restrictions, set out in 3.6.3 below, on the extent of any bank's holding of participations in non-banking institutions.

A deposit bank (one whose principal activity consists of granting and receiving sight and term deposits from the public) is not allowed to invest its sight deposits, or its time deposits due in less than two years, in property. Specific and temporary derogations may be granted by the Commission de Contrôle des Banques for both of these restrictions.[20]

A deposit bank which is principally engaged in operating on the money market may only accept deposits from the public up to a limit fixed in relation to the bank's own resources by the Conseil National du Crédit.[21] This limit was fixed by Decision 60-01 of the CNC, as the total of the bank's capital and reserves.

A long and medium-term credit bank (one whose principal activity consists of opening credits for a term of at least two years) may not, without the authorisation of the Commission de Contrôle des Banques, accept deposits due in less than two years.

3.6.2 Loans to directors

Any credits or advances, including the issue of a guarantee, by a bank in the form of a *société par actions* (see 3.4.1 above) to one of its directors or managers are governed by Law 66-537 of July 24, 1966, on Commercial Companies (Arts. 101-106 and 143-148). Broadly, this permits a bank to make such an advance in the course of its current operations conducted under normal conditions. Any special advance to a director or manager is strictly prohibited.[22]

If a bank takes a form other than that of a *société par actions*, the agreements or contracts it can make with 'connected persons' are strictly controlled. A 'connected person' is someone responsible for the management of the bank, and also any enterprise with which he is in any way connected. Agreements, including advances and credits, made in the course of the bank's current operations conducted under normal conditions are quite permissible. Any other agreement has to be reported by the bank to its auditors (see 3.3.4 above), and by them to the Commission de Contrôle des Banques at regular intervals.[23]

3.6.3 Equity Participations

A deposit bank (see 3.6.1 above) may not hold more than 20% of the capital of any enterprise other than a bank, a financial institution or a company necessary for its business and responsible for the management either of a property portfolio (patrimoine immobilier) or of technical or research services relating to the banking profession. In addition, the total of all participations in enterprises other than banks, etc., including firm subscriptions to take up shares on issue, may not exceed the total of the bank's own resources (as defined in 3.9 below). Any breach of these limits, as well as the use of sight deposits or of time deposits due in less than two years to acquire participations or property investments, is forbidden, though the Commission de Contrôle des Banques may authorise a specific and temporary derogation.[24]

A *banque d'affaires* (see 3.1 above) may not invest its sight deposits or term deposits due in less than two years in participations.[25] These banks are, however, allowed to hold 100% of the share capital of a company.

A long and medium term credit bank (see 3.1 above) is subject to the same controls as a deposit bank (see 3.1 above) on its holding of participations, though again the Commission may authorise a specific and temporary derogation.[26]

Each bank has to provide the Commission de Contrôle des Banques, along with its annual accounts and balance sheet, with a full list of all the securities it holds. This includes investments, participations and subsidiaries. The detail required includes the book and market value of the securities, their number and the percentage they represent of the capital of the issuing company (when that percentage is 5% or more).

Under Law 73-8 of January 4, 1973, as implemented by Decree 73-604, which provides for the sale of up to 25% of the shares of the nationalised banks to their staff and to certain institutional investors (5% may be sold and the remainder distributed by profit-sharing schemes), no single individual shareholder is allowed to acquire more than 500 shares in one of these banks; no single corporate shareholder, with the exception of the Caisse des Dépôts, may acquire more than 1% of the capital. The Caisse des Dépôts may acquire up to 3%.

Apart from this, there are no restrictions on the holding by one bank of a participation in another bank.

3.6.4 Mergers

The Conseil National du Crédit is empowered to approve plans for mergers between banks, on the basis of general or local economic needs, or relevance to individual banks.[27] The CNC has also, in theory, the power to impose a merger between two or more banks, if justified by general or local economic needs. In practice, this power has never been invoked.

The prior authorisation of the CNC is needed for any change in the holding of a bank's shares (or partnership capital) which will have the effect either of giving control of the bank, directly or indirectly, to one of the partners or shareholders, or to a group of partners or shareholders acting together; or of giving to any one of the partners or shareholders a stake of

20% of the bank's capital, or a stake whose cost price exceeds 10 million francs. Applications for authorisation have to be made through the Association Française des Banques (see 3.17 below) which must attach its own opinion on the application (CNC General Decision 68-01). Authorisation is deemed to be given after three months have elapsed from the time of the original application.

3.7 BANKING NAMES AND DESCRIPTIONS

No institution which is not registered on the list of banks may make use of the words 'bank', 'banker' or 'credit institution' in its name or description, or in its publicity, nor may it make use of them in any way whatever in its business.[28] This applies equally to foreign banks in France.

The names and descriptions used by banks are strictly controlled by the Conseil National du Crédit, so as to avoid any public confusion. Thus if a registered bank wishes to change its name or description, it has to seek the prior authorisation of the CNC: its application is submitted through the Association Française des Banques, which has itself to give an opinion on the application (CNC General Decision 68-01).

A bank may only use a commercial description in relation to its own business if the description has been registered along with the bank's name, and if the description is only used in a phrase following the name (CNC General Decision of November 20, 1941).

3.8 ADVERTISING

Banks are prohibited from making any mention in their correspondence or in their publicity of the powers exercised over them by the Conseil National du Crédit or the Commission de Contrôle des Banques.[29] The intention appears to be to avoid any public suggestion, even implicit, that a bank's liabilities are in any way guaranteed by the CNC or the Commission.

There are no other controls on the content of banks' advertisements.

All banks are required to keep a separate detailed account of all their publicity expenses, as well as of all payments and subventions and of all free benefits which they have granted to natural or legal persons. This account must be submitted to the Commission de Contrôle des Banques.[30]

3.9 SOLVENCY AND LIQUIDITY

3.9.1 Solvency Ratios

Banks must observe the solvency rules laid down by Decree No. 79-561 of July 5, 1979, and CNC General Decision No. 79-561 of April 24, 1979. These rules stipulate that banks must maintain a ratio of net own funds to risk assets above a certain minimum percentage. The risk assets included in the ratio calculation are loans to customers and financial intermediaries, leased assets, securities and *engagements par signature*. Different weightings are given to the various types of asset, ranging from 100% for loans to customers down, for example, to 75% for officially quoted securities, 5% for loans to financial intermediaries and to 2.5% for *engagements par signature* in favour of financial intermediaries. Guarantees received from the French Government and from certain public or semi-public bodies may be deducted from total risk assets.

For the purpose of calculating the solvency ratio, net own funds are defined to include capital, reserves, certain provisions, profits carried forward and subordinated debt (emprunts subordonnés ou participatifs created by Law No. 78-741 of July 13, 1978). From this total are subtracted any unpaid capital, losses carried forward, formation expenses, all intangible assets (except the right of leasehold) and any assets that represent the own funds or assimilated funds of banks subject to the same rules in France or of banks with their registered office in a foreign country.

Provisions may or may not be included in own funds, depending on how they are classified in the accounting regulations of the Commission de Contrôle des Banques and on their treatment for tax purposes. The accounting rules distinguish between those provisions shown as liabilities in the balance sheet and those deducted from corresponding assets. Deductible provisions include those for bad debts and those for the depreciation of share portfolios and for capital expenditure items. Only provisions recorded as liabilities may be included in own funds.

Provisions constituted out of taxed profits, which are regarded as reserves, are usually included in own funds. Tax-free provisions fall into two categories: special provisions exempt from tax by virtue of tax rules are included in own funds unless they relate to actual contingencies; other tax-free provisions are intended in principle to cover specific contingencies and are never included in own funds.

The risk asset cover rule is experimental and the new provisions will apply initially for a trial period lasting until June 30, 1982. Banks which showed a ratio of net own funds to risk assets of less than 5% on January 2, 1979, must show by June 30, 1982, that the percentage of the increase of net own funds related to the increase of their risk assets exceeds their covering ratio on January 2, 1979; by at least one percentage point, if the covering ratio was less than 3%; by at least half the difference between the covering ratio and 5%, if it was between 3% and 5%. This ratio may be calculated on the basis of consolidated figures for establishments belonging to the same group which requests such an arrangement.

3.9.2 Liquidity Ratios

The Commission de Contrôle des Banques is empowered by virtue of two decrees (No. 46-1246 and No. 46-1247) of May 28, 1946, to lay down rules that banks must observe in their management. Under these powers it has introduced a liquidity ratio and a ratio covering medium and long-term transactions.

The liquidity ratio (Rapport de liquidité) is set out in the Commission's Instruction No. 77-02-A of December 16, 1977. It applies to the activities in Metropolitan France of *banques de depôts* and *banques d'affaires*. It relates liquid and realisable assets to very short-term liabilities. Liquid and realisable assets comprise immediately cashable assets (cash, balances with the Banque de France etc.), claims on other financial intermediaries maturing within three months, any credits to customers eligible for rediscounting by the Banque de France, non-realisable claims refinanced by the bank with less than three months to run and various marketable securities.

The short-term liabilities against which these assets must be held comprise liabilities at sight and due within three months. In certain circumstances, the unused portion of credits granted by other banks established in France may be deducted from these liabilities if at least one year's notice must be given for repayment.

Banks must at all times hold liquid and realisable assets equal to at least 60% of their short-term liabilities. When foreign currency assets or liabilities make up more than 10% of a bank's balance sheet, the ratio is calculated separately for French franc items and for foreign currency items. In that case, the 60% minimum applies only to the French franc ratio. The foreign currency liquidity ratio is monitored and the Commission reserves the right to make recommendations to banks about its level. Where foreign currency-denominated assets or liabilities make up less than 10% of a bank's balance sheet, the ratio is calculated only once for French franc and foreign currency items combined.

The *coefficient d'opérations à moyen et long terme* is set out in the Commission's Instruction No. 77-03-A of December 16, 1977, and covers the activities in Metropolitan France of all registered banks. It is the ratio between, on the one hand, the total of:

medium-term credits that are not eligible for rediscounting by the

Banque de France and long-term credits and loans to financial intermediaries for an initial period of over two years

and, on the other hand:

the sum of own funds and savings resources (savings deposits and term deposits of over three months' maturity).

When more than 10% of the total assets or liabilities of a bank are denominated in foreign currency, the bank must calculate one coefficient for transactions in French francs and another for all transactions, whatever the currency.

If a bank's medium and long-term assets exceed its savings resources and own resources by a factor of more than three, then the bank must meet an alternative liquidity rule. This stipulates that 80% of the total of the following:

medium-term credits that are not eligible for rediscounting by the Banque de France, long-term credits and loans to other financial intermediaries

is covered by:

customers' deposits falling due in not less than three months, own funds and loans from other financial intermediaries falling due in not less than two years.

The Commission may allow the unused portion of standby or refinance facilities with remaining maturity longer than two years to be included in the calculation described above.

3.9.3 Loan limits

Banks must observe the rules on risk concentration laid down in Decree No. 79-561 of July 5, 1979, and in the General Decision No. 79-07 of the CNC of July 6, 1979.

These rules require, first, that no single customer may account for a risk equal to more than 75% of net own funds of a bank. However, this rule does not apply when the risk amounts to 5% or less of the bank's total exposure to its customers as a whole and to 50% or less of the customer's bank debts. Secondly, the sum of all the individual risks each amounting to over 25% of net own funds cannot be more than 10 times the amount of net own funds.

These rules apply only to risks with customers and not to those with financial intermediaries. Risks guaranteed by other financial intermediaries, the central government and certain public and semi-public bodies are deducted from the total in the calculation of risks. Customers with financial links may be regarded as a single risk for the purpose of these calculations.

A bank which provides building construction guarantees may not give a guarantee amounting to more than half the total of its capital and reserves.

Moreover, the sum of all such guarantees granted by a bank may not exceed 20 times its capital and reserves.

3.10 MONETARY AND CREDIT CONTROLS

The Conseil National du Crédit, which was established in 1945,[31] has wide powers in all matters relating to credit in the national economy. Although in principle the Banque de France is purely the executive agent of the CNC, in practice it plays a central role in the formulation and implementation of monetary policy; the focal position of the Banque de France is reflected in the fact that the Governor is normally the acting chairman of the CNC. Considerable legal powers are available to the Banque de France when it acts on behalf of the CNC but normally it prefers to act informally, an approach which is facilitated by the relatively concentrated nature of the banking system.

3.10.1 Direct Credit Controls

For an extended period considerable weight has been placed on direct credit controls. Most recently the system of 'supplementary reserves' has been in operation since 1973. This involves those institutions, whose lending exceeds the norms laid down being required to place non-interest-earning reserves at the Banque de France. The ratio for these reserves increases progressively with the amount of the excess and applies to the total outstanding credit subject to controls. The norms, which are differentiated according to the size of institutions, are fixed for six-monthly periods. Lending matched by increases in own funds and bond issues is excluded from ceiling controls and banks may carry forward unused potential credit from one six-monthly period to the next. Ceilings are applied in a highly selective manner with a variety of lending categories (e.g. export credits, subsidised housing credits and certain investment credits) benefitting from a more favourable reserve requirement.

3.10.2 Selective Credit Controls

Those credit categories are also outside the scope of the system of reserve requirements on advances (see 3.10.5 below). There are also selective elements in the Banque de France's refinancing policy - in particular certain types of export credits are rediscounted at special rates. In addition banks in France are subject to a portfolio restriction which obliges them to invest at least 5% of deposits in medium-term credits refinanceable at the Banque de France and specified bonds.

3.10.3 Regulation of Interest Rates

Currently the rates that banks may pay on deposits of less than 100,000 francs and under one year maturity are subject to official regulation. Further, banks are forbidden from paying interest on the sight deposits of individuals and non-financial companies.

3.10.4 Central Bank Accommodation

The main method of accommodation in France is market intervention rather than rediscounting. The Banque de France continues, however, to rediscount medium-term export credits to non-EEC countries and this form of accommodation has grown significantly in recent years. Market intervention takes the form of outright purchases of securities or market paper and the granting of 'pension' (purchase and resale) facilities on a day-to-day basis for maturities up to six months; pension facilities are normally made available for bills or the medium-term certificates issued by the Crédit Foncier and the Crédit National.

3.10.5 Reserve Requirements

Reserve requirements, both on banks' liabilities and advances, are in operation and the specification of these measures is subject to periodic modification. Currently banks must maintain 4% of residents' sight deposits in non-interest-earning balances at the Banque de France and the present reserve ratio on advances is 0.5%; the maximum reserve ratio against liabilities and advances authorised by the CNC is 50%. As noted in 3.10.2 above, banks are also subject to a requirement to invest in medium-term credits and specified bonds.

3.11 FOREIGN EXCHANGE

3.11.1 Authority to Deal in Foreign Exchange

Foreign exchange operations may only be carried out by authorised agents ('intermédiaires agréés') on the Ministry of Finance list: in practice only banks are so authorised. The exchange control system is administered by the Minister, who delegates certain powers of approval to the Treasury Directorate, the Banque de France, the Customs Service and the Insurance Directorate, and authorises banks with the status of approved intermediary to carry out certain transfers on their own initiative. The Customs Service has the power to police rigorously the use of these delegated powers.

3.11.2 Limits on Positions

By Decree 68-1022 of December 1968, the Minister for Finance delegated power to the Banque de France to regulate the position in foreign currencies and in francs of French banks against non-residents. This power can be used to restrain both an outflow and an inflow of currency. As at present applied, it prohibits the purchase by banks of foreign currencies on the market for the purpose of increasing their uncovered position beyond the level of September 2, 1968. For banks founded after that date, the reference level is set by the Banque de France. There are no controls on banks' covered positions.

Regular returns have to be made to the Banque de France - weekly for the large banks, monthly for other banks - setting out in detail the operations carried out since the previous report, and the closing position, both globally and by currency.

There are two other related requirements, as follows:

(i) Additional reserve requirements may be imposed against deposit liabilities to non-residents;

(ii) Banks may be prohibited from paying interest on non-resident accounts.

3.12 CREDIT INFORMATION EXCHANGE

Following General Decision No. 67-07 of June 28, 1967, of the CNC, the Banque de France is responsible for the Central Risks Service - the compilation of banking risks and credits, leasing operations and social security contributions or family allowances owed by enterprises.

The collection of information is carried out by the Central Risks Service with the object of:

(1) enabling banks to assess their customers' obligations to the banking industry as a whole;

(2) supplying the CNC and the Banque de France with information about changes in the supply of credit and the financial position of enterprises.

Declarations are made monthly or quarterly, depending on the nature of the risk. They cover all credits outstanding in excess of a certain amount (set at 350,000 francs from January 1, 1980). All facilities granted by the same branch of an institution are aggregated for this purpose. At the end of each compilation exercise, all banks reporting credit granted to a named recipient receive notification of the total credit granted to this receipient. Banks making declarations may also request the total results for branches of activity or geographical areas.

In certain circumstances, banks must inform the Banque de France of incidents arising in connection with the payment of bills of exchange; they then receive a statement summarising the incidents reported by all banks.

They must also inform the Banque de France of cheques that are not honoured; this information is recorded in a central file that banks must consult before delivering a cheque book to a new customer.

3.13 DEPOSIT INSURANCE

There is no legal requirement for a bank to participate in a deposit insurance scheme. However, the banking industry is considering the introduction of such a scheme.

3.14 SANCTIONS

3.14.1 Revocation of Authorisation

If the Commission de Contrôle des Banques establishes that a bank has infringed any banking laws or regulations, it may remove the institution from the list of banks. In theory too, the CNC may strike an institution off if, having consulted the Association Française des Banques, it considers that the bank no longer meets general or local economic needs. This power has, however, never been exercised.

The Commission can appoint a liquidator to any institution which is struck off the list of banks. If the administration or management of a bank cannot, for any reason at all, be carried on by those normally responsible, the Commission my appoint an *'administrateur provisoire'* to carry out those functions.

3.14.2 Imposition of Conditions

The Commission may also impose conditions on the institution concerned, e.g.:
(a) prohibition of certain transactions, or other limitations on the carrying out of banking operations;
(b) suspension of the responsible management, with or without the nomination of an *'administrateur provisoire'*;

3.14.3 Other Sanctions

The Commission may impose other disciplinary sanctions i.e., a warning or a reprimand, which are without prejudice to any possible penal sanctions. The Commission constitutes a Tribunal Administratif for this purpose.

3.14.4 Penalties

Penalties are prescribed by Articles 19-23 of Law 2532 of June 13, 1941, for breaches of the articles of that Law. Punitive sanctions - fines and/or imprisonment may be imposed by a Tribunal Repressif. A case before a Tribunal Repressif may be brought by the Commission de Contrôle des Banques, or by the Association Française des Banques, acting together or separately.

3.14.5 Appeals

Appeals against decisions of the Commission de Contrôle des Banques may be made to the Conseil d'Etat.

The Commission must give reasons for its decisions in all cases. These may be appealed against on grounds of *excès de pouvoir* (abuse of power) only to the Conseil d'Etat.[32]

3.15 FOREIGN BANK BRANCHES

3.15.1 Establishment

There is now no distinction in French banking law between French banks and foreign banks; the latter are subject to exactly the same laws, regulations and requirements as the former.

A foreign bank opening a branch in France has to comply with the standard formalities of registration (see 3.3 above) and has to meet the usual requirements for authorisation (see 3.4 above). It is thus subject to the CNC's assessment of the general and local economic needs for a new bank. It also has to choose the category of bank (see 3.1 above) in which it is to be registered.

Approval is automatically given for the opening of a second and subsequent branches in France (see 3.5.1 above).

Any foreign bank is required to maintain in one of its offices in France a complete record of the transactions carried out by all its branches on French territory.[33]

Under the requirements for publication of balance sheets (see 3.3.3 above), a branch of a foreign bank has to arrange for the publication both of the balance sheet of its own operations in France, and of the balance sheet of the group as a whole (in the currency of its country of origin). It has to show in its own balance sheet the amount of its endowment capital (see 3.15.2 below).

3.15.2 Earmarked Capital

Any foreign bank has to prove that it has allocated to the sum of the transactions it carries out on French territory and of its investment in France a minimum capital equal to that required by French banks (see 3.4.2 above).[34] This capital has to be invested in assets in France - property, Treasury bills, etc.

3.15.3 Nationality and Competence of Personnel

No one may take part on a regular basis in the management, administration or direction of a company in the business of banking, or of a branch of that company, nor may he sign for a bank, if he is not of French nationality or a national of another Member State of the EEC. The Minister of Finance may, however, authorise specific derogations from this restriction.[35]

Under normal commercial law, any person who is not a French national must obtain a *carte d'identité de commerçant pour les étrangers* (commercial card) before he can become the manager of the French branch or agency of a foreign company. This rule is in certain circumstances relaxed for nationals of another EEC Member State (Decree of November 12, 1938, as amended).

3.15.4 Restrictions on Business

A branch of a foreign bank is subject to the same limitations on the business it can undertake as a French bank in the same category (see 3.6 above).

3.15.5 Representative Offices

There is no restriction on the opening by a bank based outside France of a representative office in France. The office does not have to be registered as a bank (and so, of course, is prohibited from carrying out any banking business). The manager or representative will require a commercial card (see 3.15.3 above).

3.16 FOREIGN BANK SUBSIDIARIES

3.16.1 Local Ownership

There is no local ownership requirement when setting up to the same formalities of registration and has to meet the same requirements for authorisation as a French bank (see 3.3, 3.4 and 3.15.1 above).

3.16.2 Nationality of Directors

No one may take part on a regular basis in the management, administration or direction of a company in the business of banking, or of a branch of that company, nor may he sign for a bank, if he is not of French nationality or a national of another Member State of the EEC. The Minister of Finance may, however, authorise specific derogations from this restriction.[36]

Any person who is not a French national must obtain a *carte d'identité de commerçant pour les étrangers* (a commercial card) before he can become the chairman of the board or supervisory board, or a manager or general manager of a *société anonyme* or a partner in any form of partnership. This rule is in certain circumstances relaxed for nationals of another EEC Member State (Decree of November 12, 1938, as amended).

3.16.3 Guarantees from Parent Institution

There is no specific requirement that a foreign parent should guarantee the liabilities of its bank subsidiary in France. The Commission de Contrôle des Banques can, however, call for commitments or stand-by credits or can (and very occasionally has done so) require a foreign parent to make a blocked deposit in French francs to guarantee the liquidity of its subsidiary. Such measures are rare. The Commission can also require the parent institution, or of any other foreign bank of standing willing to act as guarantor, to vouch that the coefficient for medium and long-term operations (see 3.9.2 above) will be observed.

3.17 BANKING ASSOCIATIONS

3.17.1 Membership

The Association Française des Banques (AFB) (previously known as the Association Professionelle des Banques until it changed its name on April 5, 1976) was set up in 1941.[37] Every registered bank is obliged to belong to the AFB. No other professional banking association may be formed in the private sector.

In June 1980, the AFB had 392 members, of which 250 were French banks, 199 were foreign banks, 9 were banks from Monaco and the remaining 14 were from French overseas territories and departments. Of these, 289 were *banques de dépôts,* 40 were *banques d'affaires* and 63 were long and medium-term credit banks.

3.17.2 Relations with Supervisory Authorities

The AFB must keep its members informed of any regulations affecting them; the Association serves as intermediary between the banks and the CNC, and may play the same role between the banks and the Commission de Contrôle des Banques. It is also required to advise the CNC on each application for registration as a bank (cf. 3.3.2 above).

The AFB is entitled to intervene in the judicial process in every case where a bank is a party to a law suit and where the general interests of the profession are at stake.

The Commission de Contrôle des Banques may delegate to the AFB, with the agreement of the Secretary of State for the National Economy and Finances, disciplinary powers in respect of banking regulations, of CNC instructions, and of agreements reached between members.[38]

The AFB thus has a formal place in the supervisory framework of the banking industry, both as regards access to the profession and as regards the disciplining of those in the profession.

3.18 BACKGROUND SOURCES

1. Association Française (Professionelle) des Banques: Annual Reports.
2. Association Française (Professionelle) des Banques: Receuil de Textes Règlementaires interéssant la Profession Bancaire.
3. Aufricht, H.: Central Banking Legislation: Vol. II: Europe, (International Monetary Fund, Washington, D.C.), (1967).
4. Banking Federation of the European Community: Monetary Policy and the Banking System in the countries of the European Community (Brussels, 1980).
5. Banque de France: Annual Reports and Quarterly Bulletins.
6. Banque de France: Note d'Information, No. 8, (January, 1972).
7. Chaineau, A.: Le Crédit, Institutions et Techniques Françaises, (Armand Colin, Paris), (1974).
8. Conseil National du Crédit: Annual Reports.
9. Commission de Contrôle des Banques: Annual Reports.

10. Commission de Contrôle des Banques: Règlement - Dispositions Applicables aux Banques.
11. Gavalda, C. et Stoufflet, J.: Droit de la Banque, (Presses Universitaires de France, Paris), (1974).
12. Hodgman, D.R.: National Monetary Policies and International Monetary Cooperation, (Little, Brown and Company, Boston), (1974).
13. IBRO: Banking Ratios in the EEC, (A study commissioned by DG XV of the EEC Commission from the Inter-Bank Research Organisation, 1979).
14. International Monetary Fund: Annual Report on Exchange Arrangements and Exchange Restrictions, (Washington, D.C.), (1979).
15. Koszul, J.: 'Les Banques Etrangères en France', Banque, (May, 1974).
16. Stoufflet, J., Campet, Ch., Koszul, J., Moran, P. et Sarmet, M.: L'Activité des Banques Etrangères en France, (Presses Universitaires de France, Paris), (1975).
17. Vittas, D.: (ed) Banking Systems Abroad (Inter-Bank Research Organisation, London) (1978).

NOTES

1. Art. 1, Law No. 2532 of June 13, 1941, on the Regulation and Organisation of the Banking Profession.
2. Law No. 2532 of June 13, 1941, on the Regulation and Organisation of the Banking Profession, Arts. 2-5 as amended by Decree No. 72-103 of February 4, 1972.
3. Law No. 45-015 of December 2, 1945, on the Nationalisation of the Banque de France and the Large Banks, and on the Organisation of Credit.
4. Decree No. 46-1246 of May 28, 1946, on the Basic Rules on the Functioning of the Nationalised Deposit Banks.
5. Arts. 48-56, Law No. 2532 of June 13, 1941, on the Regulation and Organisation of the Banking Profession.
6. Art. 2, Decree No. 66-81 of January 25, 1966, changing certain provisions concerning the regulation of banks.
7. Law No. 45-015 of December 2, 1945, Art. 11 as amended.
8. Art. 10, Law No. 2532 of June 13, 1941.
9. Art. 16, Law No. 2532 of June 13, 1941.
10. Art. 51, Law No. 2532 of June 13, 1941.
11. Art. 6, Law No. 2532 of June 13, 1941.
12. Art. 3(2).
13. Law No. 2532 of June, 13, 1941, Art. 8, as amended by Decree No. 66-81 of January 25, 1966, changing certain provisions on the regulation of banks, and by Decree No. 72-103 of February 4, 1972.

14. Art. 7, Law No. 2532 of June 13, 1941, and Art. 16, Law No. 45-015 of December 2, 1945, as amended by Arts. 1,5, Law No. 75-601 of July 10, 1975, amending the nationality requirements for the banking profession.
15. Art. 3, Law No. 46-1071 of May 17, 1946, on the Organisation of Credit in France.
16. Art. 4, Decree No. 46-1247 of May 28, 1946 on the Basic Rules Governing the Operation of the Private Sector Banks.
17. Art. 10, Law No. 2532 of June 13, 1941.
18. Art. 11, Law No. 2532 of June 13, 1941.
19. Art. 1, Law No. 2532 of June 13, 1941.
20. Art. 5, Law No. 45-015 of December 2, 1945, on the Nationalisation of the Banque de France and the Large Banks, and on the Organisation of Credit.
21. Law No. 45-015 of December 2, 1945, Art. 5 as amended.
22. Art. 19, Decree No. 46-1247 of May 28, 1946.
23. Art. 19, Decree No. 46-1247 of May 28, 1946.
24. Law No. 45-015 of December 2, 1945, Art. 5 as amended.
25. Law No. 45-015 of December 2, 1945, Art. 5 as amended.
26. Law No. 45-015 of December 2, 1945, Art. 5 as amended.
27. Art. 34, Law No. 2532 of June 13, 1941.
28. Art. 12, Law No. 2532 of June 13, 1941.
29. Art. 8, Decree No. 46-1246 of May 28, 1946, and Art. 8, Decree No. 46-1247 of May 28, 1948.
30. Art. 2, Decree No. 66-81 of January 25, 1966.
31. Art. 12, Law No. 45-015 of December 2, 1945, on the Nationalisation of the Banque de France and the Large Banks, and on the Organisation of Credit.
32. Arts. 24-26, Law No. 2532 of June 13, 1941.
33. Art. 9, Decree No. 46-1247 of May 28, 1946.
34. Art. 9, Decree No. 46-1247 of May 28, 1946.
35. Art. 7, Law No. 2532 of June 13, 1941, and Art. 16, Law No. 45-015 of December 2, 1945, as amended by Arts. 1,5, Law No. 75-601 of July 10, 1975.
36. Art. 7, Law No. 2532 of June 13, 1941, and Art. 16, Law No. 45-015 of December 2, 1945, as amended by Arts. 1,5, Law No. 75-601 of July 10, 1975.
37. Arts. 24-26, Law No. 2532 of June 13, 1941.
38. Arts. 24-26, Law No. 2532 of June 13, 1941.

CHAPTER 4

GERMANY

4.1 INSTITUTIONS COVERED

All credit institutions are subject to State supervision and are defined in Article 1 of the 1961 Banking Law[1] as 'enterprises engaged in banking transactions where the scope of those transactions requires a commercially organised business enterprise.' Banking transactions consist of any of the following (not all credit institutions would engage in the whole range of transactions):

(i) the receipt of monies from outside sources as deposits irrespective of the payment of interest (deposit business);

(ii) the granting of money loans and acceptance credits (credit business);

(iii) the purchase of bills and cheques (discount business);

(iv) the purchase and sale of securities for the account of others (securities business);

(v) the custody and administration of securities for the account of others (safe custody business);

(vi) the transactions set out in Article 1 of the Law on Investment Companies of April 16, 1957, as amended (investment fund business, which is confined to certain specialised institutions);

(vii) the incurring of obligations to acquire claims in respect of loans prior to their maturity;

(viii) the assumption of guarantees and other warranties for others (guarantee business); and

(ix) the carrying out of transfers and clearing transactions (giro business).

The Federal Minister of Finance may, after consultation with the Deutsche Bundesbank, designate by order further transactions as banking transactions if this is accepted in the view of the business community as being justified for the purpose of supervision as laid down in the Banking Law. This power has never been exercised.

The following are not credit institutions within the meaning of the Banking Law (Art. 2):

(i) the Deutsche Bundesbank;

(ii) the German Federal Post Office;

(iii) the Reconstruction Loan Corporation (Kreditanstalt für Wiederaufbau);

(iv) the social security funds and the Federal Labour Office;

(v) private and public law insurance enterprises;

(vi) enterprises recognised as public-benefit housing enterprises;

(vii) enterprises which have been recognised as organs of government housing policy and are not primarily engaged in banking business; and

(viii) enterprises engaged in pawnbroking, to the extent that they give loans against pledges.

As regards its savings business, the German Federal Post Office is subject *inter alia* to the provisions of the Banking Law relating to savings deposits. The bodies referred to in (iv) and (v) above are subject to its provisions in respect of loans of one million deutschemarks or more. The enterprises referred to in (v) to (viii) are subject to the provisions of the Banking Law to the extent that they carry on banking business that does not form part of their customary activities.

In cases of doubt, the Federal Banking Supervisory Office (FBSO: see 4.3.1 below) has to decide whether an enterprise is subject to the provisions of the Banking Law; its decisions are binding on the administrative authorities (Art. 4).

According to the administrative criteria applied at present by the FBSO, an enterprise is deemed to be a commercially organised enterprise where it has taken more than five separate deposits totalling more than 25,000 deutschemarks, or deposits amounting to a lower total but due to more than 25 depositors; given more than 20 separate credits totalling over 1 million deutschemarks, or credits amounting to a lower total but advanced to more than 100 borrowers; carried out more than 20 separate guarantee operations totalling more than 250,000 deutschemarks, or more than 100 separate guarantee operations to a lower total; and has a combined credit and guarantee business exceeding 100 transactions or a total of 50,000 deutschemarks.

These criteria can be amended to take account of general circumstances, or of the details of a particular case.

The FBSO may determine that, with certain exceptions, the provisions of the Law are not applicable to individual enterprises, as long as, and to the extent that, they do not require supervision because of the nature of the business they conduct (Art. 2(4)).

Supervision of a credit institution by any other government office does not replace supervision by the FBSO: thus an institution may be subject to dual inspection and control (Art. 52). The savings banks, for example, are also subject to supervision by the Länder.

4.2 BASIC LAWS

The basic law is the Banking Law (Kreditwesengesetz - KWG) of July 10, 1961; it has been amended several times since 1961, the most important amendments being introduced by the Second Law amending the Banking Law of March 24, 1976, which came into force on May 1, 1976. Transitional periods for various controls strengthened by this Law extend over five years. The authoritative text of the Banking Law was published on May 3, 1976 (*Federal Law Gazette* I, p.1121). In addition, specific laws exist for specialised credit institutions, e.g. mortgage banks.

4.3 SUPERVISORY SYSTEM

4.3.1 Supervisory authority

The supervision of banks under the Banking Law is carried out by the Berlin-based Bundesaufsichtsamt für das Kreditwesen (Federal Banking Supervisory Office - FBSO), in association with the Deutsche Bundesbank.

The FBSO is established as an independent superior federal authority. Its President is appointed by the Federal President acting on a proposal from the Federal Government which consults the Deutsche Bundesbank on the matter (Art. 5). The FBSO reports to the Federal Minister of Finance.

The function of the FBSO is to supervise the credit institutions according to the provisions of the Banking Law. It is required to take action against abuses of the credit system which tend to endanger the safety of the assets entrusted to credit institutions, impair the orderly performance of banking transactions, or entail substantial disadvantages for the economy as a whole (Art. 6).

In so far as the costs of the FBSO are not covered by licence fees and other charges, 90% is paid for by the banking industry and the remainder by the Federal Government.

Under Article 23(1), the Minister of Finance may delegate to the FBSO the right to make regulations on the terms, including regulations governing rates of interest and commission, on which credits may be granted and deposits taken. This power can be exercised only by the FBSO in agreement with the Deutsche Bundesbank: the terms have to be fixed so as to support the latter's credit policy measures and to safeguard the viability of the credit sector. The power has not been exercised since 1967. Controls on interest rates were abandoned the same year.

4.3.2 Outline of system

Any person who intends to carry out any banking transactions (as defined in 4.1 above) must obtain a written licence from the FBSO. The licence may be granted subject to directions consistent with the aims of the Banking Law. It may also be limited to certain specific types of banking transactions (Art. 32). Before granting a licence to conduct a deposit-taking business, the FBSO must consult the appropriate banking association (Art. 32(3)).

Licences may be refused only on grounds of lack of adequate own funds, untrustworthiness or lack of professional qualifications on the part of the proposed managers, proprietors, etc. or if the bank does not have at least two full-time paid managers (this is known as the 'Four Eyes Principle' (Art. 33) (cf. 4.4.3 below)). A licence cannot be issued if the bank is to be organised in the form of a sole proprietorship[2] (Art. 2a). These requirements are compatible with Article 12 of the Basic Law (the Constitution), which guarantees the fundamental right to the free choice of a profession, only because of the overriding public interest in a secure banking system. Thus any more restrictive conditions, e.g. on the economic need for a bank, would infringe this fundamental right. Any applicant satisfying these requirements must therefore be granted a licence. The only exception is that a licence may be refused for a branch set up in Germany by a foreign bank if it is not considered justified in view of general economic needs (though this does not apply to banks from other EEC Member States).

The FBSO may request information and undertake investigations in order to satisfy itself about an applicant's eligibility for a licence. The appointment of a new manager must be notified to the FBSO, who must be given details of his qualifications.

A banking licence expires automatically if no use is made of it within 12 months of its receipt. It may be withdrawn if obtained through fraud or other improper means, if not exercised for any period of 12 months, if the bank is organised in the form of a sole proprietorship,[3] if untrustworthiness or lack of qualifications is proved against the management, if the 'Four Eyes Principle' is breached, or if the fulfilment of the bank's obligations to its creditors, and particularly the safety of assets entrusted to it, is endangered and if the danger cannot be averted by taking other measures under the Law (see 4.14 below). This last clause may be invoked, *inter alia*, if a bank loses half its own funds (liable funds) or loses at least 10% of its own funds in each of three years in succession (Art. 35).

The FBSO can take direct action to stop any institution carrying on business prohibited by Article 3 (see 4.6.1 below) or carrying out banking business without a licence (Art. 37). It can require information and books and records from any institution which is deemed to be a credit institution or to be conducting prohibited business (see 4.6.1 below) (Art. 44).

The Banking Law does not lay down any appeals procedure for an applicant who has been refused a licence. Refusal is, therefore, subject to the normal administrative appeals procedure involving an appeal, first to the FBSO itself. Appeals can subsequently be brought before the Administrative Tribunal in Berlin. An appeal must be lodged within one month. If a decision has not been received from the FBSO within three months of an application, the applicant can take the FBSO before the Administrative Tribunal. No appeal can be lodged after 12 months have elapsed from the date of the application.

4.3.3 Returns to Supervisory Authority

Credit institutions are required to submit a monthly return to the Deutsche Bundesbank immediately after the end of each month. If a credit institution is required to compile monthly balance sheet statistics in accordance with Article 18 of the Law establishing the Bundesbank, the filing of these statistics will rank as monthly returns. All credit institutions are required to submit to the FBSO and to the Deutsche Bundesbank their approved annual balance sheet, profit and loss account, their annual report (if any) and the auditor's report (see 4.3.4 below). Credit institutions which belong to a co-operative society audit association or which are audited by the audit office of a savings bank and giro association need submit the auditor's report only if so requested (Art. 26).

The Deutsche Bundesbank is authorised (by Article 18 of the Law establishing it) to instruct all credit institutions to compile statistics on banking and money matters. The results of these statistics may be published (though data on any individual bank are not disclosed).

The Deutsche Bundesbank is required to make available to the FBSO the results of statistical surveys carried out under Article 18 of the Law establishing the Deutsche Bundesbank (see above). It must consult the FBSO before giving any instructions regarding such surveys.

There are detailed reporting requirements for large loans. Loans granted to any one borrower which together exceed 15% of the credit institution's liable (own) funds have to be reported forthwith to the Deutsche Bundesbank; this does not apply to large loans in respect of which the amount promised or taken is not greater than 50,000 deutschemarks, unless the loan exceeds 75% of the credit institution's own funds. Large loans already reported have to be reported anew if they are increased by more than 20% of the amount last reported, or if brought to a level exceeding 75% of own funds. In addition the FBSO may order banks to submit once a year a list of large loans subject to the reporting requirements. This demand is in fact the regular practice. The Deutsche Bundesbank sends the reports with its comments to the FBSO. In calculating large loans, certain guarantees and warranties, as well as loans extended through the purchase of bills eligible for discount at the Deutsche Bundesbank, are counted at only half their value. The reporting requirements apply to loans promised and to loans drawn (Art. 13).

Banks must also report to the Deutsche Bundesbank by the tenth day of February, April, June, August, October and December (i.e. six times annually) those borrowers whose indebtedness amounted to one million deutschemarks or more at any time during the two calendar months preceding the reporting date. In the case of syndicated loans of one million deutschemarks or more, this applies even if the share of the individual bank does not amount to one million deutschemarks. The report must indicate the amount of the borrower's indebtedness (drawing) at the end of the month preceding the report. If the borrower is a group, the report must also indicate the indebtedness of each of the enterprises making up the group. The Deutsche Bundesbank notifies the FBSO of reported loans (Art. 14(1) and (3)).

Credits are defined as including money loans of all kinds; money claims purchased; acceptance credits; claims in respect of registered bonds other than registered mortgage bonds and communal bonds; the discounting of bills and cheques; the prolongation for a period beyond that customary in trade of claims in respect of non-banking commercial transactions, especially commodity transactions; a bank's guarantees and other warranties on behalf of others; the obligation to be liable for the fulfilment of money claims sold or to repurchase them at the request of the purchaser; and a bank's participation in a borrower's enterprise (any holding of not less than 25% of a company's shares is deemed to be a participation, regardless of the duration of such a holding). Securities furnished to and credit balances maintained with the credit institution by the borrower are not deducted from the total of credits (Art. 19).

A 'single borrower' covers all enterprises which belong to the same group or which are linked by agreements which provide that the administration or the entire profits of one enterprise are subject to the control of, or are paid to, another enterprise; it also covers a partnership and all its personally liable partners; persons and enterprises for whose account a loan is raised, together with the party who raises the loan in his own name (the 'man of straw' clause). In the case of purchases of money claims, the seller of the claim shall be regarded as a borrower if he is answerable for the fulfilment of the claim sold or if he has to reacquire it at the request of the purchaser; otherwise, the debtor of the liability shall be regarded as the borrower (Art. 19).

4.3.4 Auditing requirements

A credit institution must draw up its annual balance sheet and profit and loss account within three months of the end of the financial year, unless a shorter period is prescribed under other statutory provisions. They must be submitted immediately in draft and subsequently as approved, together with the annual report (if any) to the FBSO and the Deutsche Bundesbank (Art. 26). The annual accounts must be audited within five months of the end of the financial year.

If an additional audit has taken place in connection with the deposit insurance scheme set up by a banking association (see 4.13 below), the auditor shall submit the report of this audit to the FBSO and to the Deutsche Bundesbank immediately (Art. 26).

In addition to the above requirements, all banks must publish their annual accounts. The form of the annual accounts is prescribed in detail in the regulations issued by the Minister of Justice under Article 161 of the Aktiengesetz (Companies Act) of September 6, 1965 (the Minister must first consult the Minister of Economics). The current regulations are set out in an Order of December 20, 1967, as amended by an Order of May 27, 1969. The content of each item in the annual balance sheet is prescribed by the FBSO in its Notice 1/68 of July 22, 1968. In addition, banks are subject to special valuation provisions (Art. 26(a)), a violation of which can lead to the appointment of special auditors and, in extreme cases, to the invalidation of the annual accounts (Art. 26(b)). The form and content of the monthly balance sheet statistics (monthly returns) are prescribed in detail by the Deutsche Bundesbank.

For the purpose of ensuring compliance with bank supervisory regulations, the FBSO also avails itself of the services of the credit institution's auditors. Under Article 28 of the Banking Law, banks must notify the FBSO of the auditor they have appointed immediately after making the appointment. Within one month of receipt of the notification, the FBSO may request the appointment of a different auditor if this is necessary to achieve the purpose of the audit. When auditing the annual accounts, the auditor is also required, in accordance with Article 27 of the Banking Law, to look into the bank's financial circumstances and to ascertain whether it has complied with the various reporting requirements e.g. for large loans, loans of one million deutschemarks and loans to company officers or their dependants, for participations (see 4.6.3 below) and for changes in management (see 4.4.3 below), and with the requirement to disclose its financial circumstances; his findings must be included in the auditor's report (Art. 29(1) of the Banking Law).

The FBSO has published, in its Notice 2/68 of December 20, 1968, detailed guidelines for the contents of audit reports.

The report on the audit of the annual accounts (auditor's report) has to be submitted to the FBSO and to the Deutsche Bundesbank, together with the annual accounts and the annual report (Art. 26(1) of the Banking Law). If, in the course of his audit, the auditor learns of facts which might warrant the qualification or refusal of the certificate of audit, endanger the bank's existence or gravely impair its development, or which indicate that the managers have seriously violated the law, the articles of association or the partnership agreement, he must report this to the FBSO and to the Deutsche Bundesbank immediately, i.e. in the course of the audit. At the request of the FBSO or the Deutsche Bundesbank, the auditor must explain this report to them and communicate any other facts which have come to his notice in the course of the audit and which suggest that the business of the bank has not been properly conducted (Art. 29(2) of the Banking Law).

Credit institutions which conduct securities business, or hold securities in safe custody for clients, are subject to a special annual audit, under Article 30. The FBSO has laid down detailed rules on the nature, scope and timing of the safe custody account audit in a Notice of December 16, 1970 (*Federal Gazette* No. 239). The auditors of safe custody accounts are appointed by the FBSO. In special cases, the FBSO may delegate its right to appoint auditors to the Deutsche Bundesbank (Art. 30).

4.3.5 Inspection

The FBSO has the power to enquire into all the business matters of a bank, to require the production of books and records, and to carry out audits even if there is no special reason for them. In the case of banks set up in the form of a body corporate, the FBSO may also send its own representatives to shareholders' meetings and supervisory board meetings, with the right to address such meetings, and request a bank to convene meetings of its management or supervisory boards which may be attended by representatives of the FBSO. Under the Banking Law the Deutsche Bundesbank also has the right to demand any information it requires on all business matters, including the production of books and records (Art. 44). Inspections are, as a rule, carried out, not by its own auditors, but by auditors appointed by it (Art. 8 of the Banking Law).

The FBSO may also inspect and demand information from an unlicensed institution which is thought to be carrying on a banking business.

4.4 CRITERIA FOR AUTHORISATION

4.4.1 Legal Form

Article 2(a) lays down that a bank may not take the form of a sole proprietorship (*Einzelkaufmann*). Existing one man banks are exempt from this provision. Permissible legal forms include an *Aktiengesellschaft* (AG) (a public limited company); a *Gesellschaft mit beschränkter Haftung* (GmbH) (a private limited company); a *Kommanditgesellschaft auf Aktien* (KGaA) (a partnership partially limited by shares and with one or more general partners with unlimited liability); a *Kommanditgesellschaft* (KG) (a limited partnership with one or more general partners with unlimited liability); an *Offene Handelsgesellschaft* (OHG)[4] (a general commercial partnership); or an *Eingetragene Genossenschaft* (a registered co-operative society).

Public sector credit institutions - e.g. savings banks or *Girozentralen* - are, generally speaking, set up under public law (e.g. as public corporations or institutions).

A change in a bank's legal form must be reported immediately to the FBSO and to the Deutsche Bundesbank (Art. 24). This Article does not, in practice, apply very often, since any material change in the corporate form of a bank or, in the case of partnerships, any material change in the circumstances of the responsible partners requires the issue of a new licence.

4.4.2 Minimum Capital

The Banking Law states that a licence may be refused if the resources necessary for the conduct of business, in particular adequate own funds (haftendes eigenkapital), are not available in the Federal Republic of Germany or West Berlin (Art. 33). However, it does not go on to define 'adequate' - this is left to the FBSO to decide.

In general the FBSO requires a bank involved in deposit business (see 4.1(i) above) to have a minimum capital of six million deutschemarks before a licence is issued. Stricter requirements are imposed on mortgage banks and Bausparkassen. If no deposits are taken, a minimum capital of three million deutschemarks is required. Existing banks must comply with the principles relating to capital resources (see 4.9.1 below).

A bank must immediately report to the FBSO and to the Deutsche Bundesbank certain changes in its capital, in particular the loss of 25% or more of its own funds (Art. 24).

4.4.3 Management Qualifications

A licence may be refused on the grounds of untrustworthiness, or lack of professional qualifications on the part of the applicant or the proposed managers, proprietors, etc. Generally speaking, each person involved as proprietor or manager has to be fully qualified.

Professional qualifications for directing a credit institution are ordinarily assumed to exist if three years' management experience in a German credit institution of a comparable size and type is proved.

A licence may also be refused if the bank does not have at least two responsible full time managers. The purpose of this 'Four Eyes Principle' is to ensure that banks are at all times under expert and responsible management (Art. 33).

Managers are defined as those persons who are appointed to conduct the business of and to represent credit institutions (Art. 1).

Each bank must immediately report to the FBSO and to the Deutsche Bundesbank the appointment of any manager or the authorisation of any person to represent the bank in all aspects of its business, together with sufficient information to judge his trustworthiness and qualifications: it must also report the termination of such appointments (Art. 24).

A manager of a bank must inform the FBSO and the Deutsche Bundesbank immediately if he takes up or relinquishes a post as manager or member of the supervisory board of another bank or any other enterprise; he must also report any acquisition or disposal of a participation in any enterprise, as well as changes in the size of the participation (which in this context is normally taken as a holding of 25% or more of the capital of the enterprise in question but can apply to a smaller holding (Art. 24)).

4.4.4 Management Plans

In its application for a licence a bank is required to disclose information concerning its business intentions, its organisational structure and the number of persons it employs.

4.4.5 Other Requirements

The FBSO is not entitled to refuse a German bank a licence on the grounds that it is not justified by general economic needs (see 4.3.2 above). This can, however, be a reason for refusing a licence to a branch of a foreign bank (cf. 4.15.1 below), other than a bank having its head office in another EEC Member State.

Each bank must immediately report to the FBSO and to the Deutsche Bundesbank any move of its registered or head office and any alteration of its business name, its articles of association or partnership agreement (Art. 24).

Any bank set up as a public limited company (AG) or as a limited partnership with shares (KGaA) (see 4.4.1 above) is required by the 1965 Companies Act (Art. 150) to maintain a statutory reserve. (This applies to all companies in these forms, not just to banks). Generally speaking, this reserve is created by setting aside at least 5% of annual profits, until the reserve reaches at least 10% of the nominal share capital, or such higher proportion as is laid down in the articles of association. Any premium on the issue of shares etc. is also transferred to the statutory reserve, regardless of the size of the latter. The statutory reserve may only be used to write off losses which cannot be covered by the release of free reserves (insofar as it amounts to more than 10% of the share capital), to write off losses or increase the share capital by means of a bonus issue. The statutory reserve forms part of the bank's own funds (see 4.9.1 below).

4.5 BRANCHES

4.5.1 Restrictions on Branching in Germany

No permission is needed to open a branch, but credit institutions are required to report immediately to the FBSO and to the Deutsche Bundesbank the establishment, transfer and closing of any branch office (Art. 24).

The only occasion on which the general economic need for a new branch has to be established is in the case of an application by a non-EEC bank to open a branch in Germany.

4.5.2 Branching and Operations in Other Countries

There are no special restrictions on German banks as regards the setting up of branches or subsidiaries in other countries or the acquisition of participations in foreign banks. These activities are subject to any exchange controls or similar restrictions on the outflow of capital which may be in force.

4.6 RESTRICTIONS ON BUSINESS

4.6.1 Restrictions on Types of Business

A credit institution which grants credit totalling more than 50,000 deutschemarks to any single borrower must obtain from him a disclosure of his business situation, and in particular the submission of his annual statement of account. The credit institution may dispense with this requirement if it is clearly unnecessary, in view of the security provided, or of the guarantors. There is an exemption for credits relating to factoring (Art. 18).

Without prejudice to the validity of the transaction, credit institutions in the form of a body corporate or a partnership may grant a large credit only on the basis of a unanimous decision by all managers. This decision must, if possible, be taken before the granting of the credit; if not, it must be taken immediately afterwards. In the latter case, the FBSO and the Deutsche Bundesbank must be informed of the results within one month. If a credit already granted becomes a large credit owing to a reduction in own funds, similar provisions apply (Art. 13). As a rule, banks are allowed to carry on non-banking business. A bank is required to report immediately to the FBSO and to the Deutsche Bundesbank the commencement and termination of any business which is not banking business (as defined in 4.1 above) (Art. 24). The FBSO has, however, made certain administrative exceptions to this rule.

In addition to the restrictions on types of business outlined above, Article 3 lays down that the following business shall be prohibited:

(i) The conduct of deposit business where the depositors mainly consist of persons employed by the enterprise (employee savings banks - Werksparkassen), unless other banking business is being conducted which exceeds the scope of the said deposit business;

(ii) The acceptance of deposits where the majority of the depositors have a legal right to loans being granted to them from such deposits or to objects being made available to them on credit (savings enterprises for specific purposes - Zwecksparunternehmen); this does not apply to building and loan associations;

(iii) The conduct of credit business or of deposit business where agreement or business practice render it impossible, or particularly difficult, to withdraw in cash the amount of credit or the deposits.

The FBSO can take direct action to prevent the continuation of such business (Art. 37).

4.6.2 Loans to Directors

Restrictions are imposed on loans to connected borrowers, defined as managers, partners, directors, members of the supervisory board, officers and employees of a credit institution, their spouses or children and third parties acting on their behalf. Loans to connected borrowers may be granted only on the basis of a unanimous decision (stating the terms governing the rate of interest and the repayment of the credit) of all managers of the credit institution, and only with the express approval of the bank's supervisory board (if it has one). This is not applicable to loans granted to officers and employees, to their spouses and children under age, or to third parties acting on their behalf, provided that the credit does not exceed the monthly salary of the officer or employee (Art. 15).

Similar requirements apply to loans to corporations and partnerships, if a manager of the bank is a legal representative or a member of the supervisory board or a partner of the former, or if a legal representative or partner of the undertaking receiving a loan is a member of the supervisory body of the bank; to persons belonging to an undertaking controlled by or controlling the bank; to enterprises in which the bank or its manager 'participates', or which 'participate' in the bank, or the legal representatives or partners of which 'participate' in the bank ('participation' is defined as a holding of not less than 25% of the shares, regardless of the duration of such holding) (Art. 15).

There is a special requirement that such loans are to be reported to the FBSO (Art. 16). Any infringement of the provisions on connected borrowers may give rise to an obligation to compensate for any losses incurred (Arts. 16 and 17).

4.6.3 Equity Participations

There are no explicit limits set by the Banking Law on the extent to which banks may hold participations in non-credit institutions. There is, however, an indirect limit set by the long-term investments ratio (see 4.9.1 below) and by the own funds and liquidity ratios (see 4.9.1 and 4.9.2 below). There are also restrictions relating to large loans (see 4.9.3 below).

Banks are also subject, to a certain extent, to the provisions of the Gesetz gegen Wettbewerbsbeschränkungen (Law against Restraints of Competition) of July 27, 1957. Under certain conditions, the competent body, the Bundeskartellamt (Federal Cartel Office), may, *inter alia*, prohibit the purchase of participations in companies.

A bank must immediately report to the FBSO and to the Deutsche Bundesbank any acquisition or disposal of a participation in another enterprise: in this context a participation is normally defined as a holding of more than 10% of the capital of the company in question. (In some circumstances a smaller interest may have to be reported). Any change in the size of the bank's participation amounting to more than 5% of the capital must also be reported (Art. 24(1)).

A bank must immediately report to the FBSO and to the Deutsche Bundesbank any acquisition or disposal of a participation in another credit institution, and any change of over 5% in the size of its holding. The definitions above apply (Art. 24). This does not imply any limit to a bank's holding of such participations. The limits set by the long-term investments ratio and the own funds and liquidity ratios and the large loan rates apply equally to these participations.

4.6.4 Mergers

Any credit institution planning to merge with another credit institution must notify the FBSO and the Deutsche Bundesbank well in advance (Art. 24).

In the event of the Federal Cartel Office wishing to institute proceedings against a bank (see 4.6.2 above), it has to work closely with the FBSO.

4.7 BANKING NAMES AND DESCRIPTIONS

Unless otherwise laid down by law, the term 'bank' or 'banker', or a term in which the word 'bank' or 'banker' appears, may be used as part of the institution's name or as an addition thereto, or to describe the purpose of the business, or for advertising purposes, only by (1) credit institutions holding a licence from the FBSO; or (2) other enterprises which, at the time when the 1961 Law came into force, were using such terms with due authority in accordance with the rules in force at the time.

The designation 'Volksbank' ('people's bank') or one in which the word 'Volksbank' appears may be adopted only by credit institutions which are set up in the form of a registered co-operative society and which belong to an audit association.

When granting the licence, the FBSO may stipulate that the terms 'bank', 'banker' etc. mentioned above may not be used if the nature or scope of the credit institution's business does not justify the use of such a designation. Similar provisions apply to savings banks in order to protect the term 'Sparkasse' (savings bank).

These provisions do not apply to enterprises which use the words 'bank', 'banker' or 'savings bank' in a context which rules out the impression that they conduct banking business. In cases of doubt, the FBSO has to decide whether an enterprise is entitled to use the terms mentioned.

4.8 ADVERTISING

In order to counteract abuses in credit institutions' advertising, the FBSO may prohibit certain kinds of advertising, though it must first consult the associations of credit institutions before laying down any general measures

(Art. 23). This power has so far only been exercised once, in an order of February 18, 1977, in respect of the Bausparkassen.

4.9 SOLVENCY AND LIQUIDITY

Article 10 states that, with a view to fulfilling their obligations towards their creditors, and particularly in order to safeguard the assets entrusted to them, credit institutions must have adequate liable funds (own funds).

Article 11 requires credit institutions to invest their funds in such a way as to safeguard adequate solvency at all times.

The FBSO is required, in agreement with the Deutsche Bundesbank, to establish and publish (in the *Federal Gazette*) criteria by which banks can be assessed. It must also consult the banking associations on these principles (Arts. 10, 11).

The full text of the Principles currently in force is shown in the Appendix. Principle I establishes a capital/risk assets ratio; Principle Ia, a capital/foreign currency position ratio; Principle II, a long-term liquidity ratio; and Principle III, a short-term liquidity ratio.

The preamble to the Principles lays down that a more than negligible breach of one of the ratios, or frequent breaches, will be prima facie evidence that a bank's capital or liquidity is inadequate. It does, however, permit the FBSO to take into account any special circumstances which might justify either a higher or a lower ratio.

4.9.1 Solvency ratios

Principle I states that a credit institution's lending and participations should not be more than 18 times its own funds. Certain lower risk claims are included at only 50% or 20% of nominal value, and certain credits to the public sector are excluded altogether.

Under a separate long-term investments ratio set out in Article 12 of the Banking Law, the aggregate book values of a credit institution's permanent investments in land, buildings, ships and participations may not exceed own funds. On request, the FBSO may permit a credit institution to depart from this rule temporarily.

The definition of own funds ('haftendes eigenkapital') used in the calculation of the two solvency ratios above and the loan limits (4.9.3 below) is set out in Article 10:

(i) For (1) a public limited company (AG), (2) a partnership partially limited by shares (KGaA), or (3) a private limited company (GmbH): paid-up capital, less the amount of its own shares held by the bank, plus reserves. In addition, for (2) only, amounts contributed by the personally liable partners but not paid up as capital, less the withdrawals by and credits granted to such partners;

(ii) For (1) a sole proprietorship, (2) a general partnership (OHG), or (3) a limited partnership (KG): capital and reserves, less any withdrawals by, or credits granted to, the proprietor or the personally liable partners, less any excess of debt on the personal property of the proprietor. For (2) and (3), account is taken of paid-up capital only;

(iii) For a registered co-operative society: the amount paid in as shares plus the reserves, plus an amount to be fixed by order of the Federal Minister of Finance (after consulting the Deutsche Bundesbank) to allow for the liabilities of members. This responsibility may be delegated to the FBSO;

(iv) For a public law (and recognised private law) savings bank: the reserves;

(v) For any other public law credit institution: the paid-up endowment funds and reserves;

(vi) For a credit institution in any other legal form: the paid-up capital plus reserves.

Net profit is included in own funds to the extent that a decision has been taken to allocate it to the capital or to reserves; any losses incurred have to be deducted from own funds.

In certain circumstances, proved personal property of the proprietor or of the personally liable partners may be considered as own funds.

Reserves to be included in own funds comprise only the amounts shown as reserves (including the statutory reserve), to the exclusion of those liability items which - on the basis of tax regulations - are subject to taxation only upon realisation (Art. 10(3)). Thus only reserves which are created out of post-tax income, may be included in own funds. Provisions and hidden reserves are not included in own funds.

For want of any relevant provisions, loan capital is not regarded as forming part of a bank's own funds.

4.9.2 Liquidity Ratios

The full text of the Principles currently in force, and the Preamble, are shown in the Appendix. Principle II lays down that the sum of certain long-term (four years or more) and fixed assets (including participations) must not exceed the sum of certain long-term financial resources (including equity capital), plus a proportion of certain shorter term resources. Principle III lays down that the sum of certain short-term and medium-term assets should not exceed the sum of certain proportions of specific shorter term resources, plus the financial surplus, or less the financial deficit resulting from Principle II.

Article 16(5) of the Deutsche Bundesbank Law of 1957 provides that any minimum reserves held by banks at the Deutsche Bundesbank for purposes of monetary policy (see 4.10.2 below) shall be counted towards the liquidity reserves required under other provisions.

4.9.3 Loan Limits

Without prejudice to the validity of the transaction, no single loan (including loans promised) may exceed 75% of a bank's liable (own) funds; the bank's five largest 'large loans' (including loans promised) must not exceed three times its liable funds; and the total of all its large loans actually taken up (i.e. excluding loans promised) must not exceed eight times its liable funds. Certain guarantees, warranties and sureties are counted at half their value. What constitutes a 'large' loan and a single borrower for the purpose of these calculations is set out in 4.3.3 above. There is a partial exemption for 'central banking institutions' such as the Girozentralen (Art. 13).

4.10 MONETARY AND CREDIT CONTROLS

The formulation and implementation of monetary policy is the responsibility of the Deutsche Bundesbank. Though the Bundesbank is expected to support the general economic policy of the Federal Government, Article 3 of the Deutsche Bundesbank Law 1957 provides that the primary duty of the Bundesbank is to safeguard the currency. Direct credit controls, interest rate controls and selective credit controls are not employed by the Bundesbank. Rather, it conducts policy by operating on the liquidity of the banking system and interest rates, primarily through the system of minimum reserves and market intervention and accommodation.

4.10.1 Central Bank Accommodation

Refinancing is provided both through the rediscount channel and through secured advances. Each bank may rediscount eligible bills with the Bundesbank up to its quota. Quotas are based mainly on each bank's liable funds but also take account of the structure of institutions' business and the extent to which they hold eligible bills. The Bundesbank's rediscount rate is charged for this accommodation. The size of the rediscount quotas is modified from time to time, in order to ensure that the liquidity position of the banking system is consistent with policy objectives.

Advances from the Bundesbank (Lombard advances) are in principle available only for the bridging of short-term liquidity needs. The rate of interest on Lombard advances is often 1% higher than the discount rate. On occasion the Bundesbank imposes ceilings on each bank's Lombard advances for monetary policy purposes and in these circumstances a special Lombard facility at higher rates is sometimes made available.

Apart from rediscounting and Lombard advances, the Bundesbank influences the liquidity of the banking system through a variety of operations. In recent years the sale of 'mobilisation' and liquidity paper (of varying maturities), open market purchase and resale operations (generally in government bonds for a period of 30 days) and foreign exchange swaps have been the most important of these.

4.10.2 Reserve Requirements

The imposition of reserve requirements on the banking system is a major instrument of monetary policy. Reserves must be held in the form of balances with the Bundesbank on which no interest is paid; since March 1978, the banks' holdings of cash have been deductible from required reserves. The actual reserve ratios vary depending on the amount of the different categories of liabilities of each institution; a progressive scale sets different ratios for liabilities of: 10 million deutschemarks and under; between 10 million deutschemarks and 100 million deutschemarks; and over 100 million deutschemarks. In respect of deposit totals exceeding 100 million deutschemarks, the minimum ratios in force for sight, time and savings deposits in mid-1980 were 13.45%, 9.45% and 6% respectively. The maximum ratios for the three deposit categories are 30%, 20% and 10% respectively. As far as non-resident deposits are concerned, however, a reserve ratio of up to 100% may be fixed.

The minimum reserve system has an important element of flexibility in that requirements must be observed only on an average daily basis over the month. Thus to some extent banks may use their reserves as working balances. Reserve ratios are modified quite frequently in support of the Bundesbank's monetary objectives.

4.11 FOREIGN EXCHANGE

4.11.1 Authority to deal in foreign exchange

In principle all banks are permitted to carry out foreign exchange transactions.

4.11.2 Limits on Positions

Solvency Principle Ia (see the Appendix for the full text) lays down that a bank's net open positions in foreign currency and precious metal at the close of business each day must not exceed 30% of its own funds, for spot and all forward positions taken together; for all foreign currency positions due within one calendar month, the net open position must not exceed 40% of its own funds; and for all foreign currency positions due within half a calendar year, the net open position must not exceed 40% of its own funds. These limits must be observed on a day-by-day basis.

Banks have to report to the Deutsche Bundesbank each month full details of the spot and forward positions in individual foreign currencies and of their positions in precious metals. If the limits described above are breached, a report has to be made to the FBSO and to the Bundesbank on the next business day.

4.12 CREDIT INFORMATION EXCHANGE

The functions of a credit information exchange are performed by the Deutsche Bundesbank. If, under the reporting arrangements described in 4.3.3 above, it appears that credits of one million deutschemarks or more have been granted to one borrower by two or more credit institutions, the Deutsche Bundesbank is required to inform the credit institutions concerned, passing on only the borrower's reported total indebtedness (i.e. only amounts actually lent) and the number of credit institutions concerned. The amount of guarantees and other warranties contained in reported total indebtedness is stated separately in a single sum as well as the amount of liabilities on bills in respect of which the borrower has a right of recourse against other liable parties (Art. 14).

If the borrower is a group, the reports from the Deutsche Bundesbank have to set out the liabilities of the individual group enterprises.

As well as credit institutions and insurance companies, the social security funds and the Federal Labour Office are also obliged under Article 2 to make reports as provided for in Article 14, and thus are entitled to receive the collated results from the Deutsche Bundesbank.

A credit institution which has been asked to make a large loan is not entitled to obtain information from the Deutsche Bundesbank in advance about the borrower's outstanding large credits from other credit institutions. The Deutsche Bundesbank can only report back to lenders which have themselves granted credits of one million deutschemarks or more.

4.13 DEPOSIT INSURANCE

A non-compulsory deposit insurance scheme covering the entire Federal territory was established as early as the mid-1960s by the private banks belonging to the Bundesverband deutscher Banken e.V. Before May 1976, all deposits by private depositors of not more than 20,000 deutschemarks were covered by the scheme. The basis for assessing the annual contributions payable by the member banks to the insurance fund was initially the balance-sheet total, but this was subsequently replaced by the amount of liabilities towards non-banks (deposits).

Similar insurance schemes have been set up by the other groups of institutions engaged in credit business; in the case of the cooperative banks and the savings banks, the insurance arrangements were, from the outset, designed to ensure the stability of the institution, with the result that no restriction in respect of specific types of deposit or depositor was imposed. This principle was substantially modified as part of a reorganisation carried out by the cooperative banks in 1977, the outcome being that liabilities towards credit institutions in other groups could be excluded from the insurance arrangements.

Following discussions between the FBSO, the Federal Ministry of Finance and the Bundesverband deutscher Banken e.V., the insurance scheme for private banks was extended considerably in May 1976. Each depositor (excluding other banks and connected depositors), i.e. personal and corporate depositors, public authorities and, in so far as assets of an investment fund are concerned, investment companies together with their deposit banks, is now guaranteed repayment of his deposit with a bank which has gone into liquidation, up to an amount equivalent to 30% of the bank's own funds (as defined in Article 10 of the Banking Law). The amounts needed are drawn from the central fund, into which all banks taking part pay an annual levy equal to 0.03% of their liabilities towards non-banks (deposits). If the total amount thus collected is insufficient, the fund may borrow the shortfall. In this case, a further levy of 0.03% may be imposed. Membership of the insurance scheme is not compulsory, but in practice all members of the Bundesverband deutscher Banken e.V. are expected to participate.

There are only a few banks in the Federal Republic of Germany that still accept deposits and are not members of an insurance scheme.

4.14 SANCTIONS

4.14.1 Revocation of authorisation

Among the range of sanctions available to the FBSO is the power to revoke a bank's licence if it was obtained through fraud or other improper means, if the relevant business is not carried on for a period of 12 months, if untrustworthiness or lack of professional qualifications on the part of a proprietor or manager becomes known, if a bank is organised in the form of a sole proprietorship (but there is an exemption for existing sole proprietors, see 4.4.1 above), if the 'Four Eyes Principle' is breached (subject to exemptions see 4.3.2 above), or if the funds entrusted to the bank are placed at risk (particularly if a bank loses half its own funds or loses more than 10% of its own funds in each of three consecutive years) and if such risk cannot be averted by any of the other measures provided for in the Law (see below) (Art. 35).

When revoking a licence, or if a licence expires, the FBSO may, in the case of bodies corporate and partnerships, require the bank concerned to be liquidated (such a decision shall have the effect of a winding up order). At the FBSO's request, the Registergericht (court of registration) must appoint a liquidator (Art. 38).

4.14.2 Imposition of Conditions

Instead of revoking a bank's licence, the FBSO may in certain circumstances require the dismissal of a manager who has been found to be untrustworthy or unqualified, who is responsible for the risk to the fulfilment of the bank's obligations towards its creditors (see 4.3.2), or who, despite a warning, continues, wilfully or negligently, to violate the Banking Law and Regulations in force; in the case of credit institutions set up as bodies corporate, the FBSO may forbid the manager to carry out his duties (Art. 36).

If a bank does not have (a) adequate own funds, or (b) sufficient liquidity, and fails to make good the deficiency within a stipulated period, the FBSO may limit or forbid withdrawals by the proprietors or partners and the distribution of profits or the granting of credits. It may also, in the case of (b), prohibit the bank from making certain permanent investments (see 4.9 above) (Art. 45).

If the fulfilment of a bank's obligations towards its creditors and, in particular, the safety of depositors' funds are thought to be at risk, the FBSO may take temporary measures to avert such risks; in particular, it may issue instructions with regard to the conduct of the bank's business; it may prohibit or restrict the taking of deposits and the granting of credits; it may prohibit the proprietors or managers from carrying out their duties entirely or it may impose restrictions on their activities; or it may appoint supervisors to the bank (Art. 46).

4.14.3 Other sanctions

Under Article 46 (a), (b) and (c), which was introduced by the Second Law amending the Banking Law, the FBSO may, in order to avert the bankruptcy of a credit institution, declare a moratorium. The purpose of the above provision is to supplement the measures provided for in Article 46 (see 4.14.2 above), since the latter have often proved inadequate in the past as a means of restoring sound business conditions. Declaration of a moratorium is particularly appropriate where the various creditors are protected by a deposit insurance scheme operated by the association of credit institutions (see 4.13 above) and where, once it has satisfied the creditors' claims, the scheme takes the place of the creditors.

Where a bank is in danger of becoming insolvent, the FBSO may temporarily ban sales and payments by the bank, order the bank to be closed for business with customers and prohibit the acceptance of payments not intended for the discharge of debts to the bank, unless the deposit insurance scheme operated by a banking association undertakes to satisfy in full all those entitled to satisfaction. While these measures are in operation, execution of judgements, attachments and temporary injunctions against the assets of the bank may not be granted. The FBSO may apply to the court for new managers to be appointed to run a bank when the measures mentioned above have been ordered and when the previous managers have been removed (Art. 46a).

If a bank becomes insolvent or excessively indebted, the managers must immediately report the fact to the FBSO, with this taking the place of any obligation on them under other legislation to enter a petition for winding up. The FBSO alone may apply to the court for a winding up order, which the court must grant (Art. 46b).

If financial difficulties are threatening any bank which might seriously endanger the whole economy, the Federal Government may by statutory order declare a moratorium for that bank; or suspend some or all banking transactions at some or all banks; or close the Stock Exchange. Before taking any of these steps the Federal Government must consult the Deutsche Bundesbank (Art. 47).

4.14.4 Penalties

Fines and/or imprisonment are laid down as the penalties for conducting banking business without a licence and for transgressions of the reporting and other requirements imposed by the Law (Arts. 54, 56, 59).

4.14.5 Appeals

Measures taken by the FBSO are subject to the standard legal appeals system except that there can be no appeal against the court's decision on the FBSO's request for a winding up order under Article 46b (see 4.14.3 above). The lodging of an appeal cannot delay the measures listed in 4.14.2 above or the declaration of a moratorium above. Appeals are made in the first instance to the FBSO itself and where necessary, an appeal may then be made to the Verwaltungsgericht (Administrative Court) in Berlin.

4.15 FOREIGN BANK BRANCHES

4.15.1 Establishment

Branches of foreign banks are normally treated in the same way as domestic credit institutions. Every individual branch set up in Germany by a foreign bank thus needs a licence from the FBSO. This is granted subject to the same requirements as are applied to a domestic bank (see 4.4 above) except that the licence may be refused if it is not considered to be justified on the grounds of general economic needs. By virtue of EEC Directive 73/183 on Freedom of Establishment for Banks (Art. 53), this latter criterion does not, however, apply to banks having their head office in other Member States of the EEC. Moreover, in the case of a branch set up by a bank having its head office in a Member State of the EEC, only the first such branch needs a licence, while the opening of any further branch has only to be notified in accordance with Article 24(1) of the Banking Law.

One or more branches set up in Germany by a foreign bank are treated as forming one credit institution. Each such credit institution (or single branch, if there is only one in Germany) must have at least two natural persons resident in the Federal Republic of Germany who are authorised to manage the business and to represent the bank. These persons shall be deemed to be managers (Art. 53).

Separate books must be kept for the business done by the branch(es) and for the transactions with the bank's head office. When submitting their annual accounts (see 4.3.3 above) branches must also provide the annual accounts etc. of the foreign bank (Art. 53).

4.15.2 Earmarked Capital

A branch's liable (own) funds are defined as the operating capital made available by the foreign enterprise, plus any operating surpluses left with the branch to increase its capital resources, less any net balance on inter-company account, all as shown in the latest monthly return.

The FBSO requires minimum own funds of six million deutschemarks where deposit business is to be conducted, or own funds of three million deutschemarks where deposits are not accepted, before licensing a branch (or branches) of a foreign bank (see 4.4.2 above). This figure is not laid down in the Banking Law, and can be increased if necessary.

4.15.3 Nationality and Competence of Personnel

The requirements are normally the same as those applied to the responsible personnel of a German bank (see 4.4.3 above). Both managers must meet the qualifications criteria and have a command of the German language. As regards competence, it is generally deemed sufficient for one manager to have at least three years' management experience with a German bank and for the other manager to have, in addition to several years' management experience with a bank abroad, at least one year's experience of bank-related business in Germany. German citizenship is not required.

4.15.4 Restrictions on Business

Foreign bank branches are subject to the same limitations on business as German banks (see 4.6 above).

4.15.5 Representative Offices

There are no restrictions in the Banking Law relating to the opening of a representative office in Germany by a foreign bank. As a rule, however, such an office is subject to the provisions of the Industrial Code. This requires any non-EEC bank which is established as a registered company to obtain a trade licence from the competent Land (State) authority before opening such an office; for a bank having its head office in another Member State of the EEC no licence is required. The granting of a licence is a mere formality. The office will also have to be entered in the Commercial Register and be registered with the local tax office.

The establishment, transfer or closure of a representative office must be notified by the manager of the office to the FBSO and to the Deutsche Bundesbank immediately. Such notification must, according to an FBSO instruction, give *inter alia* the exact description and address of the business carried on by the representative office, and the name, head office and address of the foreign bank. Evidence of the authorisation to trade, a declaration to the effect that no bank business within the meaning of Article 1(1) is to be carried on, and the latest annual report of the foreign bank, together with its annual accounts, must be attached to the notification.

These requirements are imposed in order to facilitate supervision by the authorities and to ensure that representative offices confine themselves to their usual sphere of activity.

4.16 FOREIGN BANK SUBSIDIARIES

4.16.1 Local Ownership

There is no restriction or requirement as to the degree of local ownership of any credit institution, since independent subsidiaries of foreign banks rank as German credit institutions.

4.16.2 Nationality of Directors

There are no requirements as to the nationality of directors. The management are subject to the usual requirements as to competence (cf. 4.15.3 above).

4.16.3 Guarantees from parent institution

Guarantees are not required by law.

4.17 BANKING ASSOCIATIONS

4.17.1 Membership

The main associations of credit institutions are organised on a State (Land) basis. These state associations in turn have central bodies, at Federal level, viz.:

(i) Bundesverband deutscher Banken e.V. (Association of German Banks) which comprises the 11 state associations and the Verband privater Hypothekenbanken e.V. (the Private Mortgage Banks Association) and the Verband deutscher Schiffsbanken e.V. (the Private Ship Banks Association). The Bundesverband deutscher Banken e.V. is the central organisation of the private sector credit institutions. Membership of the state (Land) associations is voluntary and open to all privately owned banks (very few are not members);

(ii) Bundesverband der deutscher Volksbanken und Raiffeisenbanken e.V. which is the central organisation representing the state (Land) and regional associations of the agricultural and industrial co-operative banks;

(iii) Deutscher Sparkassen und Giroverband e.V., which is the central organisation representing the regional savings banks associations as well as the Verband der Deutschen Freien Offentlichen Sparkassen e.V. (Association of German Free Public Sector Savings Banks). Membership of the regional association is compulsory.

There are other central associations, including:

(iv) Verband öffentlicher Banken e.V., which represents the Girozentralen of the savings banks and other public law credit institutions;

(v) Verband der gemeinwirtschaftlichen Geschäftsbanken, which represents banks connected with the trade union movement and consumer co-operative societies.

(vi) Bankenfachverband Konsumenten - und gewerbliche Spezialkredite (BKG) e.V., which represents the credit institutions specialising in instalment finance.

4.17.2 Relations with Supervisory Authorities

The various associations' duties include representing the interests of their member institutions, advising the authorities in matters relating to money, credit and the capital market, carrying out public relations work and maintaining contacts with associations abroad. In matters of common interest, the associations work together in committees or working groups.

The FBSO is obliged by the Banking Law to consult the associations representing the credit institutions before it establishes the principles concerning banks' solvency and liquidity (see 4.9 above) and before it lays down general rules on advertising by banks (see 4.8 above). It must also consult the appropriate association before granting a licence for a deposit-taking business (see 4.3.2 above).

Moreover, the auditing bodies of the savings banks and giro associations take part in the regular supervision of savings banks and co-operative banks (prior checking of notices, issuing of expert opinions). The representative organisations referred to in 4.17.1 (i)-(iii) and (v) also play an important role in the deposit insurance schemes for member credit institutions (cf. 4.13 above).

The Bundesverband deutscher Banken e.V. is responsible for organising the deposit insurance fund (see 4.13 above), and has also set up an auditing association to assist in the provision of auditing advice and services to member banks.

4.18 BACKGROUND SOURCES

1. Aufricht, H.: Central Banking Legislation: Vol. II: Europe, (International Monetary Fund, Washington, D.C.), (1967).
2. Banking Federation of the EEC: Monetary Policy and the Banking System in the Countries of the European Community (Brussels) (1980).
3. Beeny, J.H.: European Financial Reporting: 1. West Germany, (Institute of Chartered Accountants in England and Wales' General Educational Trust), (1975).
4. Bundesverband deutscher Banken, e.V.: Annual Reports.
5. Bundesverband deutscher Banken, e.V.: Rules of the Deposit Insurance Scheme.
6. Deutsche Bundesbank: Monthly Reports and Annual Reports.
7. Elstob, M. (Ed): Banking Structures and Sources of Finance in the European Community (Banker Research Unit, London) (1979).
8. Gesetz über das Kreditwesen vom 10 Juli 1961 in der Fassung vom 3 Mai 1976 (English translation: Deutsche Bundesbank), (1976).
9. IBRO: Banking Ratios in the EEC (A study commissioned from the Inter-Bank Research Organisation by DG XV of the EEC Commission) (1979).
10. International Monetary Fund: Annual Report on Exchange Arrangements and Exchange Restrictions, 1979 (Washington, D.C.).
11. Jura Europae, Droit Bancaire et Boursier/Bank - und Borsenrecht, (Editions Techniques Juris-Classeurs, Paris), (C.H. Beck, Munich), (1974).
12. Peltzer, M. and Nebendorf, K.: Banking in Germany, (Fritz Knapp Verlag, Frankfurt am Main), (1973).

NOTES

1 Unless otherwise specified, references in this Chapter to Articles are to Articles in the Banking Law (Kreditwesengesetz - KWG) of July 10, 1961 (*Federal Law Gazette* I, p.881, as last amended by Article 72 of the Law to introduce the Tax Order of December 14, 1976 (*Federal Law Gazette* I, p.3341).

2 This does not apply to banks organised as sole proprietorships as at May 1976, which can take advantage of a five-year transitional period, allowing certain exemptions.

3 This does not apply to banks organised as sole proprietorships as at May 1976, which can take advantage of a five-year transitional period, allowing certain exemptions.

4 Banks taking the form of an *Einzelkaufmann*, a KG or an OHG are called Privatbankiers (private banks).

APPENDIX

PRINCIPLES CONCERNING THE CAPITAL AND LIQUIDITY OF BANKS
(Grundsätze über das Eigenkapital
und die Liquidität der Kreditinstitute)

of January 20, 1969

as amended up to
January 16, 1980[1]

1. The Federal Banking Supervisory Office (Bundesaufsichtsamt für das Kreditwesen), acting in accordance with sentence 3 of Article 10(1) and sentence 3 of Article 11 of the Banking Law (Gesetz über das Kreditwesen) of July 10, 1961 (*Federal Law Gazette* I, page 881), hereby announces the Principles, drawn up in agreement with the Deutsche Bundesbank and after consultation with the central associations representing the banks, according to which it will normally assess whether a bank's capital and liquidity are adequate (Article 10(1) and 11 of the Banking Law).

2. If a bank exceeds the upper limits laid down in the Principles by more than an insignificant amount or repeatedly, then there is normally reason to suppose that the bank does not possess the necessary capital (Principles I and Ia) or that its liquidity is unsatisfactory (Principles II and III). When assessing the adequacy of a bank's capital and liquidity, special conditions which, depending on circumstances, justify lower or higher requirements may be taken into consideration.

3. Public mortgage banks, instalment credit institutions and banks exclusively conducting banking business within the meaning of Article (1), items 7 and 8 of the Banking Law are subject to Principles I and Ia only.

4. Private mortgage banks which do not exercise their right to conduct extended business in accordance with Article 46(1) of the Mortgage Bank Act (Hypothekenbankgesetz), ship mortgage banks, building and loan associations and central securities depositories (Wertpapiersammelbanken) are subject to Principle Ia only.

5. The Principles do not apply to investment companies.

6. The Principles in the text of January 20, 1969, will first be applied in January 1969. Announcement No. 1/62 of the Federal Banking Supervisory Office of March 8, 1962 (*Federal Gazette* No. 53 of March

---

1.   This translation was prepared in the Deutsche Bundesbank for the convenience of English-speaking readers. It is not official, the only authentic text being the German one published in the *Bulletins* of the Deutsche Bundesbank.

16, 1962), as amended by Announcement No. 1/64 of August 25, 1964 (*Federal Gazette* No. 161 of September 1, 1964), is hereby revoked.

Principle I

1. The loans and participations of a bank, less provisions for losses on loans and advances and less fees booked but chargeable to subsequent accounting years in instalment credit business, must not exceed 18 times its liable capital (haftendes Eigenkapital). The following are to be regarded as loans:

(i) bills of exchange in the bank's portfolio and bills sent for collection prior to maturity from the bank's portfolio,

(ii) balances with banks and loans and advances to customers (including the trade receivables of banks conducting business in goods),

(iii) contingent claims in respect of
- (a) bills drawn by the bank, discounted and credited to borrowers, in circulation,
- (b) endorsement liabilities on rediscounted bills,
- (c) guarantees, guaranteed bills and cheques and other warranties.

2. Of the loans specified in 1(ii), the following are to be counted at only half their value:

(i) long-term loans serving as cover for bonds or granted against charges on real estate in the course of credit transactions secured by real property within the meaning of Article 20(2)1 and 4 of the Banking Act or against corresponding charges on ships,

(ii) loans and advances to customers as referred to in 1(ii) if guaranteed or secured in some other way by domestic legal persons governed by public law,

(iii) contingent claims on customers as referred to in 1(iii)(c),

(iv) loans as referred to at 1(ii) to foreign banks.

3. Loans as referred to at 1(ii) to domestic banks (including the domestic branches of foreign enterprises within the meaning of Article 53 of the Banking Law and banks which are domestic legal persons governed by public law) are to be counted at 20% of their value.

4. Loans to domestic legal persons governed by public law (other than banks) and to a Special Federal Fund are not to be counted when calculating total lending.

Principle Ia

1. At the close of business each day, the difference between a bank's assets and liabilities in foreign currencies and in gold, silver or platinum metals (precious metals), irrespective of their maturity, must not exceed 30% of its

liable capital. Assets and liabilities within the meaning of the first sentence comprise the following items in foreign currencies or in gold, silver or platinum metals in an unprocessed state (ie. excluding products made of these precious metals):

A. assets

(i) balances with banks, loans and advances to customers and balances in foreign currency accounts with the Deutsche Bundesbank,

(ii) bills of exchange,

(iii) Treasury bills and discountable Treasury bonds,

(iv) securities, other than shares and other participatory securities,

(v) delivery rights arising from spot and forward transactions,

(vi) holdings of

    (a) gold,

    (b) silver,

    (c) platinum metals

(vii) rights and contingent rights to the return of items listed under assets (i) to (vi) above which have been sold for subsequent repurchase, if these items are not included in these assets;

B. liabilities

(i) liabilities to banks and customers,

(ii) bonds,

(iii) own acceptances and promissory notes in circulation,

(iv) delivery obligations arising from spot and forward transactions,

(v) obligations and contingent obligations to return items listed under assets (i) to (iv) above which have been bought for subsequent resale, if these items are included in these assets.

The difference is obtained from the aggregate balances of assets and liabilities, determined separately for each currency and precious metal; amounts in different currencies and precious metals must not be set off against each other. When converting assets and liabilities in foreign currencies into deutschemarks, the middle rates are to be used for other currencies. Assets and liabilities in gold are to be converted into deutschemarks in accordance with the quotation of the Frankfurt Gold Exchange for 12.5 kg bars (1 kg 32 ounces). Assets and liabilities in silver and platinum metals are to be converted in accordance with the quotations per ounce on the London Metal Exchange.

2. At the close of business each day, the difference between a bank's assets and liabilities in foreign currencies maturing in any calendar month must not exceed 40% of its liable capital. Sentences 2 to 4 of paragraph (1), in so far as they refer to assets and liabilities in foreign currencies, apply as appropriate.

3. At the close of business each day the difference between a bank's assets and liabilities in foreign currencies maturing either in the first half or in the

second half of any calendar year must not exceed 40% of its liable capital. The second to fourth sentences of paragraph 1, in so far as they refer to assets and liabilities in foreign currencies, apply as appropriate.

Principle II

A bank's assets in the form of

1. balances with banks and loans and advances to customers with agreed maturities or periods of notice of four years and over,

2. unlisted securities,

3. participations,

4. shares in a controlling company or a company holding a majority interest,

5. land and buildings,

6. furniture and equipment

less provisions for losses on loans and advances, must not exceed the sum of the long-term financial resources specified below.

The following are to be regarded as long-term financial resources:

1. capital and reserves,

2. liabilities (other than savings deposits) to banks and customers with agreed maturities or periods of notice of four years and over,

3. 10% of liabilities (other than savings deposits) to customers payable on demand and with agreed maturities or periods of notice of less than four years,

4. 60% of savings deposits,

5. bonds outstanding and bonds sold prior to issue with maturities of more than four years,

6. 60% of bonds outstanding and bonds sold prior to issue with maturities of four years and under,

7. 60% of provisions for pensions,

8. 20% of amounts due to affiliated banks with agreed maturities or periods of notice of six months and over but less than four years (only for the regional institutions of savings banks and credit cooperatives).

Principle III

1. 20% of balances with banks with agreed maturities or periods of notice of three months and over but less than four years,

2. loans and advances to customers with agreed maturities or periods of notice of less than four years (including the trade receivables of banks conducting business in goods),

3. bills of exchange drawn by the bank, discounted and credited to borrowers, and promissory notes drawn by borrowers, discounted and

credited to them, in the bank's portfolio (except promissory notes of the Bank for International Settlements and the Import and Storage Agencies (Einfuhr - und Vorratsstellen)* and promissory notes drawn for the purpose of taking up loans of the Export Credit Company (Ausfuhrkredit-Gesellschaft mbh) and the Industrial Plant Financing Company (Gesellschaft zur Finanzierung von Industrieanlagen mbH), and contingent claims in respect of such bills and notes in circulation,

4. listed shares and investment fund units.

5. 'other assets' (including stocks of goods held by banks conducting business in goods)

less provisions for losses on loans and advances, must not exceed the sum of the financial resources specified below.

The following are to be regarded as financial resources:

1. 10% of liabilities to banks payable on demand and with agreed maturities or periods of notice of less than three months, other than loans and advances to customers on behalf of the bank,

2. 50% of liabilities to banks with agreed maturities or periods of notice of three months and over but less than four years, other than loans and advances to customers on behalf of the bank,

3. 80% of liabilities to banks in respect of loans and advances to customers on behalf of the bank,

4. 20% of savings deposits,

5. 60% of other liabilities to customers payable on demand and with agreed maturities or periods of notice of less than four years,

6. 80% of liabilities in respect of business in goods and trade payables, other than the liabilities of banks conducting business in goods included in 8 below,

7. 20% of bonds outstanding and bonds sold prior to issue with maturities of four years and under,

8. 80% of own acceptances and promissory notes in circulation and of bills drawn by the bank, discounted and credited to borrowers and promissory notes drawn by borrowers, discounted and credited to them, in circulation (except promissory notes of the Bank for International Settlements and the Import and Storage Agencies* and promissory notes drawn for the purpose of taking up loans of the Export Credit Company and the Industrial Plant Financing Company)

plus the financial surplus or less the financial deficit in Principle II, as the case may be.

---

*   *Renamed Federal Office for Agricultural Market Organisation (Bundesanstalt für landwirtschaftliche Marktordnung).*

CHAPTER 5

GREECE

Introduction

This chapter provides a summary of banking regulation in Greece, incorporating developments up to the middle of 1980. At the time of writing, Greek banking regulation is in a considerable state of flux: accession to the European Communities in January 1981 will bring substantial changes, while at home there is increasing pressure for reform.

One area where considerable change is bound to take place is that of controls on the foreign exchange business of banks. This is because the Greek authorities have undertaken, through a declaration on monetary questions annexed to the Accession Treaty, to set up a foreign exchange market in Athens before accession to the European Communities as well as to take measures to ensure that the drachma is officially quoted in at least one of the foreign exchange markets of existing Member States.

Wide-ranging changes may also be required with regard to certain regulations that may be in conflict with EEC directives on the establishment and operation of credit institutions (in particular, directives 73/183 and 77/780). These include provisions discriminating against banks from other EEC countries such as those relating to the nationality of board members and the extent of foreign ownership of Greek banks, the work permit requirements and quota system for senior foreign officials of branches of foreign banks, the criterion of economic need for new branches and the earmarked capital requirement for branches of foreign banks.

In response to domestic pressures, various proposals for a fairly radical reform of the Greek monetary and banking system have also been under discussion for some time. Reform proposals such as those set out in the recommendations of the report of the Committee on the Working of the Greek Financial System would, if implemented, alter significantly the system of controls applied on banks for monetary and credit policy purposes (e.g. interest rate controls, selective credit controls, etc.).

At the time of writing, plans have been announced for the setting up of an inter-bank foreign exchange market to be organised along the lines of the Paris inter-bank market. No indications are, however, available as to the scope or timing of any further reform measures.

5.1 CATEGORIES OF INSTITUTIONS COVERED

Banks are defined in Greece as those enterprises whose customary business, irrespective of any other business conducted by them, is to take deposits of currency or other funds (Art. 10 of Law 5076/1931 on joint stock companies and banks). Such enterprises, commonly known as 'commercial banks', are subject to the special provisions of Law 5076/1931 and most of the legislation applying to banks is directed at them. However, according to the definition used in Law 1665/1951 on the operation and control of banks, the term 'bank' refers, for control purposes, not only to banks as defined above (including their branches and agencies) but also to other institutions such as the Post Office Savings Bank, the Consignments and Loans Fund, the Agricultural Bank, the Hellenic Industrial Development Bank, the investment banks and the mortgage banks, that engage in banking business, (but only in respect of that business).

These other institutions have been authorised by virtue of special decrees to take deposits and/or engage in banking activities; they are exempt from the special provisions of Law 5076/1931 (Art. 18(2)) as well as from several of the regulations imposed on commercial banks. Special terms and conditions also apply to the establishment and operation of so-called offshore credit units which can be set up by Greek and foreign banks (see 5.15.5 below).

It should be noted that no ordinary savings banks (privately or municipally owned), credit cooperatives, building societies or credit unions operate in Greece. In the agricultural sector, however, a number of cooperatives receive global loans from the Agricultural Bank of Greece which they subsequently distribute among their members under their own responsibility.

The scope of this chapter is limited to commercial banks.

5.2 BASIC LAWS

The two basic banking laws are Law No. 5076 of June 30, 1931, on joint stock companies and banks (Arts. 10-18bis) and Law No. 1665 of January 27, 1951, on the operation and control of banks. Other laws and legislative decrees governing the operations of banks are as follows:

(i) Law 2190/1920 on Joint Stock Companies (as codified by Royal Decree 174/1963) (section on banks);

(ii) Legislative Decree 588/1948 and Law 1387/1950 on the Control of Credit;

(iii) Law 1837/1951 on the Operation of the Currency Committee and

Law 400/1976 on the Organisation of Cabinet and Government Departments (sections on Economic and Currency Committees);

(iv) Law 2292/1955 on Bank Mergers;

(v) Legislative Decree 3745/1957 on the Issue of Treasury Bills;

(vi) Law 128/1975 relating to the Functioning of the Financial System;

(vii) Law 236/1975 on the Appointment of Temporary Commissioners;

(viii) Law 431/1976 amending the Regulations governing the Operation and Control of Banks.

5.3 SUPERVISORY SYSTEM

5.3.1 Supervisory Authority

The regulation and supervision of banks and other financial institutions are vested in the Currency Committee (Nomismatiki Epitropi). This was initially set up in 1946 (Law 1015/1946), but its functions have been reaffirmed by Law 400/1976 on the organisation of the cabinet and government departments.

The Currency Committee is an inter-ministerial committee under the chairmanship of the Minister of Coordination. Other members are the Ministers of Finance, Agriculture, Commerce and Industry and Energy, one of the Deputy Ministers of Coordination and the Governor of the Bank of Greece. The Currency Committee has very wide-ranging powers over monetary, financial and foreign exchange matters. It is the main supervisory body for the financial system as a whole, covering not only the commercial banks but also all other institutions engaging in banking activities as well as certain aspects of insurance companies, pension funds, the securities markets, etc. Most of these other institutions are, however, also subject to supervision by other bodies. The Currency Committee is assisted by, and operates through, the Bank of Greece (Trapeza tis Ellados) which is the nation's central bank.

The supervisory powers of the Currency Committee are set out in Law 400/1976. It is, in particular, authorised:

(i) to control, together with the competent organs of the Bank of Greece and in accordance with the provisions of Law 1665/1951, all banks and credit institutions operating in Greece, including branches of foreign banks, and to ensure the maintenance of banking prudence;

(ii) to supervise, with the Bank of Greece, the application of the law and regulations on matters of foreign exchange;

(iii) to issue regulations on the level of bank capital in relation to the size of deposits or on the ratios between different assets or liabilities, including the right to impose a compulsory increase in bank capital within a specified period, in relation to the level, type and kind of risks assumed;

(iv) to issue regulations covering the activities of insurance companies operating in Greece in relation to the provision of finance or the collection and utilisation of savings;

(v) to issue regulations on the terms and conditions of issuing shares and bonds for public subscription and on the regular trading of any type of securities outside the Stock Exchange;

(vi) to control joint stock companies that raise funds by public subscription;

(vii) to control the investment of funds of public institutions, in accordance with the provisions of Law 1611/1950;

(viii) to approve the financing programmes of the State, public institutions and public corporations, on a monthly and yearly basis.

The Currency Committee is assisted by a Secretariat which is a separate department of the Bank of Greece and which is staffed by employees of the latter. The Currency Committee has set up a number of sub-committees, among which the Credit Sub-Committee is of particular importance. This is chaired by the Governor of the Bank of Greece and consists exclusively of senior officials of the Bank including its two deputy governors, the economic adviser of the Bank and the director of the Secretariat of the Currency Committee. Its main functions are to examine all matters relating to credit policy and control that come before the Currency Committee and to put forward proposals for action.

Much of the day-to-day work is, however, entrusted to other sub-committees, such as the Sub-Committee on Loans and Foreign Exchange, the Sub-Committee on Foreign Exchange Control and the Sub-Committee on Control of Infringements of Credit Regulations. There are also about 30 sub-committees, mostly based in branches of the Bank of Greece throughout the country, dealing with credits to small businesses. These sub-committees are responsible for implementing the decisions of the Currency Committee and for ensuring the compliance of the banking industry with the existing rules and regulations. The Currency Committee has also set up a General Inspectorate of Banks which is staffed by employees of the Bank of Greece and is authorised to inspect the books and records of banks and call their chairmen, directors and employees to give oral or written evidence to it.

The day-to-day supervision of the banking system is thus carried out by the Bank of Greece, mainly through the various sub-committees set up by the Currency Committee for specific subjects (credit control, exchange control, etc.). However, the Currency Committee has the ultimate responsibility for the orderly functioning of the banking system as well as for the formulation and implementation of monetary and credit policies. Its powers and responsibilities in the monetary field are covered in section 5.10 below.

5.3.2 Outline of System

For the establishment of a new bank in Greece, a licence from the Currency Committee is required. Every bank applying for a licence must submit all the information required by the Currency Committee. The latter has full discretion to approve or reject an application (Art. 2 of Law 1665/1951). The requirements for authorisation and the conditions for withdrawal of a licence are set out in decisions of the Currency Committee and are published in the *Official Gazette*. No amendment of a bank's articles of association is valid without the Committee's approval.

Appeals against a Currency Committee decision refusing authorisation can be made to the Council of State on the grounds of administrative irregularities (see below 5.14.5).

Compliance with the decisions and regulations of the Currency Committee is compulsory. The Committee has the power to impose sanctions on any bank that violates the law or its decisions, ranging from the issuing of specific orders to the appointment of a commissioner and the revocation of the bank's licence.

5.3.3 Returns to Supervisory Authority

Under Article 5 of Law 1665/1951 banks are required to submit to the Currency Committee any reports, statements of accounts and information required by it. The frequency and detail of the returns made by banks are determined by decisions of the Currency Committee. The basic return is a detailed balance sheet analysis. This is supplemented by other returns on specific subjects, especially for credit control purposes. The balance sheet and most other returns are submitted every month but foreign exchange returns are submitted at more frequent intervals while other returns are requested on a quarterly or annual basis.

Article 17 of Law 5076/1931 states that the Minister of National Economy (now the Minister of Commerce) may, after consulting the Bank of Greece, issue a decree prescribing a standard form for the preparation of the balance sheets and financial statements of Greek banks, as well as a special form for the financial statements on the operations in Greece of foreign banks. In fact, banks are currently free to choose the form of their balance sheets and profit and loss accounts, but the technical form of other returns is prescribed by the Currency Committee. Foreign banks are not required to publish or submit to the authorities separate profit and loss accounts for their operations in Greece.

5.3.4 Auditing requirements

There are no special auditing requirements for banks.

5.3.5 Inspection

The Currency Committee is vested with very wide powers of inspection and examination of bank books and records. It is also empowered to call for oral or written evidence from the governors, members of the board of directors and employees of a bank. The purposes of inspection are threefold: to verify compliance with the banking laws and regulations; to check the accuracy of the reports and returns submitted; and to investigate any suspected irregularities in the running of the bank. The powers of inspection extend beyond a bank to the books and records of its customers.

Article 3 of Legislative Decree 588/1948 on the control of credit prescribes that the granting and use of credits shall be controlled by employees of the Bank of Greece. Such control may also be assigned to civil servants of the Ministries of Finance and Commerce acting jointly with employees of the Bank of Greece. However, the Currency Committee has set up a General Inspectorate of Banks (Decision 550 of December 20, 1951) which is staffed by employees of the Bank of Greece. This is now the main inspection body in Greece responsible for carrying out detailed examinations and audits of bank books and records and for verifying their compliance with the existing prudential, credit and exchange controls.

The frequency of inspection is at the discretion of the General Inspectorate of Banks. Inspections are carried out at regular and fairly short intervals; however, irregular inspections may also take place in response to particular circumstances.

5.4 CRITERIA FOR AUTHORISATION

5.4.1 Legal Form

Banks, as defined in Article 10 of Law 5076/1931, must be set up as joint stock companies. Commercial banks can only issue registered shares (Arts. 3 and 11a of Law 2190/1920 on joint stock companies), ordinary or preference; they may not issue non-voting ordinary shares, but preference shares may be without voting power.

5.4.2 Minimum Capital

The Currency Committee is empowered to prescribe the minimum level of registered capital required for the establishment of a new bank. Currently, the minimum level of registered capital is set at 500 million drachmas (Decision of Currency Committee 153/8 of March 2, 1977, and Presidential Decree 529 of June 20, 1977) and has to be fully paid up at the time of application. The registered capital has to be deposited in full with the Bank of Greece, and a receipt for the amount must be attached to the application submitted to the authorities. The amount of capital thus deposited may only be withdrawn after the establishment of the new bank (Art. 14 of Law 5076/1931) or after an application is rejected.

5.4.3 Management Qualifications

There are no requirements in the two basic Banking Acts (Laws 5O76/1931 and 1665/1951) regarding the competence or nationality of personnel in control of banks. Any such requirements are laid down by decisions of the Currency Committee. Decision 1360/5 of March 3, 1965 states that the majority of the members of the board of directors of a Greek bank have to be Greek nationals residing permanently in Greece (see, however, 5.16 below for exceptions to this rule).

5.4.4 Management Plans

The Currency Committee specifies the information that banks have to submit to it when applying for authorisation. Management plans are covered by these requirements although no set form is specified.

5.4.5 Other Requirements

As stated above (5.3.2), the Currency Committee has full discretion to approve or reject an application for the establishment of a new bank. In practice, the Currency Committee takes into account the general or local economic need for a new bank. In the case of foreign banks setting up operations for the first time in Greece, account is also taken of the possible benefits to the Greek economy from the import of foreign exchange as well as of other less tangible benefits (greater competition, application of modern banking techniques, etc.).

5.5 BRANCHES

5.5.1 Restrictions on Branching in Greece

A licence from the Currency Committee is required for the opening of each branch or agency of existing banks. The Currency Committee has full discretion in granting or refusing a licence, after considering the particulars submitted by the bank concerned (Art. 2 of Law 1665/1951). Although not stated clearly in the relevant section of the law, the Currency Committee takes into consideration the social and economic need for the proposed branch. This can be construed from Article 3(2) of Law 1665/1951 which states that the operating licence for branches that pre-dated the introduction of this law can be extended if in the opinion of the Currency Committee there is a social and economic need for this.

5.5.2 *Branching and Operations in Other Countries*

There are no statutory or published restrictions on the opening of branches or the establishment of subsidiaries abroad by Greek banks. It is, however, unlikely that any bank will open a branch abroad and expand its activities overseas without first seeking the approval of the authorities. In addition, the banks are subject to exchange control regulations regarding the remittance and investment of funds overseas.

5.6 RESTRICTIONS ON BUSINESS

5.6.1 *Restrictions on Types of Business*

Banks are prohibited from carrying on commercial or industrial business on their own account (Art. 16(1) of Law 5076/1931). Moreover, Legislative Decree 400/1970 on private insurance companies prohibits the banks from directly engaging in insurance activities. Limitations are also placed on the equity participations which banks may hold.

5.6.2 *Loans to directors*

Restrictions are also placed on the granting of any type of credit to members of the board of directors of a bank without sufficient collateral security. Such loans to directors require a special resolution of the general meeting of shareholders, and the time limit of the credit may not be extended beyond the financial year in which such a resolution was adopted (Art. 16 (6) of Law 5076/1931).

5.6.3 *Equity Participations*

Banks are forbidden to invest more than 20% of their capital (share capital and reserves) in the shares of any one enterprise without the permission of the Currency Committee (Art. 16(3) of Law 5076/1931). No restriction is imposed on the size of participations in relation to the capital of such enterprises and no limit is imposed on the total of all participations in other enterprises in relation to the capital of the bank. Moreover, the Law states (Art. 16 (5)) that the above limitation shall not apply to participations in companies established abroad or which depend in any way on Greek banks or have as their object the fostering of the business of Greek banks. Thus, participations in other banks are exempt from this limitation.

The law is unclear on the position of participations in other financial institutions whether these engage in activities directly related to banking (e.g. factoring and leasing) or not (e.g. insurance). The approval of the Currency Committee is normally required before a bank can acquire a participation in another financial institution.

In practice, commercial banks have accumulated substantial and extensive interests in commercial and industrial companies. Moreover, the big commercial bank groups actually own the largest insurance companies and maintain, through them, a dominant position in the insurance market.

5.6.4 Mergers

There are no restrictions on mergers and takeovers of banks in the two basic Banking Acts but approval of the Currency Committee is in practice required. However, Law 2292/1953 on bank mergers empowers the Minister of Commerce to bring about the merger of two or more banks at the request of shareholders representing 20% of the paid-up share capital and with the consent of specified majorities of the shareholders of each bank concerned (Art. 1 (1-3)). The merger of two or more banks may also be imposed by decree issued following a decision of the Cabinet and without a resolution of a general meeting of each bank concerned (Art. 10).

5.7 BANKING NAMES AND DESCRIPTIONS

The name of each bank must be approved by the Minister of the National Economy (now the Minister of Commerce) (Art. 10(2) of Law 5076/1931). Only companies authorised under Article 2 of Law 1665/1951 and some types of institution set up by special decrees (such as the mortgage banks, the investment banks, etc.) are allowed to use the term 'bank' in their name. Individuals, general or limited partnerships or companies or associations of any other kind engaged in banking business are prohibited from using the terms 'bank' and 'banker' in the name of their firm (Art. 12).

5.8 ADVERTISING

There are no restrictions in the two basic Banking Acts (Laws 5076/1931 and 1665/1951) on advertising or the contents of advertisements issued by banks.

5.9 SOLVENCY AND LIQUIDITY

The Currency Committee is required to ensure the maintenance of sound and prudent banking practices and is empowered to issue regulations regarding specific solvency and liquidity ratios. In practice, however, the extensive use of direct controls has rendered unnecessary the use of solvency and liquidity ratios. Nevertheless, there has been, in recent years, a growing tendency to refer to the need to maintain sound banking practices, especially in those areas (e.g. inter-bank deposits, foreign exchange business) where greater freedom of action has been conferred on banks.

5.9.1 Solvency Ratios

The Currency Committee is empowered to issue regulations regarding the level of capital of a bank in relation to the size of its deposits. Moreover, it has the right to impose a compulsory increase in the capital of a bank within a specified period taking into consideration the extent of the risks assumed by the bank concerned.

No specific capital-based solvency ratios are currently applied. However, as noted in 5.14 below, if the share capital of a bank plus any reserves from the issue of shares above par (but excluding reserves from retained earnings) is less than one seventieth of its total deposit liabilities, the bank may, under certain circumstances, be compelled to double its registered capital.

Commercial as well as investment banks were until recently subject, in common with other joint stock companies, to the limitation that bonds and other marketable debt instruments could not exceed twice their equity. A recent change in legislation (Law 1046/1980) has exempted all banks from this limitation, provided the debt instruments issued are of maturities not exceeding five years and their issue is approved by the Currency Committee.

5.9.2 Liquidity Ratios

The Currency Committee is empowered to issue regulations setting limits in the ratios between different assets or liabilities. Article 15 of Law

5076/1931 also requires all banks operating in Greece to keep liquid assets in drachmas bearing a certain relationship to the total of their sight and savings deposits. However, the liquidity ratio provisions of this article are not currently enforced though it has never been specifically repealed.

Ratios between liquid assets and deposits are now exclusively set by Currency Committee decisions, primarily for monetary purposes. However, Currency Committee Decision 1509 of September 14, 1968 (Chapter IV, Section V) establishes a ceiling on loans with maturity of over four years. These cannot in total exceed an amount equal to 25% of a bank's total deposits plus an additional 25% of time deposits, savings deposits with three-month notice, capital and reserves and long-term loans to the bank with maturity in excess of four years.

5.9.3 Loan Limits

Banks may not grant loans or other credit facilities (including letters of guarantee and credit acceptances) to the same party exceeding 20% of their capital (share capital and reserves) (Art. 16 (2) of Law 5076/1931). However, the Minister of Commerce with the approval of the Currency Committee is empowered to authorise exemptions from this rule in special cases. This prohibition does not apply to transactions between domestic banks or with banks overseas, to loans to central and local government, public corporations and charitable institutions, or to advances on wheat, tobacco or raisins (Art. 16(5)).

5.10 MONETARY AND CREDIT CONTROLS

The Currency Committee has very wide powers over monetary and credit matters and has the ultimate responsibility for the formulation and implementation of monetary and credit policies. However, the Currency Committee is required to ensure that its policies are devised and implemented in such a way as to promote the aims of the overall economic policy of the government, both with regard to the monetary and budgetary state of the economy and to the financing requirements of particular sectors of economic activity.

Although the Bank of Greece is in principle the executive agent of the Currency Committee, in practice it exerts considerable influence in the formulation and implementation of monetary and credit policies. The Governor of the Bank of Greece is a member of the Currency Committee while many of the sub-committees consist of senior officials of the Bank.

In the monetary and credit control field, the Currency Committee is more specifically authorised:

(i) to decide on matters of monetary and credit policy and exercise control of credit operations in accordance with the provisions of Legislative Decree 588/1948 as subsequently amended. (The Currency Committee is authorised by Article 4 of Law 128/1975 to set the rates of interest on deposits as well as on loans or credit facilities of any type or purpose and to fix the amount and nature of any type of commission or expenses to be charged by banks and other credit institutions for the services provided by them).

(ii) to approve the issue of interest-bearing bills by the State and their terms of issue, in accordance with the provisions of Legislative Decree 3745/1957.

(iii) to decide on matters of foreign exchange and foreign exchange policy in accordance with the provisions of Law 1837/1951, as subsequently amended.

(iv) to determine the terms and conditions for hire-purchase sales and to control, with the General Inspectorate of Banks, the application of its rulings as provided in Legislative Decree 3838/1958.

(v) to approve, irrespective of any other legislation, the terms of issue of bonds and other securities of public corporations and financial institutions for public subscription.

5.10.1 Direct Credit Controls

Ceilings on the amount of credit extended by commercial banks had been imposed by the monetary authorities for a number of years prior to the mid-1970s. Credits extended to sectors of high priority had, however, been exempt from such ceilings. Since the mid-1970s the authorities have set annual targets for the growth of monetary and credit aggregates but these have in general tended to be exceeded.

5.10.2 Selective Credit Controls

Credit policy is highly selective. Banks are required to earmark stated proportions of their deposits for the financing of productive activities and for lending to small-scale industry, while considerable restrictions are imposed on the financing of import and domestic trade. Special credit regulations also apply to the size and maturity of credits to other sectors of the economy such as housing. The authorities also determine the maximum level of interest rates for each type of loan. A policy of differentiating interest rates in favour of sectors of high priority has been applied for a very long period. Sanctions can be imposed on bank customers for contraventions of the terms and conditions attached to each credit facility, as set out by relevant decisions of the Currency Committee. Under Article 2 (5) of Legislative Decree 588/1948 (as amended by Legislative Decree 979/1971), banks must ensure that each credit facility contains a penalty clause in favour of the Greek State which is invoked on the discovery of a contravention by the Currency Committee, following an inspection by the General Inspectorate of Banks or at the suggestion of the bank that granted the credit facility. Currency Committee Decision 157/9 of March 30, 1977, sets out in detail the terms and conditions for the application of the penalty clause. In addition, any amounts outstanding under the credit facility concerned become immediately due for repayment while the Currency Committee can deny the customer concerned any further credit facilities for a specified or indefinite period.

5.10.3 Regulation of Interest Rates

For an extended period the Currency Committee has been setting the rates of interest on all types of deposit and credit. In recent years, however, some rates have been left to be determined in the market. These include the rates of interest on inter-bank deposits in drachmas and foreign currency and on foreign currency deposits of non-residents. A differentiation of interest rates in favour of larger and longer-term deposits has also been introduced in recent months.

5.10.4 Central Bank Accommodation

The Bank of Greece accommodates the commercial banks by rediscounting commercial paper and by refinancing special medium and long term credits. However, the main channel of accommodation is the use of overdraft facilities on current accounts maintained by the commercial banks with the Bank of Greece. Penalty rates are applied to such overdrafts in relation to the banks' deposits. There are no organised markets in treasury bills, short-term monetary claims or foreign exchange, though a market for inter-bank deposits has evolved in recent years and an inter-bank foreign exchange market is due to be set up before accession to the Community (see 5.11 below).

5.10.5 Reserve Requirements

At present, commercial banks are required to place on an interest-bearing compulsory deposit with the Bank of Greece 7% of the total sum of their deposits in drachmas from the private sector and of their deposits in foreign currency that have been converted into drachmas at the Bank of Greece. (Currency Committee Decision 143/12 of December 15, 1976), with the exception of so-called 'special time deposits' - a new category of deposits introduced in June 1980 that pay interest on a rising scale with the size of deposit. The compulsory reserve requirement for these deposits has been set at the level of 5% (Currency Committee Decision 275 of June 21, 1980).

Banks are also required to invest 34% of such deposits in treasury bills and other public sector securities - e g., economic development bonds and bonds of public corporations (Currency Committee Decision 249/14 of September 27, 1979). Of this requirement, no less than 5.5% but no more than 12% must be invested in bonds. The exact percentage applicable is not based on liquidity considerations, but is mainly a monetary policy variable influenced by the requirements for financing the government budget.

Banks are further required to channel 15% of their total drachma deposits into medium and long-term credits for the financing of productive activities. Any shortfall is compulsorily deposited with the Bank of Greece in a special low-interest-bearing account. Part of these compulsory deposits may be invested, with the approval of the Bank of Greece, in treasury bills. Banks with total deposit liabilities in drachmas and foreign currency of less than 2000 million drachmas are subject to a 5% requirement only. Moreover, branches of foreign banks, except those of American Express International Banking Corporation, are not subject to this requirement.

Banks, including branches of foreign banks, are also required to set aside 7% of the increase in their total drachma deposits above their level at the end of 1965 for credits to small businesses. (Currency Committee Decision 282 of August 14, 1980). Any shortfall is again compulsorily deposited in a special low-interest-bearing account with the Bank of Greece. Each loan falling under this category must not exceed 20 million drachmas and its terms and conditions are set by decisions of the Loans and Foreign Exchange Sub-Committee.

Banks operating in Greece, including branches of foreign banks, are also subject to reserve requirements calculated on their loans. Some loans are subject to reserve requirements while others give rise to a right of release. The main purpose of these requirements has been to equalise the effective yields to the banks of high-interest and low-interest loans, although the latest amendments, effected in September 1979 and June 1980, have in fact brought about a differential in effective yields in favour of loans with low nominal rates of interest. Effective yields are further affected by compulsory contributions to special accounts, which differ by type of loan. These accounts are used to fund the rebates payable to banks to cover any difference between the interest they are allowed to charge on some types of highly desirable loans (e.g. foreign currency loans to domestic enterprises) and the interest they have to pay on the corresponding deposits.

Currently, the reserve and release ratios for different categories of loans are as set by Currency Committee Decision 275/13 of June 21, 1980, and range from a reserve requirement of 27% for high-interest loans to a release ratio of 52% for low interest loans. There are some categories of loans that are not subject to this scheme. These include loans funded by the Bank of Greece and loans in foreign exchange or with a foreign exchange clause.

Reserve and release requirements are calculated on the basis of outstanding balances at the end of the preceding month. Compulsory reserves are held on a non-interest bearing account with the Bank of Greece. If releases exceed the level of compulsory reserves, the difference is covered by a deposit placed in a non-interest bearing account by the Bank of Greece with the commercial bank concerned at the request of the latter.

5.11 FOREIGN EXCHANGE

5.11.1 Authority to Deal in Foreign Exchange

For a very long period, there has been no organised foreign exchange market in Greece. Banks have engaged in foreign exchange transactions not for their own account but as agents of the Bank of Greece. They have been required to surrender regularly to the Bank of Greece any surplus of foreign exchange receipts over disbursements by currency and have been entitled, in turn, to obtain any shortfall from the Bank of Greece. However, banks have been allowed to maintain working balances in foreign currencies with their correspondent banks overseas. Such funds have originated from certain categories of foreign exchange deposits which they have not been obliged to surrender to the Bank of Greece. The buying and selling rates of exchange for a number of currencies, for which official quotations are maintained, have been set daily by the Bank of Greece.

Banks have been authorised to issue import and export licences, make exchange settlements relating to permitted trade and invisible transactions and grant residents a standard travel allowance. However, in several cases, approval by the Bank of Greece has also been required. Banks have not been allowed to trade foreign exchange among themselves, while forward exchange cover for trade transactions has only been provided by the Bank of Greece and only in or through US dollars.

Greece has undertaken to set up a foreign exchange market before accession to the Community in January 1981 and to take measures to ensure that the drachma is quoted in at least one of the foreign exchange markets of the Community. At the time of writing, plans have been announced for the setting up of an organised inter-bank market for foreign exchange. Under the proposed rules, authorised banks will be allowed to engage in foreign exchange transactions for their own account with their customers, other banks and the Bank of Greece. The Bank of Greece will also cease to set the rates of exchange on a daily basis as hitherto. The market will be organised along the lines of the Paris inter-bank foreign exchange market.

5.11.2 Limits on Positions

At present, the banks are not allowed to have open positions in any foreign currency. Under the proposed new rules, the Bank of Greece will be authorised to issue regulations setting limits on the foreign currency positions of banks.

Under existing rules, commercial banks may, however, borrow convertible currencies abroad, provided they lend corresponding amounts in foreign currency (or in drachmas but with a foreign currency clause) for periods of at least five years to productive enterprises established in Greece. The interest rates charged on such loans are regulated by the Greek monetary authorities but commercial banks are entitled to a rebate covering any difference between interest paid and interest received.

Banks have also been authorised to operate convertible sight or time deposit accounts in drachmas or in foreign currencies for foreign and Greek nationals permanently residing abroad as well as for Greek nationals working abroad on a temporary basis, including seamen. They have also been allowed to take foreign currency deposits from other banks in Greece. Initially, the terms and conditions (interest rates, maturities, notice of withdrawal) for most categories of foreign currency deposits were set by the Currency Committee. Banks were also required to convert these deposits into drachmas at the Bank of Greece. Such drachma proceeds had to be used locally and were subject to the same reserve requirements as ordinary drachma deposits of residents.

Under new regulations introduced gradually in 1980, banks have been allowed to negotiate freely the terms and conditions of their foreign currency deposits. Moreover, the requirement to convert foreign currency deposits into drachmas has been lifted completely for some categories of deposits (e.g. deposits from other banks or from shipping companies) or replaced by a requirement to redeposit them, in full or in part, in foreign currency accounts with the Bank of Greece at rates set periodically by the latter in accordance with prevailing inter-bank deposit interest rates in the international money markets. The requirement to convert into drachmas has, however, been retained for some categories of deposits. Freely disposable foreign currency funds are subject to a provision that no more than 30% of such funds may be placed in local markets or abroad for maturities exceeding one year. The rules governing foreign currency deposits have been subject to continuous review and further changes are very likely.

5.12 CREDIT INFORMATION EXCHANGE

The Currency Committee has powers to require the reporting of any type of loan under the provisions of Legislative Decree 588/1948 on the control of credit. Banks and other credit institutions have to report to the Currency Committee all credit facilities including letters of guarantee granted to any one borrower if either the total outstanding of credits drawn exceeds 10 million drachmas or the sum of credits drawn and letters of guarantee issued exceed 20 million drachmas per borrower (Currency Committee Decision 180/2 of May 8, 1978).

A service for the monitoring of bank credit facilities to individual enterprises has been in operation in Greece since 1957 when it was set up by Currency Committee Decision 1015/6 of August 2, 1957. The functions of this service, which is based at the Bank of Greece, are similar to those of central risks bureaux in other countries. Within the first fortnight of each month, individual branches of banks and other credit institutions have to submit directly to the Currency Committee, rather than through their head offices, detailed returns on official forms provided by the authorities covering the amounts outstanding at the end of the preceding month for all customers whose credit facilities exceed the limits mentioned above. The monthly information includes the name and branch of economic activity of the borrower and the types of credit facilities granted, classified by maturity and purpose. Credits in arrears for more than six months, letters of guarantee issued and blocked deposits or state guarantees held as collateral for letters of guarantee are also shown.

The monthly reports are collated by the monitoring service and each reporting bank is entitled to receive information on its customers' overall borrowings from the banking sector. The monthly reports are also used for credit control purposes and for assessing the credit risks of particular borrowers. The system is also used to provide detailed analyses of credits by sectors or sub-sectors of economic activity for macroeconomic and credit policy purposes.

5.13 DEPOSIT INSURANCE

There is no legal or other requirement for deposit insurance in Greece.

5.14 SANCTIONS

5.14.1 Revocation of Authorisation

If a bank's capital has decreased as a result of losses or if it is considered inadequate for its needs, the Currency Committee can call upon the bank to restore its capital to its original level or to raise it to the desired level within a minimum period of 60 days. The Committee can also order the suspension of dividend payments and the transfer of profits to capital reserves.

Failure to comply with such an order provides grounds for revocation of the bank's licence by the Currency Committee. Other grounds for revocation include refusal to co-operate and a breach of the law or decision of the Committee. The Committee then has a choice between revoking the bank's licence and putting the bank into liquidation or appointing a commissioner (Art. 8 of Law 1665/1951 see below 5.14.2 - 5.14.3).

5.14.2 Imposition of Conditions

The Currency Committee may also impose conditions on a bank that has infringed any banking laws or regulations. These may include the prohibition of certain transactions or other limitations on the carrying out of banking operations or the suspension of the responsible management and the appointment of a commissioner or a temporary commissioner.

Thus under Article 5 of Legislative Decree 588/1948, the Currency Committee can revoke for a specified or indefinite period the authorisation for conducting foreign exchange operations and/or prohibit the financing of the bank concerned by the Bank of Greece. These sanctions are supplemented by the provisions of Article 1 of Law 1387/1950 which empower the Currency Committee to impose an increase in the ratio of compulsory deposits held by the offending bank with the Bank of Greece and/or to raise the rate of interest charged on its borrowings from the latter.

Some of these sanctions are restated in Law 1665/1951 (Art. 11) on the operation and control of banks. Under this article, the Currency Committee can forbid the granting of credits to any offending bank by the Bank of Greece and/or debar it from conducting foreign exchange operations. It can also exclude it from the loans distributed to the banks by the Bank of Greece out of the deposits compulsorily held with the latter by public corporations and institutions. (These institutions are required by Law 1611/1950 to place with the Bank of Greece their accumulated reserves in excess of working balance requirements; investment of their accumulated reserves in any other form requires the prior approval of the Currency Committee).

Before appointing a commissioner, the Currency Committee notifies the bank concerned in writing about the alleged infringement and the latter has the right to make representations within a month. The Committee may also call the management of the bank to give oral evidence to the Committee.

Once a commissioner is appointed, no decisions can be taken by the management or administration without his consent. The commissioner is required to submit to the Committee within a stipulated period a report on the financial, accounting and administrative position of the bank. If the Currency Committee considers on the basis of this report and other information that the activities of the bank cannot continue under its existing management, it can assign the administration of the bank to the same commissioner or another. The commissioner is subject to the control and supervision of the Currency Committee and can be replaced or his appointment terminated by a decision of the Committee.

The Currency Committee is also empowered by Law 236/1975 to appoint a temporary commissioner if it considers that this is required either by the urgent nature of the matter under consideration or in order to protect the public interest, to safeguard the interests of the bank, the State or other parties or to avoid any adverse repercussions on the money market and the economy. The decision to appoint a temporary commissioner takes effect immediately and is not subject to the procedure (written notice, representations within a month) set out above. The task of the temporary commissioner is terminated on the appointment of a commissioner who assumes the management of the bank.

Banks whose management is repeatedly placed under a commissioner or temporary commissioner and whose share capital plus reserves from issuing shares above par are less than one seventieth of their total deposit liabilities may be required to double their share capital (Law 431/1976): 90% of the newly issued shares have then to be offered to public law corporations and institutions (pension insurance funds, etc) and the Post Office Savings Bank. The subsequent disposal of shares held by such public law entities is subject to the approval of the Currency Committee. The effect of these provisions is to bring the offending bank under indirect state control.

5.14.3 Other Sanctions

A bank may be put into liquidation by a resolution of the Currency Committee if its licence is revoked or if it is unable to meet its liabilities towards its creditors. One or more liquidators may be appointed by the Committee to take over the administration of the bank, subject to the control and supervision of the Currency Committee. As from the notification of the decision of liquidation, the bank is forbidden to take deposits while the Currency Committee may also restrict other activities of the bank. A bank in liquidation may not be declared bankrupt and any procedure for bankruptcy that may have begun must be suspended as from the publication in the Official Gazette of the decision concerning liquidation.

5.14.4 Penalties

Punitive sanctions for bank officials who contravene legal and control requirements are laid down in several laws and legislative decrees.

Thus, Article 2 of Law 1387/1950 states that breaches of the provisions of Legislative Decree 588/1948 on the control of credit and of any related decisions of the Currency Committee are punishable by imprisonment up to five years and/or by fines up to 500,000 drachmas. These sanctions can be imposed not only on those employees of a bank that commit the offence but also on its governor or managing director and on the appointed divisional or departmental directors who are held jointly and severally reponsible for the infringement.

Under Article 10 of Law 1665/1951, the governor, directors, auditors, managers and the employees concerned of a bank can be punished by imprisonment and fines if (a) they do not keep regularly the books and records prescribed by law as well as those ordered by the Currency Committee, (b) they omit the entry of any transaction in the books, (c) they submit to the Currency Committee or to its control bodies false or inaccurate reports or supply false or inaccurate information and (d) they fail to cooperate with the supervisory authorities.

Article 3 of Law 236/1975 on the appointment of a temporary commissioner also states that penal sanctions (imprisonment and fines) can be imposed on the governors, directors, managers and employees of a bank who obstruct the task of the temporary commissioner or do not provide him with all relevant books, records, etc.

The penal sanctions provided for in these laws are imposed by special courts set up by Law 710/1945. Article 4 of Law 710/1945 set up special chambers of the Magistrates' Courts in various major cities. Each of these chambers is composed of three judges of first instance who are appointed for terms of six months, that can in certain cases be extended for up to a year. The cases brought before these courts by the Currency Committee refer to violations of exchange control laws as well as banking laws and related Currency Committee decisions.

5.14.5 Appeals

Appeals against a Currency Committee decision imposing sanctions or revoking a licence can be made to the Council of State but only on the grounds of administrative irregularities. The Council of State examines whether the Currency Committee adequately explains the reasons for its decisions but does not question the factual economic considerations behind them. In the case of sanctions or a revocation of a licence, representations to the Currency Committee can be made within a month of receiving written notification of the decision.

Penal sanctions (above a certain minimum) imposed by the special court set up by Law 710/1945 (Art. 4) are subject to the normal appeals procedure of the Greek legal system.

5.15 FOREIGN BANK BRANCHES

5.15.1 Establishment

Branches of foreign banks are subject to the banking legislation in the same way as domestic institutions and have to comply with all the regulations, decisions and rulings issued by the Currency Committee. The opening of branches requires authorisation by the Currency Committee. Foreign banks must publish a separate balance sheet, though not a profit and loss account, for their operations in Greece. They are also required to submit all the returns prescribed by the monetary authorities for control purposes. Foreign banks can also set up offshore credit units which are subject to special terms and conditions and enjoy various fiscal and other advantages (see 5.15.5 below). However, no such units have been established yet.

5.15.2 Earmarked Capital

For the establishment of a branch in Greece by a foreign bank, an amount of not less than 10 million US dollars, or the equivalent in other convertible foreign currency, must be imported and earmarked as the branch's capital for the duration of its operation in Greece. For each additional branch a further 10 million US dollars, or equivalent in other convertible foreign currency, must be imported under the same conditions as above. Earmarked capital must be deposited with the Bank of Greece as a foreign currency deposit or used for long-term foreign currency financing of the Greek State, public corporations and investment banks. The size of earmarked capital for branches of foreign banks, like the minimum level of capital of Greek banks, can be altered by a decision of the Currency Committee. The branches of American Express International Banking Corporation are exempt from this requirement by virtue of the fact that this bank was established in Greece long before the requirement for earmarked capital for foreign branches was introduced. This bank is, however, subject to other requirements that are normally imposed on domestic banks only.

5.15.3 Nationality and Competence of Personnel

The only requirement regarding senior officials of foreign banks is that they must be resident in Greece. A work permit has to be obtained from the Ministry of Labour before a position can be taken up and a quota system of foreign nationals applies for each bank.

5.15.4 Restrictions on Business

Branches of foreign banks are, by and large, subject to the same restrictions as Greek banks as far as types and range of activity are concerned. Branches of foreign banks, with the exception of those of American Express International Banking Corporation, are not, however, subject to the requirement to utilise 15% of their deposit liabilities for medium-term and long-term loans for the financing of productive activities. Instead, their operations are subject to the requirement that their loans for working capital cannot exceed four times the sum of their foreign currency deposits with the Bank of Greece and the total of their long-term lending to the Greek State, public corporations and investment banks. Long-term loans are defined as those with an original maturity of five years or more.

5.15.5 Representative Offices

No provisions are laid down in the basic banking legislation on the opening of representative offices. Representative offices are covered by the provisions of Law 89/1967 which regulates the establishment of offices of foreign companies whose sole purpose is to carry out business outside Greece. Offshore offices benefit from fiscal and other incentives, including a simpler procedure for issuing work and residence permits for foreign personnel and exemption from tax on the income of such personnel from offshore activities. The permission of the Currency Committee is required to set up a representative office which is prohibited from carrying out any banking activity in Greece.

Law 89/1967 was amended in 1979 to allow offshore credit units to be established in Greece and to engage in offshore banking activities. Under the terms and conditions for the establishment of such units, as set out in Currency Committee Decision 238/23 of May 24, 1979, a licence from the Minister of Coordination issued with the approval of the Currency Committee is required. Offshore credit units may engage in banking activities with foreign or Greek nationals residing permanently abroad, with offshore companies operating in Greece under Law 89/1967, with Greek and foreign banks operating in Greece and with the Greek Government and the Bank of Greece.

Among the offshore banking activities permitted are the acceptance of deposits in foreign currency in minimum amounts of 100,000 US dollars or equivalent in other currencies, the issuing and negotiation of debt instruments in foreign currency with a minimum nominal value per instrument of 100,000 US dollars or equivalent, the granting of loans and participation in loans in foreign currency for financing activities carried out outside Greece, the investment in and negotiation of securities whose value is expressed in foreign currency and whose original proceeds were used for financing activities carried out outside Greece, the issuing of letters of guarantee or opening of documentary letters of credit and handling of all values in foreign currency for projects or transactions outside Greece and the undertaking of financial transactions of all kinds with the Greek Government and the Bank of Greece.

In addition to enjoying various fiscal and other advantages (exemption from all kinds of tax, free transfer of profits, etc.) offshore credit units are also exempt from reserve requirements or other credit restrictions on their activities. Companies, including Greek banks, applying for a licence to establish an offshore credit unit must provide evidence that their capital base (share capital and reserves) is substantial (a minimum of 75 million US dollars or the equivalent in other currencies may be required) and that they enjoy a high reputation and standing in their country of origin and have considerable experience in international banking activities. Offshore credit units are subject to supervision by the Currency Committee and are required to submit regular returns to the Committee covering their activities and in particular their foreign currency exposure. Finally, the operations of offshore credit units must at all times be kept totally separate from the operations of any branch of the same financial institution engaging in banking activities in the domestic market.

5.16 FOREIGN BANK SUBSIDIARIES

5.16.1 Local Ownership

By a decision of the Currency Committee (1360/5 of March 3, 1965), the participation of expatriates in the capital of a bank established in Greece cannot exceed 40%. Expatriates are defined as legal persons that have their head office abroad or natural persons that reside permanently abroad, irrespective of their nationality. An exception to this rule has been granted to the Arab Hellenic Bank which is only 40% owned by Greek interests. More recently, another exception has been granted to a new bank to be set up by an American corporation (the Hellenic American Development Corporation) which is controlled by Americans of Greek origin. The new bank, to be known as International Hellenic Bank, is subject to the requirement that 40% of its share capital should be covered by natural or legal persons of Greek nationality, residing or having their head office permanently in Greece, while the remaining 60% should be covered by importing the corresponding foreign exchange by natural persons of Greek origin, irrespective of their place of permanent residence, or by corporations or foundations based abroad, provided they have been established and are controlled by natural persons of Greek origin. Otherwise, there are no foreign-owned or controlled banking subsidiaries of foreign banks in Greece, though foreign banks may have minority participations in Greek banks.

5.16.2 Nationality of Directors

The majority of the members of the board of directors of a Greek bank must be Greek nationals, permanently resident in Greece. An exception to this rule has been granted to the Arab Hellenic Bank and the International Hellenic Bank (see above).

5.16.3 Guarantees from Parent Institution

No requirements are laid down for such guarantees.

5.17 BANKING ASSOCIATIONS

5.17.1 Membership

All banks established in Greece and foreign banks which maintain a branch in Greece may become members of the Hellenic Banks' Association. Membership is not compulsory. In fact, of the foreign banks operating in Greece, only American Express International Banking Corporation is a member of the Association. Total membership of the Association was 18 commercial and investment banks in June 1980.

5.17.2 Relations with Supervisory Authorities

The Hellenic Banks' Association does not play any formal part in the supervisory system. The role of the Association is at present limited - it is not, for example, usually consulted on policy developments - but its importance and activities are expanding especially vis-à-vis European Community institutions and the Fédération Bancaire of which it became a full member on accession to the EEC. Minimum commission rates for various types of banking services are, however, set under the auspices of the Hellenic Banks' Association.

5.18 BACKGROUND SOURCES

1. Aufricht, H. (ed.): Central Banking Legislation, Vol. II, (International Monetary Fund, Washington, D.C.) (1967).
2. Bank of Greece: Annual Reports.
3. Charissopoulos, N.B.: Report of the Committee on the Working of the Greek Financial System, (Bank of Greece, Athens) (1980).
4. Common Market Reporter - Doing Business in Greece (Loose-leaf service), (Commerce Clearing House, Inc: Chicago) (1979).
5. Elstob, M. (ed.): Banking Structures and Sources of Finance in the European Community, (The Banker Research Unit, London) (1979).
6. Halikias, D.J.: Money and Credit in a Developing Economy: The Greek Case, (New York University Press, New York) (1978).
7. International Monetary Fund: Annual Report on Exchange Arrangements and Exchange Restrictions, 1979 (Washington D.C.).
8. Lassados, V.: Currency Committee: A Code of Provisions in Force (in Greek), (Bank of Greece, Athens) (1979).
9. Tax and Trade Guide, Greece, (Arthur Andersen & Co: Chicago) (1978)
10. Tragakis, G.E.: Banking Law and Practice in Greece (in Greek), (Nomiki Vivliothiki, Athens), (1980).
11. Tragakis, G.E.: Summary of Greek Banking Legislation (in Greek) (unpublished manuscript) (Bank of Greece, Athens) (October 1977).
12. Vittas, D.: The Structure of the Financial System in Greece and in Some Member States of the EEC, Study for the Committee on the Working of the Greek Financial System, (in Greek), (unpublished manuscript), (Bank of Greece, Athens and Inter-Bank Research Organisation, London), (December 1978).

CHAPTER 6

IRELAND

6.1 INSTITUTIONS COVERED

All banks and other bodies engaged in 'banking business' in the Irish Republic must be licensed and must also maintain a deposit with the Central Bank of Ireland in accordance with section 13 of the Central Bank Act 1971. 'Banking business' is defined by section 2 of the Act as:

(i) the business of accepting deposits payable on demand or on notice or at a fixed or determinable future date; or:

(ii) the business aforesaid and any other business normally carried on by a bank.

Irish banks may be divided into two basic groupings: Associated Banks (i.e. clearing banks) and non-Associated banks. The term 'Associated' derives from the Central Bank Act 1942 which gave such banks a special relationship with the Central Bank. The non-Associated banks are sub-divided into four sub-groups for statistical purposes: merchant banks, North American banks, industrial banks and other banks (including European banks).

The regulatory provisions apply to all Associated and non-Associated banks.

Under the Central Bank Act 1971(s. 7(4)) the following bodies are excluded from the licensing and supervision procedures and are not covered here:

(i) the Agricultural Credit Corporation Limited;

(ii) the Industrial Credit Company Limited;

(iii) the Post Office Savings Bank;

(iv) trustee savings banks certified under the Trustee Savings Banks Acts 1863 to 1965;

(v) building societies;

(vi) industrial and provident societies;

(vii) friendly societies;

(viii) credit unions;

(ix) investment trust companies;

(x) managers of unit trust schemes in respect of the business of such trusts.

6.2 BASIC LAWS

The Central Bank Act 1971 amends and extends the Currency Act 1927 and the Central Bank Acts of 1942 and 1964. The four Acts together form the basis of Irish currency and banking legislation, and may be supplemented by regulations made by the Minister of Finance and the Central Bank. The Currency Act 1927 and the Central Bank Act of 1942 had provided for the collection of statistics on a regular basis from certain financial institutions, thereby enabling their activities to be monitored.

The 1942 Act also gave the Central Bank the role of regulating the banking system in the interest of the public at large, but the need for more formal control was answered by the 1971 legislation, which conferred extensive licensing and supervisory powers on the Central Bank. Proposals for additional legislation, which would further strengthen the Central Bank's powers in relation to the supervision of banks, are under consideration.

6.3 SUPERVISORY SYSTEM

6.3.1 Supervisory Authority

The Central Bank of Ireland is designated as the Control Authority for the licensing and supervision of banks in Ireland under the Central Bank Act 1971. Until September 1, 1971, responsibility for licensing banks had rested on the Revenue Commissioners.

The Central Bank of Ireland was established on Febuary 1, 1943 (by virtue of the Central Bank Act 1942), and took the place of the Currency Commission which had been set up under the Currency Act 1927. The whole of the capital stock of the Central Bank is owned by the Government.

Under the Central Bank Act 1942, as amended by the 1971 Act, the Bank is controlled by:

(i) a Governor who is appointed by the President on the advice of the Government;

(ii) two Banking Directors, who are appointed, after consultation by the Minister with the Governor, from among the directors of the Associated Banks (s. 53, 1971 Act); and:

(iii) a further number of directors not exceeding six (s. 53, 1971 Act), appointed by the Minister of Finance. This number shall not include at any one time more than two service directors, i.e. directors who are in the permanent service of the State. One such service director is usually the representative of the Minister of Finance.

By section 53(3) of the Central Bank Act 1971, if a Banking Director ceases to hold office as a director of an Associated Bank, he is disqualified from holding the office of Banking Director.

The Central Bank determines and applies monetary policy (see 6.10 below) in the context of the economic policy of the country and acts:

(i) as banker to the Government and other banks;

(ii) as the central note-issuing authority;

(iii) as agent of the Government for the issue and regulation of Government securities and the administration of exchange control;

(iv) as licensing authority for banking establishments;

(v) as compiler and issuer of statistics on monetary matters; and

(vi) as the authority responsible for monitoring charges for all bank services and for consumer protection in banking.

6.3.2 Outline of System

Under the Central Bank Act 1971, no one may carry on banking business (see 6.1 above) or hold himself out to be a banker, unless he is the holder of a licence and maintains a deposit with the Central Bank.

The Central Bank has discretionary power to grant a licence to any applicant (s. 9, 1971 Act) and may impose such conditions when granting a licence as it feels will promote the orderly and proper regulation of banking (see below 6.14.2).

Subject to the provisions of section 9 of the Central Bank Act 1971, the Central Bank may, in its discretion, grant or refuse to grant an applicant a licence authorising the holder to carry on banking business. The refusal of a licence does, however, require the Minister's consent.

Whenever the Central Bank proposes to refuse to grant a licence to a person:

(i) it shall notify the person in writing that it intends to seek the consent of the Minister of Finance to the refusal and of its reasons for the refusal and that the person concerned may, within 21 days after the date of the giving of the notification, make representations in writing to the Minister in relation to the proposed refusal;

(ii) the person may make such representations in writing to the Minister within the time aforesaid; and

(iii) the Minister shall, before deciding to give or withhold his consent, consider any representations duly made to him under this subsection in relation to the proposed refusal (s. 9, Central Bank Act 1971).

There is no right of appeal from the Minister's decision (but see 6.14.5 below).

As far as the criteria for licensing are concerned, the Central Bank issued in autumn 1971 a set of guidelines which it uses in assessing applications for licences. These guidelines were revised in spring 1975 and since they are not statutory conditions, they may be amended again at any time (see 6.4 below).

The standards expected of licensees are obviously based on normal commercial considerations, but are also prompted by the consideration that the control of money and credit should remain primarily in Irish hands and be administered in the interest of the community as a whole. Although the latter is an important aim, account has also to be taken of the obligations imposed by EEC membership (see 6.4.3, 6.15 and 6.16 below).

Under section 9(5) of the 1971 Act, the grant of a licence to a person shall not constitute a warranty as to the solvency of the person to whom it is granted and the Central Bank shall not be liable in respect of any losses incurred through the insolvency or default of a person to whom a licence is granted.

The Central Bank must publish the names of licence holders at least once a year and in practice does so in its Annual Report. The Central Bank must also keep the Registrar of the Supreme Court and officers of the lower courts informed of their names (s. 12, 1971 Act).

6.3.3 Returns to Supervisory Authority

Under the 1971 Act, a licence holder:

(i) shall keep such books and records as are specified by the Central Bank (s. 17 of the Central Bank Act 1971);

(ii) shall furnish, as required, such information and returns as the Central Bank may specify (s. 18);

(iii) shall publish statements in respect of its business as specified by the Central Bank (s. 19); and

(iv) shall display such statements in its offices and branches (s. 20).

The information above must be supplied by the licence holder as and when the Central Bank specifies. In practice the main returns have to be completed monthly. Different forms may be specified by the Central Bank for the purposes of sections 19 and 20 of the Act in relation to different holders of licences. In the case of information required under sections 17 and 18, no specific form is laid down by the Act.

6.3.4 Auditing requirements

There are no special auditing requirements for banks.

6.3.5 Inspection

Under section 17(3) of the Central Bank Act 1971, a Central Bank officer or accountant authorised by the Bank Governor, may at all reasonable times inspect and take copies of, or extracts from, the books and records kept by licence holders in accordance with Central Bank requirements. The licence holder must produce the records at the request of the inspector and give him any information he may reasonably require.

Inspections are carried out as and when the Central Bank deems necessary.

6.4 CRITERIA FOR AUTHORISATION

6.4.1 Legal Form

An applicant for a new banking licence must be a company constituted under the laws of any Member State of the EEC and must have a legal form acceptable to the Central Bank.

Before the incorporation of a company under the Companies Act 1963, which, if incorporated, would, in the opinion of the Registrar of Companies, be holding itself out as a banker, the Registrar shall not give a certificate of incorporation to the company unless and until the Bank indicates its willingness to grant a licence to the company or to exempt it under section 8 of the 1971 Act, (see 6.7 below).

6.4.2 Minimum Capital

As from 1975, a minimum paid-up share capital of Irish £1 million is required. Existing licence holders which do not meet the requirement (nine banks out of a total of 44 licence holders) have been allowed a period of time to comply. The minimum capital requirement is fixed at the discretion of the Central Bank.

6.4.3. Management Qualifications

Banks must comply with the following requirements in respect of their directors, managers and auditors (Central Bank Annual Report 1975):

(i) A majority of the Board of Directors must be Irish or nationals of other Member States of the EEC.

(ii) The Central Bank must be satisfied in regard to the management structure of a licensed bank. Directors and management executives must be persons of integrity and should have suitable experience in banking, industry or commerce.

(iii) The effective management of the day-to-day operations of the branch offices in Ireland of a licence holder shall be carried out by persons resident in Ireland.

(iv) The Central Bank must be satisfied that there is provision for adequate management succession, particularly in the smaller banks.

(v) The auditor of a licence holder shall not be appointed to the bank in any capacity other than that of auditor, consultant, share registrar, receiver or liquidator.

6.4.4 Management Plans

An applicant must satisfy the Central Bank that it has clearly defined objectives which have been adequately researched (Central Bank Annual Report 1975).

6.4.5 Other Requirements

Other requirements are:

(i) An applicant for a banking licence must satisfy the Central Bank that its objectives are consistent with the aims of economic and monetary policy, the safety of depositors' funds and fair trading in banking.

(ii) The liabilities of a licensed bank which is a subsidiary company, must be guaranteed to the satisfaction of the Central Bank by the parent banking company. (Central Bank Annual Report 1975).

(iii) A bank must maintain a deposit with the Central Bank under section 7 of the 1971 Act. Such a deposit must amount to 5% of the total deposits (including deposits on current accounts) held at the domestic offices of the licence holder, but must not be less than Irish £20,000 nor more than Irish £500,000 (s. 13(1), 1971 Act). Since the 5% figure is fixed by statute, it can only be amended by legislation. The amount of the deposit is calculated by the Central Bank at the time of the licence application and is recalculated twice yearly by reference to the returns made by the licence holder to the Central Bank.

The deposit carries interest at the rate determined by the Central Bank. The rate may not be less than the Central Bank's minimum rediscount rate for the time being for exchequer bills fixed under section 7(1)(g) of the Central Bank Act 1942.

6.5 BRANCHES

6.5.1 Restrictions on Branching in Ireland

A licence holder must, in relation to the number and location of any branches, offices or sub-offices in Ireland, conform to the policy approved from time to time by the Central Bank. This requirement was first published by the Central Bank in 1975 (Central Bank Annual Report 1975).

6.5.2. Branching and Operations in Other Countries

There are no statutory or published restrictions on the opening of branches abroad by Irish banks. However, the Central Bank is consulted before the opening of such branches (cf. 6.5.1 above).

6.6 RESTRICTIONS ON BUSINESS

6.6.1 Restrictions on Types of Business

There are no specific legal restrictions on the types of business which can be undertaken by banks in the Republic, but limitations are placed on the use of bank funds (see 6.9.3. below) and on the types of participation banks may hold.

The general guiding principle is that a licence holder must ensure that its activities are consistent with the aims of economic and monetary policy, safety of depositors' funds and fair trading in banking (Central Bank Annual Report 1975).

6.6.2 Loans to directors

A licence holder should not employ more than 2% of risk assets with any one of its directors or any one business in which it or any one of its directors has what is considered by the Central Bank to be a major interest. Beneficial ownership of 15% of the equity, together with membership of the board of the business, would be considered by the Central Bank to be a major interest. In relation to an individual director, the aggregate of such accommodation must not exceed 8% of risk assets (Central Bank Annual Report 1975).

6.6.3 Equity Participations

A licence holder may not, without the prior approval of the Central Bank, make an investment in voting shares of another company in excess of 20% of such shares (Central Bank Annual Report 1975).

The aggregate of all investments in the voting shares of other companies must not exceed 30% of a bank's risk assets.

The rules governing equity participations in other banks operate effectively as a merger control. Any one shareholder, or what is deemed by the Central Bank to be an associated group of shareholdérs, may not hold more than 20% of the shares of any class in a bank without the written consent of the Central Bank (Central Bank Annual Report 1975).

6.6.4 Mergers

There are no statutory provisions regulating bank mergers and changes of ownership with the exception of the Bank of Ireland Act 1929. Section 2 (i-j) of that Act prohibits the absorption of the Bank of Ireland by any other company and provides that it, in turn, cannot acquire another bank without the consent of the Minister for Finance. As mentioned above in 6.6.3, the rules on equity participations operate as a merger control on licence holders.

6.7 BANKING NAMES AND DESCRIPTIONS

Only licensed banks are authorised to use the words 'bank' or 'banker' as part of their name (s. 7 of the Central Bank Act 1971). The Central Bank may, however, grant an exemption from this provision under section 8 of the Act on the grounds that, in the opinion of the Central Bank, the person does not in fact carry on or propose to carry on banking business and does not otherwise hold himself out or represent himself as a banker, or as carrying on banking business.

The Registrar of Business Names shall notify the Central Bank of any proposed change of business name, if, in his opinion, the company would, by virtue of the change, be holding itself out as a banker (s. 16, 1971 Act).

6.8 ADVERTISING

Under section 22 of the 1971 Act, the Central Bank may give a direction in writing to a holder of a licence in relation to the information which the holder shall include in any advertisement to be published by him, or on his behalf, or in any statement to the public to be made by him or on his behalf.

The Central Bank may give a direction to a holder of a licence to refrain from publishing or continuing to publish, during such period as shall be specified in the direction, an advertisement inviting deposits from the public. The Bank shall not give a direction under this section unless it is satisfied that it is desirable to do so in the interest of the orderly and proper regulation of banking.

Any person who is not a licence holder (or the representative of a licence holder) or an exempt body (see 6.1 above) is forbidden to advertise for or solicit deposits (s. 27, 1971 Act).

6.9 SOLVENCY AND LIQUIDITY

Section 23 of the 1971 Act gives the Central Bank wide powers to impose ratios. The Central Bank may require all licence holders, or holders in one or more specific categories, to observe a specified ratio (or a minimum or maximum ratio) between their assets and liabilities, in total or in specific parts. The Act does not require the Central Bank to state the motive or justification for these ratios; thus they can be applied for prudential or monetary policy reasons or both. At present section 23 is used for monetary policy rather than prudential purposes (see 6.10.5 below).

6.9.1. Solvency Ratios

As part of the Central Bank's non-statutory licensing and supervision requirements, a uniform solvency ratio was imposed on all non-Associated banks by the Central Bank in 1971. This stipulated that free resources (paid-up share capital, capital and revenue reserves and a proportion of subordinated loan stock, less fixed, intangible and fictitious assets) should be not less than 10% of risk assets (all assets other than cash, Central Bank balances, balances with other banks, money at call or short notice and government bills, fixed assets, securities and guarantees). The proportion of subordinated loan stock that may be included in free resources is subject to the approval of the Central Bank. No particular ceiling has been published.

A free resources ratio of 10% is still regarded as the norm for most banks, but since 1975 the Central Bank exercises discretion in its application in determining the specific level appropriate to the circumstances of different banks (Central Bank Annual Report, 1975).

The Central Bank applies a different solvency test to the Associated Banks. They are expected to maintain own funds (paid-up share capital, capital and revenue reserves and subordinated loan stock (as above)) at not less than 6½% of their total gross assets.

The Central Bank also takes a close interest in banks' profitability. It is known to have developed criteria for assessing profitability, though the criteria used at present have not been published (see Central Bank Annual Report, 1980).

6.9.2 Liquidity Ratios

At present there is no formal prudential liquidity ratio, but every licence holder is required to "observe such liquidity standards as may be determined by the Central Bank from time to time" (Central Bank Annual Report, 1975). The Central Bank has not published any such standards to date. Liquidity ratios currently required to be observed are imposed for monetary policy purposes (see 6.10 below).

6.9.3 Loan Limits

A number of controls designed to limit the concentration of risk are set out in the Central Bank's Annual Report, 1975:

(i) A licence holder must not employ more than 8% of risk assets with any one individual or firm or what is deemed by the Central Bank to be an associated group of individuals or firms. The ten largest borrowings under these heads shall not account for more than 40% of risk assets. Again, these requirements may be waived by the Central Bank in special cases.

(ii) A licence holder must not have more than 20% of risk assets concentrated in any one sector of business or economic activity which is subject to a common predominant risk factor.

(iii) The aggregate of all investments by a licence holder in the voting shares of other companies must not exceed 30% of its risk assets.

(iv) A licence holder should not grant an advance, loan or credit facility against the security of its own shares or the shares of any subsidiary, fellow subsidiary or parent company unless such shares are quoted on a stock exchange.

(v) A licence holder should not employ more than 2% of risk assets with any one of its directors or any one business in which it or any one of its directors has what is considered by the Central Bank to be a major interest. In relation to an individual director, the aggregate of such accommodation shall not exceed 8% of risk assets.

(vi) A licence holder must not owe more than 10% of total private and commercial deposits to any one depositor, or what is deemed by the Central Bank to be an associated group of depositors. The ten largest private and commercial deposits shall not exceed 40% of such deposits and the deposit portfolio in general should be widely spread. The Central Bank may waive these requirements in special cases.

6.10 MONETARY AND CREDIT CONTROLS

In Ireland, both direct credit restrictions and measures designed to influence the liquidity of the banking system, including the imposition of minimum liquidity ratios, are employed for the control of global credit and the monetary aggregates. In addition, a variety of instruments are used to influence the allocation of bank lending, and the interest rates of the Associated Banks are subject to official constraints.

6.10.1 Direct Credit Controls

Up to 1972 the main method of credit regulation was a system of lending ceilings; initially these controls were imposed only on the Associated Banks but in 1969 they were extended to other banks. In 1972 ceilings were suspended and more emphasis was placed on the control of bank liquidity. However, the Central Bank has found it necessary to reintroduce direct controls from time to time, most recently in 1978. These ceilings remain in operation.

6.10.2 Selective Credit Controls

Selective credit controls on the banking system are of considerable significance in Ireland. The credit ceilings mentioned above have frequently had a selective dimension in recent years and on several occasions the Central Bank has directed that the banks should not add, by their personal lending policies, to consumer demand. In addition the Central Bank has, from time to time, issued guidance requesting that bank lending be channelled into uses which are directly productive and not into projects of a 'non-productive' or speculative nature. Further, the secondary liquidity ratio (described below) may be considered as a selective measure since its primary purpose is to facilitate the flow, and reduce the cost, of funds to the Government.

6.10.3 Regulation of Interest Rates

The lending and deposit rates of the Associated Banks are fixed by a consultative process between the banks and the Central Bank. Either party may initiate discussions when it is considered that an adjustment of rates is required.

6.10.4 Central Bank Accommodation

Until recently the main methods of Central Bank accommodation were the rediscounting of exchequer bills and the provision of secured loans. In early 1980, however, the Central Bank introduced a short-term credit facility for the banks; access to the facility is subject to quotas for each institution. The Central Bank also provides liquidity to the banking system through purchases of exchequer bills and agricultural commodities intervention bills.

6.10.5 Reserve Requirements

Banks in Ireland are subject to a primary and secondary liquidity ratio which are calculated on the basis of each institution's 'relevant resources'. Relevant resources comprise all domestic deposits, plus any net external liability position, less balances with or lending to other licensed banks. The assets that can be held to satisfy the primary ratio are cash in tills, balances with the Central Bank and Central Bank reserve bonds. For the Associated Banks, the first 3% of relevant resources must be held in a separate account with the Central Bank and are remunerated at significantly below market rates. Secondary liquid assets comprise Irish government securities, agricultural commodities intervention bills and eligible commercial bills (up to 1% of relevant resources). Reserve ratios have been fairly stable and are not modified on a short-run basis to influence the liquidity of the banking system. The ratios in force in January 1981 are shown in Table 1.

Table 1: Minimum Reserve Ratios

Institutional Category	Primary Ratio %	Secondary Ratio %	Total %
Associated Banks	12	25	37
Merchant Banks	12	15	27
North American Banks	12	15	27
Continental Banks	12	15	27
Industrial Banks	12	13	25
Other Banks	12	13	25

6.11 FOREIGN EXCHANGE

6.11.1 Authority to Deal in Foreign Exchange

Banks must receive permission (Limited Exchange Control Approval) from the Central Bank before they can provide any foreign exchange services. Banks which have authority to provide the complete range of services are termed 'Authorised Dealers' of which there are currently 26.

The Minister for Finance has delegated the powers required for the supervision of the day-to-day operations of exchange control to the Central Bank. Specialised inspections, at very little notice, are carried out on all aspects of a bank's foreign exchange business if deemed necessary by the Central Bank.

6.11.2 Limits on Positions

Absolute limits are imposed on the exposure of banks in all foreign currencies taken together against Irish Pounds as at the close of business each day. The amount of each bank's foreign currency position (long or short) vis à vis the Irish Pound is reported on a daily basis to the Central Bank.

There are no limits on exposure in individual currencies, although details of exposures between foreign currencies (i.e. other than against Irish Pounds) are reported on a monthly basis for surveillance purposes only.

6.12 CREDIT INFORMATION EXCHANGE

There is no credit information exchange or central risks bureau in Ireland.

6.13 DEPOSIT INSURANCE

There is no deposit insurance system in operation in Ireland. However, proposals are under consideration for the establishment of a limited protection scheme for depositors in licensed banks.

6.14 SANCTIONS

6.14.1 Revocation of Authorisation

The Bank may, with the consent of the Minister of Finance, revoke a licence under section 11 of the Central Bank Act 1971:

(i) if the holder of the licence so requests;

(ii) if the holder fails or ceases to carry on banking business;

(iii) if the holder is adjudicated bankrupt;

(iv) if the holder is a partnership and the partnership is dissolved by the death or bankruptcy of any partner, or otherwise under the law of partnership;

(v) if the holder, being a company, is being wound up;

(vi) if the holder becomes unable to meet his obligations to his creditors, or suspends payments lawfully due by him;

(vii) if the holder fails to maintain a deposit with the Central Bank of an amount determined in accordance with section 13 of the Central Bank Act 1971, (see 6.4.5 above);

(viii) if the holder is convicted on indictment of an offence under any provision of the Central Bank Act 1971 or an offence involving fraud, dishonesty or breach of trust;

(ix) if, since the grant of the licence, the circumstances relevant to the grant have changed and are such that, if an application for a licence were made in the changed circumstances, it would be refused.

Whenever the Central Bank proposes to revoke a licence (other than in pursuance of a request by the holder to do so):

(i) it shall notify the holder in writing that it intends to seek the consent of the Minister of Finance to the revocation and the reasons for the revocation, and that the holder may, within 21 days after the date of giving of the notification, make representations in writing to the Minister in relation to the proposed revocation;

(ii) the holder may make such representations in writing to the Minister within the time limits above; and

(iii) the Minister shall, before deciding to give or withhold his consent, consider any representations duly made to him under this subsection in relation to the proposed revocation (s. 11, Central Bank Act 1971).

The Central Bank shall, as soon as may be after the revocation of a licence, publish notice of the revocation in such manner as it thinks fit (s. 12(2), Central Bank Act 1971).

6.14.2 Imposition of Conditions

When granting a licence, the Central Bank may impose such conditions as it feels will promote the orderly and proper regulation of banking. These conditions may be amended, revoked or added to, and conditions may be imposed in relation to a licence from time to time by the Bank for the same object (s. 10, 1971 Act).

6.14.3 Other Sanctions

The Central Bank may, where it is of the opinion that the holder of a licence has become, or is likely to become unable to meet his obligations, issue directions to suspend the taking of deposits or the making of payments which have not been authorised by the Central Bank, for a period of up to two months.

6.14.4 Penalties

Any person who contravenes the following sections of the Central Bank Act 1971: section 7 (carrying on a banking business without a licence), section 14 (unauthorised use of banking name or description), section 17 (failure to produce books or records), section 18 (failure to furnish information to the

Central Bank), section 27 (illegal advertising for deposits); and a holder of a licence who:

(i) contravenes section 19 (failure to publish business statements), section 20 (failure to display financial statements), section 26 (failure to comply with rules on collection of cheques etc.), section 31 (failure to observe requirements on termination of banking business), or section 33 (failure to observe rules on bank transfers);

(ii) commits a breach of a condition attached to a licence;

(iii) fails to comply with a direction under sections 21 or 22 of the Act, or a requisition under section 23 of the Act; or

(iv) contravenes regulations under section 24 (power to require deposits from licence holders) or section 25 (powers in respect of clearances of licence holders) of the Act

will be guilty of an offence and will be liable on summary conviction, to a fine not exceeding £100, or on conviction on indictment to a fine not exceeding £5,000.

If the contravention, breach or failure in respect of which he was convicted is continued after the conviction, he will be guilty of a further offence and shall be liable on conviction on indictment to a fine not exceeding £250 for each day on which the contravention, breach or failure was so continued (s. 58, Central Bank Act 1971). An offence under the Act which is being tried summarily may be prosecuted by the Central Bank (s. 59).

6.14.5 Appeals

There is no statutory right of appeal to the court against the Minister's decision to revoke a licence (see 6.14.1 above). The institution may, however, in some circumstances be able to take advantage of administrative law remedies to review the decision of the Minister. Similarly a bank may be able to challenge conditions imposed under section 10 of the Central Bank Act 1975 by the Central Bank, although again there is no statutory right of appeal.

A licence holder which has received directions from the Central Bank to suspend the taking of deposits or the making of payments (see 6.14.3 above) can apply to the High Court for an order setting aside the direction (s. 21(3) of the Central Bank Act 1971).

Convictions under section 58 of the 1971 Act (see 6.14.4 above) are subject to the usual rights of appeal in the Irish courts.

6.15 FOREIGN BANK BRANCHES

6.15.1 Establishment

EEC banks may be permitted to establish branches in Ireland. Whether or not non-EEC banks can establish locally on a branch basis is at the discretion of the Central Bank. The rules for foreign bank branches are the same as for domestic banks except where stated below.

6.15.2 Earmarked Capital

The requirements in relation to earmarked or endowed capital are:
  (i) it should not be less than Irish £1 million;
  (ii) the first Irish £1 million shall be non-interest bearing and the balance shall attract a rate of interest which shall be agreed with Central Bank;
  (iii) the level to be maintained will be determined in accordance with the Central Bank's published standard relating to a free resources ratio.
  The stated purpose of the earmarked or endowed capital requirement is primarily to ensure that banks establishing locally on a branch basis do not enjoy a competitive advantage over locally incorporated banks.

6.15.3 Nationality and Competence of Personnel

The Central Bank's agreement to the establishment of foreign banks in Ireland on a branch basis is subject to certain requirements in relation to the establishment of a local supervisory board for the branch.
  This supervisory board should consist of at least four persons, including the person in the bank's head office (or his nominee) having responsibility for the Irish branch, together with at least two businessmen with qualifications satisfactory to the Central Bank and, possibly, the manager of the branch. The board's duties and responsibilities should be defined in a form similar to that found in the articles of association in relation to company's board of directors, and should be set out in a formal document.

6.15.4 Restrictions on Business

Branches of foreign institutions are subject to the same limitations as Irish banks in this respect (see 6.6 above).

6.15.5 Representative Offices

There is no legal bar to the establishment of a representative office, but in practice the consent of the Central Bank would have to be obtained.

6.16 FOREIGN BANK SUBSIDIARIES

6.16.1 Local Ownership

In the case of non-EEC-owned banks, what is deemed by the Central Bank to be an appreciable part of the share capital must be in beneficial Irish ownership (Central Bank Annual Report 1975). There is no requirement as to local ownership for EEC-owned banks.

6.16.2 Nationality of Directors

A majority of the Board of Directors of an EEC-owned bank must be Irish or nationals of other EEC Member States (Central Bank Annual Report 1975). Non-EEC-owned banks would be required to have a majority of Irish directors on the Irish board.

6.16.3 Guarantees from Parent Institution

The liabilities of a licensed bank which is a subsidiary company must be guaranteed to the satisfaction of the Bank by the parent banking company (Central Bank Annual Report 1975).

6.17 BANKING ASSOCIATIONS

6.17.1 Membership

The Irish Banks Standing Committee is composed only of representatives of the four Associated Banks, while all licence holders may apply to join the Irish Bankers Federation. In June 1980, 42 of the 44 licensed banks were members. The Irish Finance Houses Association has 20 members, 10 of them being licensed banks and the remainder being non-deposit-taking instalment credit companies.

6.17.2 Relations with Supervisory Authorities

The Central Bank is under no statutory obligation to consult the Irish Banks Standing Committee on any matter. It does, however, as a matter of practice consult the Committee on points of detail and principle - particularly those relating to new developments or techniques.

Neither the Standing Committee nor the Irish Bankers Federation play any part in the supervisory system.

6.18 BACKGROUND SOURCES

1. Aufricht, H.: Central Banking Legislation, Volume II: Europe, (International Monetary Fund, Washington, D.C.), (1967).
2. Banking Federation of the EEC, Monetary Policy and the Banking System in the Countries of the European Community (Brussels, 1980).
3. Central Bank of Ireland: Quarterly Bulletins and Annual Reports.
4. EEC Monetary Committee: Monetary Policy in the Countries of the European Economic Community: Institutions and Instruments. Denmark, Ireland, United Kingdom (Supplement 1974) (An expanded and updated version of this paper was printed in the Central Bank of Ireland's 1975 Annual Report).
5. Elstob, M.: (ed.), Banking Structures and Sources of Finance in the European Community (Banker Research Unit, London) (1979).
6. International Monetary Fund: Annual Report on Exchange Arrangements and Exchange Restrictions 1979 (Washington, D.C.).
7. Whitaker, T.K.; (former Governor of the Central Bank of Ireland): 'The Central Bank and the Banking System'. (Central Bank Quarterly Bulletin), (Winter, 1971).

CHAPTER 7

ITALY

7.1 INSTITUTIONS COVERED

Article 1 of the Banking Law 1936[1] states that the accepting of savings from the public and the granting of credit are matters of public concern, and are regulated by the Law. Such functions may only be exercised by chartered public banks, banks of national interest, savings banks and institutions, banks, companies and private enterprises authorised accordingly.

Article 5 of the Banking Law defines as credit institutions (aziende di credito) the following institutions and persons, who alone are entitled to accept short-term deposits:

(i) credit institutions incorporated under public law (known as chartered public banks) and banks of national interest (those banks which are in the form of joint stock companies, have branches in at least 30 provinces of Italy and have by decree been recognised as banks of national interest);

(ii) banks and credit institutions in general, however constituted, including People's Cooperative Banks, which accept sight or short-term deposits from the public, on savings account, on current account or in any other form;

(iii) branches in Italy of foreign credit institutions;

(iv) savings banks;

(v) pledge banks;

(vi) rural and artisans co-operatives.

All these credit institutions are controlled by the Banca d'Italia.

Institutions accepting medium and long-term deposits are defined in Article 41: they are also controlled by the Banca d'Italia. They are not within the scope of this study. (The distinction between institutions taking short-term deposits and those taking medium and long-term deposits is of considerable importance in Italy: it is discussed more fully in 7.6 below).

All credit institutions under Article 5 of the Banking Law are within the scope of this study. Savings banks, People's Cooperative Banks and rural and artisans cooperatives, apart from being subject to the Banking Law, are also subject to specific provisions dealing with their structure and/or business.

7.2 BASIC LAWS

The following laws and decrees apply to the banking sector as a whole:

(i) Royal Decree Law No. 375 of March 12, 1936 (the Banking Law);

(ii) Law No. 141 of March 7, 1938, amending Royal Decree Law No. 375 of March 12, 1936;

(iii) Law No. 933 of June 10, 1940, amending Royal Decree Law No. 375 of March 12, 1936;

(iv) Legislative Lieutenancy Decree No. 226 of September 14, 1944, amending Royal Decree Law No. 375 of March 12, 1936;

(v) Legislative Decree of the Provisional Head of State No. 691 of July 17, 1947, establishing the Inter-Ministerial Committee for Credit and Savings (CICR);

(vi) Decision of the Comitato Interministeriale per il Credito e il Risparmio (Inter-ministerial Committee for Credit and Savings (CICR) of May 16, 1962, on the establishment of a Central Risks Bureau;

(vii) Decision of the CICR of January 28, 1963, on the definition of short, medium and long-term savings;

(viii) Directive of the CICR of June 23, 1966, 'temporarily' precluding the authorisation of additional banks;

(ix) Ministerial Decree of March 23, 1972, allowing banks to lend specified amounts at medium term (later amended by a decision of the CICR of June 4, 1976).

Other provisions apply to particular categories of credit institution:

(i) Legislative Decree No. 105 of February 10, 1948, on the People's Cooperative Banks and subsequent amendments;

(ii) Royal Decree No. 967 of April 25, 1929, on the Savings Banks Consolidation Act, and subsequent amendments;

(iii) Royal Decree No. 1706 of August 26, 1937, amended by the Law of August 4, 1955 - the Rural and Artisans Cooperatives Consolidation Act.

7.3 SUPERVISORY SYSTEM

7.3.1 Supervisory Authority

The Banca d'Italia (Bank of Italy) is the supervisory body for all public and private law institutions accepting deposits from the public and extending credit. The department of the Bank which carries out this function is the Supervisory Office of Credit Institutions (Servizio Vigilanza sulle Aziende di Credito). The Banca d'Italia carries out the functions attributed by the Banking Law to the Ispettorato per la difesa del risparmio e l'esercizio del credito (Inspectorate for the Protection of Deposits and Credit Activities) by virtue of Legislative Decree No. 691 of July 17, 1947 (Art. 2) which amended Article 12 of the Banking Law. The Governor of the Banca d'Italia carries out the functions and duties of the head of the Ispettorato in accordance with directives from the Comitato Interministeriale per il Credito e il Risparmio -CICR (Inter-Ministerial Committee for Credit and Savings).

The Banca d'Italia was established by Law No. 449 of August 10, 1893, and has been the sole bank of issue since 1926. Under the Banking Law, it ceased to be a private joint stock company of limited duration and became an institution incorporated under public law of unlimited duration (Art. 20): its capital, which is subdivided into 300,000 registered 'participations' of 1,000 lire each, may be held only by savings banks, public law banks, banks of national interest, social security agencies and insurance companies. The administrative body of the Banca d'Italia is the Board of Directors which consists of the Governor and 13 directors who are elected at the General Meetings convened at the Bank's regional main offices.

The main functions of the Banca d'Italia are:

(i) banker to the Treasury;
(ii) note issue;
(iii) supervision of the banking system;
(iv) implementation of monetary policy;
(v) regulation of the capital market;
(vi) regulation of the foreign exchange market.

Controls over individual banks are exercised by the Banca d'Italia partly from its head office, and partly through its regional offices - thus, for example, a number of statistical returns have to be submitted in duplicate, one copy going to the Banca d'Italia's head office and one to its local office in the region containing the reporting bank's head office.

7.3.2 Outline of system

Banks may not be set up, commence activity or open new branches, in Italy or abroad, without prior authorisation (Art. 28). Public law banks can be established by express or general legal provision. For public law banks and banks of national interest it is the Minister for the Treasury who, after consulting the CICR, adopts the measures approving their charters (Art. 27). Authorisation for other commercial banks is given by the Banca d'Italia.

The Banca d'Italia maintains a register of all banks (Art. 29). This records the latest information on the name of the bank, its legal form, its capital or endowment fund and reserves on the basis of the latest balance sheet, and the location of its head office and branch offices.

The main requirements laid down by the Banca d'Italia for authorisation of a commercial bank relate to the minimum capital (see 7.4.2 below), the competence of personnel in control (see 7.4.3 below), and the provision of management plans (see 7.4.4 below). The Banca d'Italia also has to approve a bank's articles, and so the type of business it can carry out. Even when all these requirements are met, the Banca d'Italia retains a considerable amount of discretion in deciding whether to authorise the establishment of a bank. One of its major considerations is the 'economic need' for a new bank in the place (whether town, city or province) proposed.

This 'economic need' criterion has in fact been used to withhold the authorisation of any new Italian-based banks since 1966. A Directive of the CICR of June 23, 1966 asked the Banca d'Italia to suspend temporarily the granting of authorisations for new banks: this request was based on the CICR's wish to avoid any increase in the number of banks in the country and to rationalise banking operations. Although described as a temporary measure the request has not been withdrawn. (It does not apply to branches in Italy of banks based in foreign countries). Furthermore, the setting up of new Rural and Artisans Cooperatives has subsequently been allowed under a Directive of May 1971 in places where there are no bank branches.

Appeals against refusal of authorisation may be made within one month to the CICR (Art. 19). There is no provision for any further appeal.

The Banca d'Italia has considerable powers of control over the activities of banks - see, for example, 7.6 below on the types of business a bank may undertake and on its equity participations, and 7.9 below, on ratios for solvency and liquidity purposes. The Banca d'Italia is entitled to summon a special general meeting of the shareholders of a bank and it is entitled to apply a range of sanctions (see 7.14): the ultimate sanction is the Banca d'Italia's right to advise the Minister for the Treasury to revoke a bank's authorisation.

7.3.3 Returns to Supervisory Authority

Under Article 31 of the Banking Law, all banks are obliged to submit to the Banca d'Italia periodic statements and balance sheets, together with all other information and statistics for which the Banca d'Italia asks. 'One-man' banks are also obliged to give the Banca d'Italia all information on their non-banking activities (Art. 31).

The frequency and detail of the returns made by banks depend basically on their size. The basic return is a detailed balance sheet analysis, which is supplemented by other returns on specific subjects. For the major banks, the balance sheet and some other returns are required every month, with the remaining returns on a quarterly or annual basis; for the other banks the balance sheet return is required every quarter, with rather fewer accompanying returns on a quarterly or annual basis.

7.3.4 Auditing requirements

Article 32 of the Banking Law gives the Banca d'Italia the power to determine the technical form of balance sheets and other returns. In fact, banks are now free, subject to the requirements of the Civil Code, to choose the form of their balance sheets, but the technical form of prudential returns is prescribed by the Banca d'Italia. The form of the profit and loss account is laid down for all credit institutions in a Ministerial Decree of November 19, 1975.

7.3.5 Inspection

The Banca d'Italia can order inspections of banks, giving officials the right to inspect all documents and other matters. In the case of 'one-man' banks, the inspections may also be extended to business done by the owners outside the banking field (Art. 31). There are two main types of inspection: the general inspection and the sectoral inspection. A general inspection covers all a bank's activities, while a sectoral inspection will only be concerned with specific areas, for example, the foreign currency sector. Inspections of individual branches are also carried out.

The frequency of inspection is at the discretion of the Banca d'Italia. General inspections take place, on average, every four or five years. Sectoral inspections take place in response to particular circumstances. On the spot inspections are carried out at short notice in response to specific developments or rumours of an institution in difficulty.

7.4 CRITERIA FOR AUTHORISATION

7.4.1 Legal Form

The commercial banking system consists of three groups of banks: the chartered public banks, banks of national interest and other commercial banks. It should be noted, however, that the other credit institutions mentioned in Article 5 carry on banking business in a way analogous to the so-called commercial banks; the operational differences between the various credit institutions are steadily disappearing.

The chartered public banks are public corporations incorporated under public law. Banks of national interest are joint-stock companies having branches in at least 30 provinces, recognised as banks of national interest by the President of the Republic on the proposal of the Minister for the Treasury (Art. 25). Other commercial banks must be established as *società per azioni* (joint stock companies) or *società in accomandita per azioni* (limited partnerships with shares) (Art. 30). Some 'one-man' banks do still exist; these were in operation before the Banking Law. These latter institutions may continue in operation by being passed on from one generation to the next.

A credit institution can only be inscribed on the Company Register if it provides the written authorisation of the Banca d'Italia (Art. 28).

7.4.2 Minimum Capital

Article 28 of the Banking Law gives the Banca d'Italia the power to prescribe the minimum capital or endowment fund required for the establishment of any new credit institution. No explicit rules regarding minimum capital exist; rather the Banca d'Italia decides on the minimum capital required on a case by case basis.

The Civil Code requires all joint stock companies (including banks in this legal form) to allocate 5% of net profits to reserves until reserves are equal to 20% of nominal capital. The minimum allocation of profits to reserves for the public law banks is specified in the charter of each bank. Article 32 of the Banking Law allows the Banca d'Italia to require further allocation of profits to reserves. The power, however, is not invoked.

7.4.3 Management Qualifications

The respectability of administrators, managers and directors of credit institutions must be assured, whether they are Italian or foreign citizens. Foreign citizens, who are managers or directors of Italian or foreign banks established in Italy, must be resident in Italy. No minimum qualifications are laid down.

Article 38 of the Banking Law states that managers, directors, liquidators or members of the supervisory boards of credit institutions may not contract any obligations, whatever their nature, or engage in purchase or sale transactions, with the institution they administer, direct or supervise, except with the unanimous approval of the board of directors and the supervisory board.

Article 9 of the Banking Law states that no senior bank official may hold a similar position in other banks or companies without the authorisation of the Banca d'Italia. The purpose of this provision is to prevent conflicts of interest. Where no potential conflict of interest exists, however, authorisation is generally granted. Article 9 also states that officials of the Government or Government-controlled institutions may not occupy administrative or directoral positions in credit institutions, except by express authorisation of the CICR.

Article 39 of the Banking Law empowers the Banca d'Italia to require managers, managing directors, department heads and directors of branch offices to furnish a special bond *(cauzione speciale)* which must be deposited with the Banca d'Italia under such terms as it may prescribe. A decision of the CICR of May 14, 1971, left the imposition of this requirement to the discretion of individual institutions and the practice is now uncommon. However, Article 2387 of the Civil Code requires that all members of the board of directors of all joint stock companies (including those banks in this legal form) must provide a guarantee of 2% of the nominal capital of their company with a ceiling of 200,000 lire.

7.4.4 Management Plans

An institution seeking authorisation must provide the Banca d'Italia with detailed management plans in order to demonstrate that there is an economic need for the new bank.

7.4.5 Other Requirements

It should also be mentioned that the Banca d'Italia enjoys considerable discretionary powers in granting authorisations. It is free to refuse authorisation even when all the conditions prescribed are fulfilled. This enables the Banca d'Italia to apply the economic need criterion.

Changes in the articles of association of banks of national interest and chartered public banks must be approved by the Minister for the Treasury, after consulting the CICR (Art. 27). Articles of other banks can only be modified with the approval of the Banca d'Italia, which has to approve the original articles (Art. 28).

7.5 BRANCHES

7.5.1 Restrictions on Branching in Italy

The opening of branches of institutions already operating, as well as of new institutions, requires the authorisation of the Banca d'Italia. The stated purpose of this is to avoid a multiplicity of banks disproportionate to the needs of the financial market in any one place, with the harmful consequences of duplication of operating costs and of competition so keen as to prove detrimental to the financial soundness of the banks concerned.

The current guidelines on the territorial competence of credit institutions were set by a Decision of the CICR of June 4, 1976. This determined the areas within which banks can operate:

(i) Credit institutions with liabilities on savings deposits and on current account of more than 3,600 milliard lire: the entire national territory;

(ii) Credit institutions with liabilities of between 1,200 and 3,600 milliard lire: the region[2] in which their head office is located, adjacent regions and regions in which they have a fully functioning branch in a provincial chief town;

(iii) Credit institutions with liabilities of between 360 and 1,200 milliard lire: the region in which their head office is located, in adjacent regions only those provinces where they already have branches, and, in other regions only those provinces where they have fully funtioning branches (even if these are not in the provincial chief town);

(iv) Credit institutions with liabilities of between 36 milliard lire and 360 milliard lire: the provinces in which they have fully functioning branches and the adjoining provinces (even if these are in another region);

(v) Credit institutions with liabilities of less than 36 milliard lire - the municipality where their head office or fully functioning branches are located, and also adjoining municipalities so long as they are not the chief town of the region.

For the purpose of determining the areas where it can operate, the actual amount of a bank's liabilities on savings deposits and on current account is increased by a predetermined percentage, whose value ranges from 0% to 50% according to the ratio between the bank's own funds and the above-mentioned liabilities.

Banking operations in this context are defined as the granting of credit to customers located within the area where the bank can operate. Banks, however, are allowed to continue existing credit arrangements to customers who have moved out of the area not more than 18 months previously.

Exceptions to those limits, and a wider definition of banking operations, may be granted on an individual basis.

It should be noted that the ban on the authorisation of new banks (see 7.3.2 above) does not refer to the opening of new branches by existing banks.

Outside these limits, economic need, in the sense of ensuring an appropriate geographical distribution of branches in order to achieve higher productivity and greater uniformity of competition, is a primary criterion in assessing an application for a new branch.

7.5.2 *Branching and Operations in Other Countries*

Article 28 of the Banking Law provides that credit institutions which are subject to the control of the Banca d'Italia may not open branches abroad without its express authorisation. This is quite separate from any exchange control regulations on the remittance of funds from Italy to establish branches abroad.

7.6 RESTRICTIONS ON BUSINESS

7.6.1 Restrictions on Types of Business

The Banca d'Italia and the CICR have wide powers of control over the activities of banks. In the first place the Banca d'Italia has to approve the articles of association of every credit institution: these define the business which it may undertake, and so at an early stage the Banca d'Italia can be very restrictive. (For chartered public banks and banks of national interest - see 7.1 above - this approval has to be given by the Minister for the Treasury). In practice, the Banca d'Italia does not allow banks to conduct operations which are not defined as banking operations in the Banking Law - the acceptance of deposits from the public and the granting of credit (the operation of payments services being subsumed in this definition).

Under Article 32, the Banca d'Italia, implementing decisions of the CICR, may issue directives on the proportions of different types of investments which may be held, classified either according to their liquidity or according to the economic sector involved. Under Article 33, the CICR may decree that certain forms of investment must be positively authorised by the Banca d'Italia. Directives under these two articles may apply to all credit institutions, or to individual institutions.

A general decree has been issued under Article 33 with respect to the purchase of real estate and the purchase of shares. So far as the former is concerned, banks are generally not permitted to invest in property, other than for their own operating needs (branches, etc.) except temporarily, where the real estate is an asset of a defaulting borrower.

A more fundamental control on banking activities is set out in the Banking Law, which draws a sharp distinction between short-term deposits and medium and long-term deposits. As mentioned in 7.1 above, only those institutions defined as credit institutions by Article 5 are entitled to accept short-term deposits (defined as up to 18 months by a CICR Decision of January 28, 1963), and they are not allowed to accept medium or long-term deposits, nor until recently were they allowed to lend at more than 18 months. This latter prohibition was relaxed by a Decree of the Minister for the Treasury of March 23, 1972, and by a CICR Directive of June 4, 1976, allowing some categories of commercial banks to extend medium-term credit, with maturities ranging from 18 months to five years, up to a total of from 10 to 15% of their deposit liabilities, depending on the amount of 'own funds'. There are also specific provisions in the charters of the public law banks permitting the limited extension of medium or long-term credit.

Finally, credit institutions (as defined above) and other deposit-taking institutions require the specific permission of the Banca d'Italia before participating in the selling or underwriting of bonds (this is a matter of capital market controls, as well as of prudential controls on the issuer).

7.6.2 Loans to Directors

Strict controls are also imposed on loans by banks to their directors and managers: Article 38 forbids managers, members of the supervisory board and directors to contract any obligation whatever to their bank without the unanimous consent of the board of directors and the supervisory board.

7.6.3 Equity Participations

The powers, set out in Article 32, to control the proportions of different types of investment are described in 7.6.1 above. They have in practice never been invoked. Instead the CICR has issued a Decree under Article 33, under which all purchases of shares have to be positively authorised by the Banca d'Italia.

In general, equity participations in non-credit institutions are not permitted except in the case of economic organisations promoting the public interest, or corporations performing services complementary to the activity of the participating bank. Thus, banks have been allowed to participate in finance companies, trustee companies, companies operating in the field of electronic data processing and, recently, in SWIFT (Society for Worldwide Interbank Financial Telecommunication).

Equity participations in credit institutions also require the prior authorisation of the Banca d'Italia under the Decree mentioned above. Those participations which contribute to the soundness of the structure of the banking system or facilitate the promotion of new credit institutions with a social purpose are generally permitted. Thus, many of the larger banks have been permitted to participate in some of the smaller banks.

7.6.4 Mergers

All mergers and takeovers in the banking sector require the prior approval of the Banca d'Italia. Details of a merger can only be recorded in the Company Register on the presentation of this approval (Art. 48). Mergers between savings banks are authorised by a decree of the President of the Republic on the advice of the Minister for the Treasury, after consulting the CICR (Art. 49).

In recent years the Banca d'Italia has sought to encourage increased concentration in the banking sector both for purposes of rationalisation and to promote the soundness of the banking system.

Article 26 states that shareholders in a bank of national interest (see

7.1(i)) must be Italian citizens. This was amended by Presidential Decree No. 1655 of December 30, 1965, to allow EEC residents to become shareholders.

7.7 BANKING NAMES AND DESCRIPTIONS

Article 2 of the Banking Law states that the terms 'bank', 'banking', 'credit', 'savings', etc., may under no circumstances be used in the names of institutions or enterprises which are not subject to the control of the Banca d'Italia and which consequently have not received its authorisation.

7.8 ADVERTISING

Banks are prohibited from carrying on any business for the purpose of attracting new customers in a manner not in keeping with the dignity of banking. This prohibition refers in particular to house-to-house visits, the supply of printed and other matter free of charge, the despatch of advertising circulars and the granting of lines of credit without any specific request having been made by the person or firm concerned.

Banks are required to show, on all their letters, publications and advertisements, etc., the amount of their paid-up capital and reserves or endowment capital, as of their latest balance sheet (Art. 31).

7.9 SOLVENCY AND LIQUIDITY

7.9.1 Solvency Ratios

Under Article 32(f), the Banca d'Italia, with the approval of the CICR, may lay down a fixed ratio between own funds and total liabilities, and may control the use of the deposits accepted by banks in excess of this ratio. Under Article 35, the Banca d'Italia has the power to limit the ratio between own funds and investment in fixed assets and shares.

The Banca d'Italia has not made use of these powers to introduce any type of compulsory capital-based solvency ratio.

The definition of own funds (patrimonio netto) for supervisory purposes has recently been revised. Own funds comprise two components:

(a) 'Capital and reserve items in the strict sense'. Besides share capital or endowment funds, these include all the other reserves deriving from net profits.

(b) 'Other capital and reserves items'. These include funds of a reserve nature - usually constituted out of gross profits, that are charged to the profit and loss account before determining net profits - which are not committed to third parties (like general provisions for loan losses or the securities fluctuation fund).

Since the beginning of 1974, banks have not been allowed to have undisclosed reserves. Banks are generally not allowed to issue loan capital.

7.9.2 Liquidity ratios

Although there is no formal liquidity ratio enforced for prudential purposes, once a year the Banca d'Italia carries out a detailed examination of banks and their liquidity position. Some main aspects, and in particular those regarding liquidity are, moreover, observed on the basis of monthly returns submitted by banks.

7.9.3 Loan limits

There is a ceiling on the total amount of large loans that a bank may grant. A large loan is defined as one that exceeds 20% of a bank's own funds; all types of credit to a single customer are aggregated for this purpose. Since October 1, 1976, the total amount of such loans must not exceed a ceiling which varies between 25% and 40% of deposits depending on the circumstances of the bank concerned.

In addition, no individual customer may be granted credit by a bank to an amount exceeding the own funds of that bank, except in cases where a derogation is accorded by the Banca d'Italia. At present, the Banca d'Italia interprets these guidelines rather strictly and will authorise banks to exceed them only in exceptional cases.

These controls designed to limit the concentration of risk are applied under Article 35(ii)(b) of the Banking Law.

7.10 MONETARY AND CREDIT CONTROLS

Overall responsibility for economic policy lies with the Comitato Interministeriale per la Programmazione Economica (Inter-Ministerial Committee for the Economic Programme (CIPE)) and within the general framework established by CIPE, the Comitato Interministeriale per il Credito e il Risparmio (CICR) is responsible for monetary, credit and foreign exchange policies. The Banca d'Italia is the executive agent of the CICR in implementing monetary policy. Though the Banca d'Italia does not have an autonomous policy function, it nevertheless plays an important initiating and advisory role. The Governor of the Banca d'Italia is entitled, ex officio, to attend the meetings of the CICR and is also chairman of the Board of the Ufficio Italiano dei Cambi (Italian Exchange Office).

7.10.1 Direct Credit Controls

Credit ceilings are an important instrument of monetary policy in Italy. Except for a brief period in 1975-76, they have been in force continuously since 1973. Ceilings have to be observed by all types of credit institution except the special long-term institutions. Currently, the only credits exempt are single credits of less than 130 million lire and foreign currency credits.

7.10.2 Selective Credit Controls

Currently, selective credit controls are of limited importance in Italy. Whilst for many years the credit ceilings were applied with considerable selectivity, with lending to the electricity industry, the health services, the railways and for the support of agricultural production amongst the exempt credit categories, since 1978 a more global approach has been followed. For an extended period the banks have been obliged to invest in specified bonds. The level of this 'securities investment requirement' and the range of bonds eligible for inclusion has been modified on a number of occasions. Currently, the banks are obliged to invest a minimum of 6.5% of their deposits in the bonds of the agricultural land and building credit institutions.

7.10.3 Regulation of Interest Rates

Bank interest rates are not subject to official regulation. However the Associazione Bancaria Italiana (Italian Bankers' Association (ABI)) makes interest rate recommendations to its members, which are expected to reflect official monetary measures.

7.10.4 Central Bank Accommodation

The Banca d'Italia refinances the banking system by rediscounting and granting advances. This accommodation is at the complete discretion of the central bank and the banks do not enjoy 'as of right' access to refinancing up to specified quotas. Nevertheless, the cost of refinancing depends on the outstanding borrowing of individual institutions.

7.10.5 Reserve Requirements

The current system of reserve requirements was introduced in 1975. This obliges banks to place cash deposits with the Banca d'Italia equal to 15.75% (originally 15%) of the increase in their sight and time (lire) deposit liabilities in excess of the growth in their capital and reserves, calculated on a monthly basis. The Ministry for the Treasury can adjust the reserve coefficient by up to 5% and impose different reserve ratios on different deposit categories. Interest is paid on reserve balances (currently at 5.5%).

As noted in 7.10.2 above, the banks are also subject to a secondary reserve requirement to invest in specified bonds.

7.11 FOREIGN EXCHANGE

7.11.1 Authority to deal in foreign exchange

Only banks authorised by the Ufficio Italiano dei Cambi (Italian Exchange Office) may undertake transactions, whether commercial or financial, involving purchases and/or sales of foreign currency or movements of lire held abroad. Currently, there are 240 authorised banks.

7.11.2 Limits on positions

The Italian Exchange Office regulates on a daily basis:
(i) banks' net positions vis-à-vis non-residents in foreign currencies and lire together;
(ii) the overall position, spot and forward combined, in all foreign currencies.

Currently banks, with respect to (i), must not take up net creditor positions and, with respect to (ii), must maintain individually balanced positions in dollars, in EEC currencies taken together and in other currencies taken together. Moreover, their forward positions are strictly controlled.

These controls are applied with a view to the conservation of the national foreign currency reserves: they do not have any particular prudential implications for individual banks.

Banks are required to make a return to the Italian Exchange Office with details of their outstanding positions and contracts in individual currencies monthly or twice monthly. Forward transactions must be reported on the same day that they are effected.

7.12 CREDIT INFORMATION EXCHANGE

The Servizio per la Centralizzazione dei Rischi Bancari (Credit

Information Clearing Bureau) was established by a decision of the CICR of May 16, 1962, in accordance with Article 32 of the Banking Law. It functions as a clearing centre for banking intelligence. Banks are required to report immediately the position of customers who have borrowed from them 30 million lire or more (Regulation of the Banca d'Italia of October 31, 1971) and receive in return detailed information concerning these customers' overall positions vis-à-vis the whole of the banking sector. Separate legal entities are considered as separate customers for this purpose. The Banca d'Italia is, however, able to record information on loans to associated companies which amount to 30 million lire or more, on the basis of information which it collects from the banks. Banks can also obtain prior information about new applicants for loans, all reference to other banks that have previously granted loans to the same persons or firms being omitted. All banking institutions governed by the Banking Law, the central institutions[3] and the special credit institutions are obliged to report to the Servizio.

7.13 DEPOSIT INSURANCE

There is no legal or other requirement for deposit insurance in Italy.

7.14 SANCTIONS

7.14.1 Revocation of authorisation

In the case of grave irregularities in the administration of a credit institution, or of grave violations of the banking laws and regulations; or of a grave loss of own funds; or at the request of the credit institution concerned, the Minister for the Treasury, on the advice of the Banca d'Italia, and having consulted the CICR, may by decree revoke the authorisation of the credit institution and put it into liquidation. The liquidation procedure, which is set out in considerable detail, is effected by one or more Commissioners in Liquidation, appointed by the Governor of the Banca d'Italia, and a supervisory committee (Arts. 67-86).

If the credit institution concerned is a 'one-man' bank, the Commissioners may take over for the benefit of the creditors any assets of the owner which are not invested in the bank (Art. 67).

In the interests of the creditors, the Commissioners may carry on the business of the credit institution, but they may not, without the authorisation of the Banca d'Italia, dispose of the bank and its operations en bloc (Art. 75).

7.14.2 Imposition of Conditions

In the case of exceptionally grave irregularities, violations or losses, as referred to above, or at the request of the credit institution concerned, the Minister for the Treasury, on the advice of the Banca d'Italia and having consulted the CICR, may by decree institute a special administration for the bank concerned. This involves the dissolution of the administrative organs of the bank, and the exercise of their functions by one or more special Commissioners appointed by the Governor of the Banca d'Italia, and a supervisory committee. This special administration can last for a period of up to one year, and can, in exceptional circumstances, be extended by a further six months (Arts. 57-66).

   In exceptional circumstances, and when justified by the interests of the creditors, the Commissioners may suspend payment of the bank's liabilities for a period of one month (which can be extended to three months) (Art. 63).

7.14.3 Other Sanctions

In the case of a grave and deliberate infringement of a banking law or regulation, the Governor of the Bank may instruct the credit institution concerned to suspend from duty or dismiss the individuals concerned (Art. 91).

7.14.4 Penalties

Infringements of the banking laws or of any regulations of the CICR or the Banca d'Italia are punished by fines. The Governor brings a case before the CICR (Arts. 87-90).

7.14.5 Appeals

Appeals against a fine imposed by the Minister for the Treasury with the authorisation of the CICR (7.14.4 above) may be made to the Court of Appeal in Rome (Art. 90). An appeal against suspension or dismissal (7.14.3 above) may be made in the usual way (Art. 91).

   There is no specific provision in the banking law for appeals to be made against decisions of the Minister for the Treasury to institute a special administration (7.14.2 above) or to revoke an authorisation and place a credit institution in liquidation (7.14.1 above).

7.15 FOREIGN BANK BRANCHES

7.15.1 Establishment

Branches of foreign banks are subject to the Banking Law in the same way as domestic institutions. Furthermore, they are also subject to the provisions contained in Articles 2506-2508 of the Civil Code concerning companies established abroad and having one or more permanent branches in Italy. The provisions in force regarding the opening of branches of foreign banks (but excluding branches opened by banks from other EEC Member States) are found in Royal Decree No. 1620 of September 4, 1919, and Article 40 of the Banking Law.

The opening of branches requires the authorisation of the CICR. Relevant considerations for the CICR are the question of reciprocity for Italian banks in the country of origin of the bank concerned, and the 'economic need' for the branch. Following the implementation of the EEC Directive of June 28, 1973, on Freedom of Establishment of Banks and other Financial Institutions, a Directive of June 4, 1976, ordered that the Banca d'Italia should assess applications by EEC banks to open new Italian branches on the same basis as it would assess applications by Italian banks. Authorisation is given by the Banca d'Italia under Article 28 of the Banking Law.

Foreign banks who wish to apply for authorisation must:

(i) supply their statutes or articles of association;

(ii) indicate the level of capital they intend to earmark for their operations in Italy (Art. 1, Royal Decree No. 1620);

(iii) give the names of the persons who will direct and manage the branch;

(iv) supply information about the type of banking business and the programme of operations which the new branch proposes to undertake; and

(v) publish a separate balance sheet for the branch.

7.15.2 Earmarked Capital

A foreign bank must meet the requirements of the competent authorities (see 7.15.1 above) regarding the capital to be earmarked for a branch in Italy. Capital requirements are decided on a case by case basis. The specified capital of the branch of a foreign institution has to be invested in Italy.

7.15.3 Nationality and Competence of Personnel

Senior officials of branches of foreign banks must obey the same rules and meet the same standards as officials of Italian banks (see 7.4.3 above). In particular, they must show that they are resident in Italy.

7.15.4 Restrictions on Business

Branches of foreign banks are subject in general to the same limitations as Italian banks (see 7.6 above). However, they are subject to different rules as regards the granting of credit (e.g. the limits on large loans and operations beyond the short-term) and the operational limits with regard to geographical area. These regulations are not discriminatory as they take into account the operational peculiarities of foreign banks.

7.15.5 Representative Offices

A foreign bank may open a representative office without the permission of the Banca d'Italia, provided that it acts only as an economic observer and does not itself conduct banking business. The Banca d'Italia would nevertheless expect to be informed of the opening of the representative office.

7.16 FOREIGN BANK SUBSIDIARIES

There are no special provisions in the Banking Law concerning the establishment of Italian-registered banks owned by banks outside Italy. They are subject to the same controls as Italian-owned banks as regards their establishment and functioning. Since the issuing of the CICR directive of June 23, 1966, only one foreign bank has established a subsidiary in Italy, with the previous agreement of the CICR.

7.16.1 Local Ownership

This is decided on a case by case basis depending in part on reciprocity.

7.16.2 Nationality of Directors

This is decided on a case by case basis depending in part on reciprocity.

7.16.3 Guarantees from Parent Institution

This is decided on a case by case basis depending in part on reciprocity.

7.17 BANKING ASSOCIATIONS

7.17.1 Membership

The Italian Bankers' Association (Associazione Bancaria Italiana (ABI)) was established in 1919. Although all commercial banks do in fact belong to the Association, membership is not compulsory. Other institutions besides banks, including medium and long-term credit institutions and finance houses, belong to the Association. In June 1980 there were 819 members of the Association.

7.17.2 Relations with Supervisory Authorities

A principal function of the Association is to represent banks in their relations with the Government and with the monetary and financial authorities. The Association does not, however, play a role in the supervisory process.

As well as the ABI, there are other banking associations representing specific types of institutions. For the ordinary commercial banks the secondary association is the Associazione Nazionale Aziende Ordinarie di Credito.

7.18 BACKGROUND SOURCES

1. Associazione Bancaria Italiana: 'La legge bancaria e le altre norme essenziali in materia creditizia' (1978), Bancaria, (monthly).
2. Aufricht, H. (ed.): Central Banking Legislation, Vol. II, International Monetary Fund, (Washington, D.C.), (1967).
3. Banca d'Italia: Annual Reports.
4. Banco di Roma: The Italian Banking System, (1974).
5. Banking Federation of the EEC, Monetary Policy and the Banking System in the Countries of the European Community (Brussels, 1980).
6. Campi, C.C.: 'Italie', Droit Bancaire et Boursier, Jura Europae, (Editions Techniques Juris-Classeurs, Paris), (looseleaf).
7. De Vecchis, P: La legislazione bancaria italiana nella prospettiva della Comunita Europea, (Dott. A. Giuffrè, Milan), (1975).
8. Elstob, M. (ed) Banking Structures and Sources of Finance in the European Community (Banker Research Unit, London) (1979).
9. IBRO: Banking Ratios in the EEC (A study commissioned by DG XV of the EEC Commission from the Inter-Bank Research Organisation) (1979).

10. International Monetary Fund: Annual Report of Exchange Arrangements and Exchange Restrictions, (1979) (Washington D.C.), (1974).
11. Padoa-Schioppa, T.: 'Selective Credit Policy: Italy's Recent Experience', Banca Nazionale del Lavoro Quarterly Review, (March, 1975).
12. Ruta, G: Il Sistema della Legislazione Bancaria, (Rome), (1975).
13. Vittas, D., (ed) Banking Systems Abroad (Inter-Bank Research Organisation, London) (1978).

NOTES

1. Unless otherwise specified, references are to Articles of the Royal Decree Law No. 375 of March 12, 1936 (as amended), known as the Banking Law.
2. For administrative purposes the 20 regions of Italy are divided into provinces, each of which contains a number of municipalities.
3. These institutions provide a wide range of economic, financial and technical assistance for the benefit of their members. The institutions are the following: Istituto di Credito delle Casse di risparmio italiane; Istituto Centrale delle Banche Popolari Italiane; Istituto Centrale di Banche e Banchieri; Istituto di Credito delle Casse rurali e artigiane.

CHAPTER 8

LUXEMBOURG

8.1 INSTITUTIONS COVERED

The 1981 Banking Law provides for the uniform treatment of all 'credit institutions', defined as institutions incorporated or established in Luxembourg, whose business consists of accepting deposits or other repayable funds with a view to using them for their own account in credit or investment operations (Art. 1). The Law states which leasing and factoring operations are deemed to be credit operations. Credit institutions are divided by the Law into three categories:

(i) banks and savings institutions: these institutions may as a rule carry on all types of banking business and may accept sight or short-term deposits. This category includes the two existing public credit institutions: the Caisse d' Epargne de l'Etat (State Savings Bank), which combines the functions of a savings bank and a commercial bank with some of the functions of a central bank, and the Société Nationale de Crédit et d'Investissement (National Credit and Investment Company), whose function is mainly to contribute to the development of industry and commerce by extending financing facilities to those sectors;

(ii) agricultural savings banks: these may also accept sight or short-term deposits;

(iii) non-bank financial institutions: these may not accept funds for a term shorter than two years, except from associated companies and other credit institutions. Before the 1981 Banking Law, these institutions were known as 'credit institutions' and were subject to Article 12 of the Decree Law of June 19, 1965, but not to most of the other banking legislation.

8.2 BASIC LAWS

The basic laws and decrees are the following:
(i) Decree Law of October 17, 1945;
(ii) Decree Law of June 19, 1965;
(iii) Ministerial Regulation of September 16, 1971, on the Consultative

Council for Bank Control as amended by the ministerial regulations of March 23, 1976, and January 25, 1979;

(iv) Regulation No. 4 of the Commissaire (Banking Control Commissioner) of September 18, 1972, on the publication and lay-out of balance sheets by banks (confirmed by Ministerial Decree of October 30, 1972).

(v) Law of 1981 implementing the first EEC banking directive of December 12, 1977.

8.3 SUPERVISORY SYSTEM

8.3.1 Supervisory Authority

The Commissariat au Contrôle des Banques (the office of the Banking Control Commissioner) was created in 1945.[1] The Commissaire (Commissioner), who is appointed by the Minister for Finance, is responsible for the supervision and, in cooperation with the Minister for Finance, for the regulation of:

(i) credit institutions (as defined in 8.1 above);

(ii) investment funds and other collective investment institutions;

(iii) fiduciary representatives.

The Commissaire also has some responsibilities for:

(i) persons authorised to carry out foreign exchange transactions;

(ii) persons authorised to buy and sell transferable securities and for their offer for sale and similar operations.

The powers of the Commissaire are essentially directed towards the prudential supervision of the liquidity and solvency of credit institutions in the interests of their depositors. In addition, and in the absence of a central bank, the Commissaire has some powers to regulate domestic financial markets. He may, with the approval of the Minister for Finance, conclude agreements with the credit institutions relating to the orderly development of credit and to the liquidity policy of the banking sector.

The Conseil de Contrôle des Banques (Council for Banking Control) was established in 1971, thus formalising what had for some time been informal practice.[2] The Conseil consists of the Commissaire as chairman, the president of the ABBL (see 8.17 below) and six other members (including a number of bankers) nomiated by the Minister for Finance to serve for three years. An alternate of the Minister for Finance, the Secretary-General, and the Directors of the Commissariat's departments and its Legal Adviser also participate in the meetings of the Council. The preamble to the Ministerial regulation[3] implies that the Conseil was set up to represent the banking industry. Its main functions are to advise the Commissaire on matters of principle, particularly those relating to the solvency ratio[4] and to regulations for the orderly development of credit and the liquidity policy of the banking system.[5] The Conseil operates through specialised sub-committees. The Minister for Finance may request that the Conseil is consulted by the Commissaire on all proposals and opinions submitted to him by the Commissaire.

8.3.2 Outline of System

Under the Law of 1981, no natural or legal person can accept deposits or other repayable funds with a view to using them for their own account in credit or investment operations without written authorisation from the Minister for the Middle Classes (Ministre des Classes Moyennes). Each branch and agency of the institution in Luxembourg and abroad must be individually authorised. Authorisations may be granted by the Minister for the Middle Classes only with the approval of the Minister for Finance, and after the application has been examined by the Commissaire.

Those credit institutions which were already authorised before the Law came into force are deemed to be authorised under the new provisions and are given three years from the coming into force of the legislation to conform with the new management and audit requirements (see 8.4.3 below).

Institutions must be notified of the Minister's decision within six months of their application, provided that all the necessary information was supplied. Where this is not the case, a decision must be reached within six months of receipt of the additional information or within 12 months of the original application, whichever is the earlier. [6] Failure to reach a decision within these time limits may be treated by the applicant as a refusal. All rejections of applications may be appealed to the Comité du Contentieux du Conseil d'Etat, within three months of the notification of the decision. [7]

Authorisation is granted for an unlimited period. [8] The authorisation can be revoked if use is not made of it within 12 months of the date of issue,[9] or if the institution voluntarily stops trading for more than six months. [10]

It can be revoked on grounds of fraud, etc., or on grounds which, if present at the time of the original application, would then have justified a refusal,[11] or if it appears that the institution can no longer fulfil its obligations towards its creditors.

8.3.3 Returns to supervisory authority

Every bank must provide the Commissaire with a detailed financial statement each month. Each monthly statement must show separately the total of advances to the management. Included in the total of advances are guarantees given by the debtor in his own right, or in association with any commercial company or partnership. Included in the definition of management are administrators, members of the executive committee, all personnel of the bank who have been granted signing powers, their spouses and their children who are still minors.

The form and detail of the banks' returns are specified in the instructions attached to the Commissaire's Regulation No. 4 of September 18, 1972.

Banks are also required to report to the Commissaire every quarter any advances to one single customer of 50 million francs or more. Advances are defined as the total facilities available (rather than the amount drawn) in the form of loans, overdrafts, lines of credit, acceptances etc. If the bank's own funds are less than 500 million francs, advances to one customer amounting to 10% or more of those own funds have to be reported. [12] This requirement refers to 'un seul et même débiteur': the intention is to regard as 'one customer' all separate advances to different persons or companies which may be considered to form the same risk.

8.3.4 Auditing requirements

The balance sheet and profit and loss account must be published in the *Mémorial* (Official Gazette) within six months of the end of the financial year. A maximum of three months grace may be given by the Commissaire in special circumstances.[13]

It should also be noted that the Company Law of 1915 (as amended) requires companies to publish their annual balance sheet and profit and loss account within 15 days of their being approved by the shareholders' general meeting.

The Commissaire au Contrôle des Banques has powers to issue regulations regarding the publication and the lay out of balance sheets and accounts, and the way in which they are drawn up. He may also require any other information which is relevant to the conduct of financial policy.[14]

8.3.5 Inspection

The Commissaire has general powers of inspection under Article 2 of the Decree Law of October 17, 1945, in order to verify the accuracy of accounts and other information supplied to him by credit institutions.

There is a regular inspection of each bank at the end of each financial year, because the 'nihil obstat' of the Commissaire is required before the annual accounts may be published.[15] Apart from this inspection, the Commissaire only carries out special inspections of individual institutions if he wishes to check up on particular points.

8.4 CRITERIA FOR AUTHORISATION

8.4.1 Legal Form

A credit institution set up in Luxembourg must take the form of a *société anonyme* (public limited company), a *société en commandite par actions* (partnership limited by shares), a *société cooperative* (cooperative company) or an *association agricole* (agricultural savings bank). Credit institutions incorporated abroad must have separate own funds.

8.4.2 Minimum capital

A credit institution is required to have sufficient assets to safeguard the interests of its creditors. Precise capital requirements for individual categories of institution will be laid down by decree. Under the present requirements a new bank setting up in Luxembourg is required to have a minimum capital of 350 million francs, of which 250 million francs have to be paid up. A foreign bank branch needs separate endowment capital of at least 250 million francs. The resources of the institution must be commensurate with the type of business which it intends to carry on.

8.4.3 Management Qualifications

Responsibility for effective management and policy-making must rest in the hands of at least two persons who must be of sufficiently good repute and have the necessary experience to carry out their duties. The reputation criterion must also be met by the directors, the supervisory organs and by those shareholders or partners who are in a position to influence the running of the business to a significant extent, by virtue of their shareholding or capital contribution.

Any changes in the persons who have to satisfy the criteria set out above must be approved beforehand by the Minister for the Middle Classes. However a change in the controlling shareholders or partners need be notified only within 15 days of the date when the change becomes known to the credit institution. If no objections are made within two months, the changes are deemed to be approved.

8.4.4 Management Plans

An applicant seeking authorisation as a credit institution must disclose its management plans: in particular, details must be given of the type and volume of intended operations, together with information about the organisational structure of the credit institution.

8.4.5 Other requirements

An applicant must provide any other information which is required by the Minister, and must demonstrate that it enjoys the necessary commercial reputation and creditworthiness in the financial community to carry on its proposed business. The Commissaire must also be satisfied that each credit institution's internal and external control systems are adequate to forestall problems. In particular, the annual accounts of the bank must be audited by an independent auditor who has the necessary professional qualifications, experience and good repute for the task.

Each application is subject to an administrative tax of 2,000 - 10,000 francs.

8.5 BRANCHES

8.5.1 Restrictions on Branching in Luxembourg

Specific authorisation is required for each branch or agency of a bank inside Luxembourg (cf. 8.3.2).[16]

8.5.2 Branching and operations in other countries

Authorisation is also required for each branch or agency set up outside Luxembourg.

The setting up of branches or subsidiaries outside Luxembourg is not subject to any exchange control or similar restrictions on the outflow of capital.

8.6 RESTRICTIONS ON BUSINESS

8.6.1 Restrictions on Types of Business

There are no statutory restrictions on the type of business that a bank may undertake. There are, however, restrictions, mentioned elsewhere in this study, on the extent of certain activities relative to a credit institution's capital or resources (see, for example, 8.6.3 and 8.9 below). Non-bank financial institutions may not accept short term funds (cf. 8.1. above).

8.6.2 Loans to directors

There are no statutory restrictions on loans to directors but every monthly statement to the Commissaire must show the total advances to directors and managers separately (see 8.3.3 above).

8.6.3 Equity participations

There are no statutory restrictions on credit institutions acquiring shareholdings in Luxembourg or foreign companies. The only effective limiting factor is that, if such shareholdings are defined as participations, they must be included in the fixed assets, and hence must be fully covered by own funds (see 8.9.1 below).

Any shareholding is regarded as a participation if it was acquired for the purpose of obtaining control of the company or of gaining a commercial advantage, rather than for the exclusive purpose of providing a profitable investment.

Credit institutions have to report every three months the details of their holdings of investments and participations. [17]

8.6.4 Mergers

There are no statutory controls on mergers, but if a foreign credit institution wishes to acquire a controlling interest in the form of a major shareholding in a Luxembourg credit institution, the Commissaire will need to be satisfied as to the reputation and the competence of the foreign institution; if he is not so satisfied, and the acquisition goes through, he can recommend to the Minister for the Middle Classes that the authorisation be revoked (cf. also 8.4.3 on approval of new shareholders).

8.7 BANKING NAMES AND DESCRIPTIONS

A list of authorised credit institutions, as defined in 8.1 above, is published at least once a year by the Commissaire in the *Mémorial* (Official Gazette).[18] Only bankers and savings institutions appearing on this list may use the name 'bank', 'banker', 'savings institution', or any other description giving the impression that they carry on banking or savings business. These provisions do not apply to persons using these words in a title or description which clearly excludes such banking or savings business.[19] Branches of banks with their head office in another EEC Member State are allowed to use the name by which they are known in their country of origin, but if there is any danger of confusion, they may be required to add certain explanatory particulars to the name.

The use of the names 'agricultural bank' and 'non-bank financial institution' is similarly protected. In order to avoid confusion, non-bank financial institutions are required to use that title.

8.8 ADVERTISING

Although there are no explicit controls over the contents of advertisements, it is the usual practice for credit institutions to submit drafts of their proposed advertisements to the Commissaire before publication. Two individual controls should be mentioned:

(i) Credit institutions may not mention in any document the fact that they are controlled by the Commissaire;

(ii) The annual accounts of a credit institutions may only be published with the 'nihil obstat' of (i.e., after inspection by) the Commissaire (cf. 8.3.4 above), and any publication of the financial situation of a credit institution may be made only in the forms prescribed by him.[20]

8.9 SOLVENCY AND LIQUIDITY

8.9.1 Solvency Ratios

Article 6 of the Decree Law of June 19, 1965, authorises the Commissaire, with the approval of the Minister for Finance, to make regulations fixing a solvency ratio for credit institutions. This ratio (the coefficient de solvabilité) is defined as the proportionate relationship between a credit institution's own funds (fonds propres) and its current liabilities (passif exigible) and may be fixed by the Commissaire, with the approval of the Minister for Finance at between 3% and 10%. These limits may, however, be changed by applying Article 8 of the 1965 Decree Law (for details see 8.17.2). At present this ratio is at the minimum of 3%. Full details are shown in the Appendix.

A fixed assets ratio is prescribed in the 1965 Decree Law (Article 7). This stipulates that a credit institution's fixed assets must not exceed the total of its own funds. Full details of the definitions used in this ratio are shown in the Appendix.

8.9.2 Liquidity Ratios

The Commissaire may, with the approval of the Minister for Finance, make agreements with credit institutions designed to promote the orderly development of credit and of the liquidity policy of the banking system. These arrangements may be implemented by regulation for a maximum term of three years (for details of the scheme of arrangement with the banks, see 8.17.2 below). In practice these arrangements have so far been introduced informally: since no regulation is involved their term is unlimited.

A formal cash ratio (trésorerie) used to be applied, at 6%. This is no longer formally applied, but the Commissaire still expects every bank to observe an appropriate cash ratio: each bank's returns will continue to be scrutinised in this respect. Full details are shown in the Appendix.

In addition, the Commissaire has issued a 'recommendation' to banks requiring that their liabilities be covered to the extent of 30% by liquid assets. Details of the components of this ratio are set out in the Appendix.

8.9.3 Loan Limits

There are no formal limits on the maximum size of loan a bank may grant to one customer or on the maximum acceptable degree of concentration. However, banks must report details of large loans to the Commissaire (see 8.3.3 above).

8.10 MONETARY AND CREDIT CONTROLS

In the absence of a central bank and because of the close links with Belgium in the Belgo-Luxembourg Economic Union, the extent to which the Luxembourg authorities can pursue an independent monetary policy is inevitably very limited. Primary responsibility for monetary policy matters lies with the Commissaire who, with the approval of the Minister for Finance, may make arrangements with the credit institutions to promote the orderly development of credit and liquidity.[21] If these arrangements are agreed to by 90% of credit institutions, they may be embodied in a formal regulation. Currently, however, there are no monetary reserve requirements, selective controls, direct lending controls or interest rates regulations in force.

The Banque Nationale de Belgique, which has a branch in Luxembourg, is not directly concerned with the operation of monetary policy but it operates in close cooperation with Luxembourg institutions. Luxembourg banks are provided with the facility of discounting certain claims on the Luxembourg government, or guaranteed by the government, with the Banque Nationale.

8.11 FOREIGN EXCHANGE

8.11.1 Authority to deal in Foreign Exchange

Only banks authorised by the Institut Belgo-Luxembourgeois du Change (IBLC) are authorised to operate in the official market, where most current transactions are settled. The free market is used mainly for capital transactions and is not subject to exchange control regulations.

8.11.2 Limits on Positions

Since January 25, 1974, a ceiling has been applied to the net foreign asset position on the official market of each bank in Luxembourg (and in Belgium). The ceiling on the net creditor spot position in foreign currencies on the official market is set at 20 million Luxembourg francs for most banks, but for the major banks it is calculated on the basis of their size and their turnover. A temporary excess of 10% over the ceiling is tolerated so as not to disturb the normal operation of current transactions.

Banks were instructed in September 1973 not to allow their net external debtor spot positions (on the official market in foreign currencies, plus liabilities to non-residents in Luxembourg and Belgian francs on convertible accounts) to increase beyond specified ceilings, calculated as for the net foreign asset position ceilings above.

Banks have been instructed that their overall foreign currency position relating to the official market (spot and forward combined) should normally be close to balance and should not register a substantial debtor or creditor position.

All these controls are imposed and operated by the Institut Belgo-Luxembourgeois du Change.

All the above controls apply only to the official market. There is no formal limit on a bank's positions on free market accounts. Nonetheless, the Commissaire closely controls banks' free market operations. Frequent reports are required, and if any bank shows an open position equivalent to 30% or more of its own funds, its operations are monitored particularly closely. The information provided by banks is sufficiently detailed to allow the Commissaire to assess if the bank is over-trading; if such appears to be the case, the bank will be warned to scale down its operations.

Since November 1974 all banks have been required by the Commissaire to submit regular monthly reports on their forward dealings in all currencies where their uncovered risk exceeds 25 million francs. In addition to the reports mentioned above, the Commissaire has instructed banks to carry out daily checks at top management level on their foreign exchange operations, and to tighten up their controls on dealing records, the issue of confirmations, etc. Similar requirements apply to banks' dealings in gold.

8.12 CREDIT INFORMATION EXCHANGE

Under Article 15 of the Law of 1981, the Commissaire is authorised to set up a credit information exchange. The Commissaire is empowered to pass on to any of the institutions listed in Article 1 of the Law (see 8.1 above) information about the total credits granted to an individual or economic unit, provided that the intended recipient of the information has granted a credit to the individual or unit or has been asked to do so. In the latter case, the information may only be passed on with the consent of the prospective borrower.

8.13 DEPOSIT INSURANCE

There are no legal requirements for a deposit insurance scheme of any sort in Luxembourg.

8.14 SANCTIONS

8.14.1 Revocation of authorisation

A credit institution's authorisation may be withdrawn if it no longer continues to meet the criteria laid down in the Law of 1981 for management, directors, controlling shareholders and auditors (see 8.4.3 and 8.4.5 above), or if it no longer complies with the own funds and creditworthiness criteria (see 8.4.2 above). Authorisation may also be withdrawn if it was obtained by making false statements or by other irregular means, if the institution can no longer be relied on to fulfil its obligations to its creditors, if it has not started its business within 12 months of the date on which it was granted authorisation, or if it has stopped trading for more than six months. The authorisation granted to the branch of a foreign credit institution must be withdrawn if the supervisory authorities in the country where the credit institution has its head office have withdrawn authorisation. Where the Commissaire intends to revoke the authorisation of a credit institution with its head office in another EEC Member State, it must consult the supervisory authorities in that Member State. In very urgent cases, notification will suffice. (The same procedure must be followed in the case of a Luxembourg credit institution with a branch in another Member State.)

8.14.2 Imposition of Conditions

Conditions which are incorporated in agreements made between the Commissaire and the credit institutions may be imposed on those institutions which did not participate in the agreement if 90% of all institutions have signed the agreement (see 8.17.2 below).

8.14.3 Other Sanctions

There is at present no special legislation covering the liquidation of credit institutions, although the Commissaire has found that the ordinary company law provisions are not appropriate when dealing with the special problems of credit institutions. A bill on the liquidation of credit institutions is pending.

8.14.4 Penalties

Penalties for breach of the banking regulations may be imposed on administrators, managers and directors. Under the 1981 Law, fines ranging from 20,000 to 2 million francs and/or a term of imprisonment of up to five years may be imposed for unauthorised deposit-taking or breach of the banking names provisions. The same fines may be imposed for failure to notify changes in managers or directors.

Under the 1945 Decree Law [22] fines from 500 to 20,000 francs may be levied for the following offences:

(i) refusal to supply balance sheets, accounts and any other information requested;

(ii) supplying of incomplete, inexact or false information;

(iii) failure to observe regulations made under the Decree; or

(iv) any other serious irregularity.

Under the 1965 Decree Law [23] the same penalties may be imposed for breach of the provisions dealing with, for example, the form and publication of accounts and the solvency and fixed assets ratios.

Article 23 also provides for eight days to three months' imprisonment and/or a fine of between 501 and one million francs for a repetition within two years of any of these offences above or for breaches of the rules applicable to foreign exchange dealing.

The Commissaire has power to impose fines under the 1945 Decree Law, but the sanctions under Article 23 of the 1965 Decree Law can only be imposed by a court.

8.14.5 Appeals

An institution may appeal against decisions of the Minister to the Conseil d'Etat, Comité du Contentieux. Appeals against sanctions imposed by a court may be made to the Court of Appeal. Decisions of the Commissaire may be appealed in the first instance to the Minister.

8.15 FOREIGN BANK BRANCHES

8.15.1 Establishment

Duly authorised foreign credit institutions have the same rights and obligations as national credit institutions. [24] Nonetheless the authorisation procedure does permit the Commissaire to exercise control over the type of institution allowed to set up business in Luxembourg.

No matter what their legal form, all foreign-incorporated credit institutions or banks must publish annually in the *Mémorial* (Official Gazette) their world-wide balance sheet and profit and loss account. The balance sheet of the Luxembourg branch alone is simply submitted for inspection by the Commissaire. It does not at present have to be published in the *Mémorial* (Official Gazette). The form and lay-out of the information to be published are determined by the Commissaire.

8.15.2 Earmarked Capital

Foreign bank branches must have a minimum endowment capital of 250 million francs. They are bound by the same solvency requirements as domestic credit institutions (see 8.9.1 above). However, short-term deposits from head office are not counted as part of current liabilities of a branch in the calculation of the solvency ratio. [25]

8.15.3 Nationality and competence of personnel

The Commissaire, in order to make it difficult to establish a 'letter box' in Luxembourg while actually operating elsewhere, requires that all credit institutions must have at least one manager resident in Luxembourg who is responsible for the management of the institution and who can be easily contacted. There are no provisions regarding nationality, and the competence of personnel in control is assessed in the same way as for Luxembourg credit institutions (see 8.4.3 above).

8.15.4 Restrictions on Business

There are no limitations on the business which may be undertaken by branches of foreign credit institutions.

8.15.5 Representative Offices

There are no restrictions in the banking legislation on the establishment of representative offices. In practice, however, the establishment of a representative office is subject to a series of conditions. It must be called a 'bureau d'information'; it is not allowed to transact any business or even to serve as an intermediary between the credit institution and local customers and its role is limited to collecting and issuing information.

8.16 FOREIGN BANK SUBSIDIARIES

8.16.1 Local Ownership

There are no statutory requirements for local participation in foreign bank subsidiaries.

8.16.2 Nationality of Directors

There are no restrictions on the nationality of directors: the competence of personnel in control is assessed in the same way as for Luxembourg credit institutions (see 8.4.3 above).

8.16.3 Guarantees from parent institutions

No guarantees from the foreign parent institution are required at present.

8.17 BANKING ASSOCIATIONS

8.17.1 Membership

All banks established in Luxembourg are eligible for membership of the Association des Banques et Banquiers Luxembourgeois (ABBL). In June 1980, 89 of the 109 licensed banks were members of the Association.

8.17.2 Relations with supervisory authorities

The credit institutions collaborate with the Commissaire through the Conseil de Contrôle des Banques (see 8.3.1 above), of which the chairman of the ABBL is a 'de iure' member.

There is also provision for direct contact and discussions between the Commissaire and the banks. The Commissaire may, with Treasury approval, and with the agreement of 90% of the credit institutions, issue regulations controlling liquidity and the development of credit, which are binding on the whole credit sector for a period of up to three years. The number of votes cast by each credit institution are in proportion to its total liabilities to third parties as calculated on December 31 of the preceding year.[26]

8.18 BACKGROUND SOURCES

1. Banking Federation of the European Community: Monetary policy and the Banking System in the Countries of the European Community, (Brussels, 1980).
2. Elstob, M., Banking Structures and Sources of Finance in the European Community, (Banker Research Unit, London), (1979).
3. IBRO, Banking Ratios in the EEC, (a study commissioned by Directorate-General XV of the EEC Commission from the Inter-Bank Research Organisation, 1979).
4. International Monetary Fund: Annual Report on Exchange Arrangements and Exchange Restrictions (1979) (Washington, D.C.)
5. Meier, U.: 'La Structure du Système Bancaire au Grand-Duché de Luxembourg', Banque, (October, 1976).
6. Rapport du Commissaire au Contrôle des Banques 1945-1975.

NOTES

1. Article 1, Decree Law of October 17, 1945.
2. Ministerial Regulation of September 16, 1971.
3. Ministerial Regulation of September 16, 1971.
4. Article 6, Decree Law of June 19, 1965.
5. Article 8, Decree Law of June 19, 1965.
6. Article 10, Law of 1981.
7. Article 10, Law of 1981.
8. Article 9, Law of 1981.
9. Article 8(1), Law of 1981.
10. Article 8(1), Law of 1981.
11. Article 8, Law of 1981.

12. Article 2, Regulation No.4 of September 18, 1972.
13. Article 4, Decree Law of June 19, 1965.
14. Article 2, Decree Law of October 17, 1945; Article 5, Decree Law of June 19, 1965.
15. Regulations made under Article 2 of the Decree Law of October 17, 1945.
16. Article 2, Law of 1981.
17. Article 2, Regulation No.4 of September 18, 1972.
18. Article 17, Law of 1981.
19. Article 18, Law of 1981.
20. Article 5, Decree Law of June 19, 1965.
21. Article 8, Decree Law of June 19, 1965.
22. Article 8, Decree Law of October 17, 1945.
23. Article 23, Decree Law of June 19, 1965.
24. Article 10, Decree Law of June 19, 1965.
25. Article 8, Decree Law of June 19, 1965.
26. Article 20, Law of 1981.

APPENDIX

SOLVENCY AND LIQUIDITY RATIOS

Coefficient de solvabilité (solvency ratio)

Current liabilities must not exceed 33⅓ times own funds (i.e. current liabilities must be covered by own funds to the extent of 3%).

For the purpose of this ratio, own funds are defined (in Article 6 of the 1965 Decree) as capital, reserves, subordinated loan capital (within limits and under certain conditions, see below), legally drawn-up calculations of appreciation in the value of assets, provisions (see below), profits brought forward and undistributed profits in general (including the profits of the current year), less losses brought forward and provisions to meet costs which are clearly calculated and which at present seem likely to occur.

The only provisions included in the definition of own funds are those for general risks pertaining to banking activities.

Subordinated loan stock issued by a bank and maturing in one year from the date of calculation of the ratio is included in the total of current liabilities. For such stock maturing in more than one year, the decision is taken on a case by case basis, whether the subordinated debt may be considered as capital or not. The debt must fulfil certain conditions of form and duration, and cannot be repayable without the agreement of the Commissaire. If these conditions are met, the loan stock may be taken into account as own funds up to a maximum of 50% of paid up capital and reserves.

Current liabilities are defined as all liabilities to third parties, except comptes fiduciaries (trust accounts).

This ratio is calculated monthly in two forms: the first on the definitions referred to above, the second with the definition of own funds amended to exclude the results (profit or loss) of the current financial year.

Coefficient de couverture d'immobilisé (fixed assets ratio)

The fixed assets, which must not in total exceed the value of a bank's own funds (as defined above), are defined as property (less depreciation), furniture and equipment (less depreciation), participations, claims on affiliated non-banking companies, assets leased out, legal and similar costs of establishing and continuing the bank plus other fixed assets (e.g. equipment distrained on by the bank to satisfy bad debts).

This ratio is calculated monthly in two forms: the first uses the definition of own funds set out above; the second amends the definition of own funds to exclude the results (profit or loss) of the current financial year.

Coefficient de trésorerie (cash ratio)

For the purpose of this ratio, cash is defined to include the following assets: notes and coins, postal cheques, sight balances at the State Savings Bank and monetary reserve assets (réserve monétaire) at central banks.

The short-term liabilities against which cash must be held are defined as those liabilities, not exceeding one month on sundry coupon and similar accounts, plus sight liabilities to banks, plus term liabilities to banks, plus liabilities to non-bank financial institutions, plus current accounts, plus sight deposits, plus monetary notes issued, plus 20% of liabilities on savings books, plus sundry sight liabilities (including trade creditors).

There is no longer a fixed minimum for this ratio. The Commissaire now expects each bank to maintain an appropriate ratio in the light of its own particular circumstances.

Recommandation de liquidité (Liquidity ratio)

The numerator of this ratio includes cash assets as defined above, plus assets in course of collection, plus term claims (i.e. over one month) on banks, plus sight and term claims on non-bank financial institutions, plus certain short-term advances, plus public sector securities eligible for rediscounting with the Banque Nationale de Belgique or with similar institutions, plus negotiable financial paper, plus rediscountable commercial paper.

The denominator includes the liabilities in the cash ratio above, except that all liabilities on savings books are included, plus liabilities to privileged or guaranteed creditors (including taxes and excise duties), plus term deposits, plus certificates of deposit, plus bonds issued by the banks, plus sundry term liabilities, plus the contingent liability on partly paid securities.

The Commissaire recommends that banks maintain a minimum coefficient of 30% for this liquidity ratio.

CHAPTER 9

THE NETHERLANDS

9.1 INSTITUTIONS COVERED

The credit institutions covered by this chapter are those institutions which are subject to the control, for both prudential and monetary purposes, of the Nederlandsche Bank. They are licensed and registered under the provisions of the Act on the Supervision of the Credit System 1978 (Arts. 2, 12 and 13).

Credit institutions are defined as those institutions 'whose business is to obtain the disposal of funds withdrawable at less than two years notice' and 'to grant credits and make investments on their own account'.

Credit institutions are sub-divided into certain categories:

(i) Universal banks: defined as 'credit institutions except banks organized on a cooperative basis, security credit institutions, savings banks and central credit institutions.' They have a wide range of business, including dealing on the stock exchange, and underwriting share issues. Although 84 institutions were registered as universal banks at the end of 1979, 60% of their total resources was accounted for by the two largest banks, and approximately 75% by the three largest banks.

(ii) Banks organized on a cooperative basis: defined as 'credit institutions having the legal form of a cooperative society (coöperatieve vereniging) which are affiliated on a cooperative basis with a central credit institution, as well as the incorporated credit institutions created by them which, for the purpose of encouraging saving, make it their main business to obtain the disposal of savings and do not have as their object the disbursement of profits other than for a charitable or social purpose'. These institutions were originally formed as farmers' co-operatives and are principally concerned with the promotion of saving. There were, at the end of 1979, 992 co-operatives grouped together in a central organisation, the Coöperatieve Centrale Raiffeisen Boerenleenbank (the Rabobank) (see (v) below), and a further 991 affiliated savings banks. The number has been reducing rapidly (though not the number of branches) mainly due to the merger of two central credit institutions to form the Rabobank in 1972. Co-operative banks have recently widened their range of business considerably, both in the personal field and in the field of business financing.

(iii) Security credit institutions: defined as 'credit institutions whose business is mainly to act as intermediaries in security transactions on the stock exchange'. Dealing in stocks and shares is their main business but they also take money on deposit and lend to their clients. However, they are not regarded as being an important part of the banking system. There were 22 such institutions registered at the end of 1979.

(iv) Savings banks: defined as 'incorporated credit institutions which, for the purpose of encouraging saving, make it their main business to obtain the disposal of savings and do not have as their object the disbursement of profits other than for a charitable or social purpose, with the exception of banks organized on a cooperative basis'. These banks have been broadening their range of business in recent years and now offer current accounts and personal loans to their customers. At the end of 1979, 78 of the 92 savings banks were members of the Association of Savings Banks, which has established its own commercial bank, the Bank der Bondsspaarbanken, to operate in the money market and use savings banks' funds to make business loans to customers which could not be made by individual savings banks.

(v) Central credit institutions: defined as 'credit institutions which jointly determine the policy of a group of credit institutions'. There is at present only one central credit institution, the Rabobank, formed by the co-operatives (see (ii) above): it has a number of functions including issuing its own directives to its members. A relatively small number of co-operatives which are not members are controlled directly by the Nederlandsche Bank.

There are a number of institutions which lend money but which do not come within the definition of a credit institution, because they raise funds by the issue of bonds rather than by taking deposits.

By a Royal Decree based on Article 30, the most important of these institutions, the mortgage banks, have been brought under the control of the Nederlandsche Bank for prudential purposes, but not for monetary purposes. They have been entered in a separate section of the register. Within the near future more so-called capital market institutions will be brought under the prudential control of the Nederlandsche Bank.

The Nederlandsche Bank is exempted from the Act. Also specifically excluded from the definition of a credit institution are the Post Office Savings Bank, the services within the scope of the Giro Act 1936, the Postal Cheque and Giro Services, and offices, branches, agencies or permanent representatives in the Netherlands of other central banks (Art. 1). Although they are not credit institutions, the Postal Cheque and Giro Services, the Post Office Savings Bank and the services within the scope of the Giro Act 1936 are subject to control for monetary purposes, although not for prudential purposes.

9.2 BASIC LAWS

The basic banking laws in the Netherlands are the following:
    (i) The Bank Act 1948, which is the charter of the Nederlandsche Bank;
    (ii) The Act on the Supervision of the Credit System of April 13, 1978.
    The 1978 Act was originally submitted to the Dutch Parliament in 1970. It was considerably delayed, mainly because of changes of government, the tightening up of attitudes towards prudential controls, and the wish to bring the new law in line with the EEC proposals to harmonise banking law. A revised version was put before Parliament in July 1975, and was approved by Parliament on April 11, 1978. The Act entered into force on January 1, 1979.

9.3 SUPERVISORY SYSTEM

9.3.1 Supervisory Authority

The Nederlandsche Bank N.V. (the Central Bank) is responsible for enforcing the Act and for the overall control of banks. Certain of its powers relating to the supply and verification of information required under solvency and liquidity controls have been delegated to the Rabobank and the Association of Savings Banks (see 9.9. below).

    The Nederlandsche Bank is a limited company, whose shares are owned by the Government; it was founded in 1814 and nationalised by the Bank Act 1948. It is controlled by a Board of Commissaries (supervisory board), which has 12 members appointed by the Government, and which is responsible for the supervision of the management of the Bank and for the establishment of the annual balance sheet and profit and loss account; by the Governing Board (management board), which has between five and seven members appointed by the Crown, and which is responsible for the administration of the Bank in the fullest sense of the word; and by a Royal Commissioner, appointed by the Crown, who is responsible for supervising the Bank's actions on behalf of the Government. There is also a Bank Council, which has the task of advising the Bank and the Minister of Finance on the policy to be followed by the Bank and also on any changes to the banking laws. Finally, the Minister may issue directions to the Governing Board, after consulting the Bank Council, for the purpose of coordinating the Government's monetary and financial policy and the policy of the Bank. The Governing Board may object to such directions, but, if they must be implemented, both the direction (supported by a statement of reasons) and the objection will be published in the *Nederlandse Staatscourant* (Official Gazette).

The functions of the Nederlandsche Bank, as set out in Article 9 of the Bank Act 1948, are:

(i) to regulate and stabilise the value of the Netherlands currency in such manner as shall be most conducive to the country's welfare;

(ii) to supply the money in circulation and facilitate the money transmission system in the Netherlands and with foreign countries;

(iii) to supervise the credit system on the basis of the provisions of the Act on the Supervision of the Credit System.

The Nederlandsche Bank may recover from credit institutions the costs incurred in supervising the credit system (Art. 48 of the Act), but in practice this power is not used.

9.3.2 Outline of System

The Act (Art. 2) provides for a compulsory authorisation system for all credit institutions. If a credit institution (as defined in 9.1 above) meets the necessary requirements regarding minimum own funds (see 9.4.2 below), competence of personnel (see 9.4.3 below), and certification by a registered accountant of the annual accounts, it will be granted a licence and will be subject to supervision by the Nederlandsche Bank. Otherwise it will not be allowed to carry on business. An institution which has been refused a licence may appeal against the decision of the Nederlandsche Bank to the Minister of Finance. A further appeal may be made to the Administrative Court for Trade and Industry, an administrative judicial tribunal set up by Law No. 416 of September 16, 1954. There is no appeal from the decision of this court.

A credit institution which has obtained a licence is entered in the register. The register has, by Royal Decree, been divided into the following sections:

Section I Universal banks
II Banks organised on a cooperative basis
III Security credit institutions
IV Savings banks
-subsection associated savings banks
-subsection non-member saving banks
V Central credit institutions
VI Financial institutions placed under prudential control pursuant to section 30
-subsection mortgage banks

An entry in more than one section is not permitted. The entry of an enterprise or institution whose licence has been revoked is cancelled. The register is maintained by the Nederlandsche Bank but it has delegated this task to the Rabobank and to the Association of Savings Banks (see 9.17 below) in respect of their members (Art. 12).

The system of compulsory licensing has been influenced by a number of factors, among others the first EEC directive on the harmonisation of banking law. The Nederlandsche Bank may obtain, or cause to be obtained, any information necessary from an enterprise or institution which, in the Bank's view, might be a credit institution, and such information must be provided and verified by the enterprise in question.

9.3.3 Returns to Supervisory Authority

Each bank is required to submit a detailed monthly return, in balance sheet form, to the Nederlandsche Bank as at the end of each month. These returns are used both for prudential purposes in relation to each individual bank, and for aggregation into macro-economic statistics.

The Nederlandsche Bank has the right to demand consolidated returns from any credit institution which holds a participation in another credit institution (Art. 19). These consolidated returns may replace or be in addition to the returns of the individual institutions. A participation is defined in this context as a holding of more than 10% of the own resources of the institution concerned: consolidation will be pro rata to the size of the participation.

The balance sheet and profit and loss account have to be submitted to the Nederlandsche Bank, duly audited, not later than six months after the end of the credit institution's accounting year (Art. 11). The Nederlandsche Bank prescribes the form of the balance sheet and profit and loss account and all returns in consultation with the representative organisations.

In accordance with its powers set out in Article 18 to obtain information from banks the Nederlandsche Bank also requires all commercial banks to report all large credits monthly. Large credits are defined as credits with a line of at least one million guilders, or amounting to 5% or more of the bank's own resources (capital and reserves). The aggregate figures from all banks are used for macro-economic purposes, classified by borrowing sector.

The Nederlandsche Bank also uses these figures to check on banks' lending policies and on the total loans granted to one borrower for the purpose of the 25% requirement (see 9.9.3 below).

9.3.4 Auditing requirements

The Act (Art. 11(3)) stipulates that a credit institution shall give the accountant appointed to audit its annual accounts written authority to supply the Bank with all the information which it requests and which may reasonably be deemed necessary for the Bank to carry out its duties. A representative of the credit institution has the opportunity of being present when such information is supplied.

9.3.5 Inspection

The Nederlandsche Bank is authorised to obtain, or to cause to be obtained, from every credit institution all the information which it thinks is necessary under the Act; and every such institution is required to allow the Bank, or any body or person designated by the Bank to verify for themselves by inspection the accuracy of the information supplied (Art. 18). Thus the Bank has full powers to inspect every credit institution with a view to verifying the statistical and other returns received.

The Nederlandsche Bank inspectors make regular visits to banks, sometimes by appointment, but unannounced if they feel the situation requires it. The Rabobank and the Association of Savings Banks (see 9.17 below) inspect their members and report any problems to the Nederlandsche Bank which has ultimate control.

9.4 CRITERIA FOR AUTHORISATION

9.4.1 Legal Form

A universal bank or a security credit institution (as defined in 9.1 above) may take the form of a *rechtspersoon* (a body corporate), a *vennootschap onder firma* (a general partnership), a *commanditaire vennootschap* (a limited partnership) or a *natuurlijk persoon* (an individual: this is only allowed on a temporary basis in the case of a partnership where one of the partners has died). A bank organised on a cooperative basis must take the form of a *coöperatieve vereniging* (a cooperative society). A savings bank must take the form of a *rechtspersoon* (a body corporate) (Art. 1).

9.4.2 Minimum Capital

The Minister of Finance may decide what is the minimum amount of *eigen vermogen* (own resources) which must be possessed by credit institutions before they can be granted a licence. The Minister must define what is to be regarded as 'own resources' for this purpose: the definition may vary according to the different legal forms involved (Art. 10). The minimum capital required before a licence can be granted has been fixed at 500,000 guilders.

Credit institutions are forbidden to reduce their issued or paid-up capital without first obtaining a declaration from the Nederlandsche Bank that it has no objection (Art. 25(i)(a)).

In the case of those credit institutions whose liabilities are guaranteed by another credit institution to the satisfaction of the Nederlandsche Bank, the Act provides that the Nederlandsche Bank may exempt them from the licensing requirements in respect of minimum capital, management qualifications and accounts. This exemption may be made subject to conditions (Art. 8).

9.4.3 Management Qualifications

The Act stipulates that the day-to-day business of a credit institution must be controlled by at least two persons: and that any credit institution in the form of a public or private company with limited liability must have at least three non-executive directors (Art. 9(2)). It also lays down minimum standards of technical competence of the management and trustworthiness of the persons who determine or help to determine the policy of the credit institution.

The power of exemption mentioned under 9.4.2 above may be extended to the requirement for two managers.

9.4.4 Management Plans

Institutions applying for a licence to operate as a credit institution must include in their application a programme of operations, in accordance with the provisions of Article 3 (4) of the EEC Banking Directive.

9.4.5 Other Requirements

The Nederlandsche Bank may require any enterprise or institution to provide and to verify any information which can reasonably be regarded as necessary for the purpose of deciding whether the enterprise or institution should be licensed.

9.5 BRANCHES

9.5.1 Restrictions on branching in the Netherlands

There are no statutory restrictions on the opening of branches by Dutch banks. Foreign banks have to obtain a licence before opening a branch in the Netherlands (see 9.15 below).

9.5.2 Branching and operations in other countries

There are no restrictions in the Act on the setting up by Dutch banks of branches or subsidiaries in other countries. These activities are, of course, subject to any exchange control or similar restrictions on the outflow of capital which may be in force.

The solvency regulations (see 9.9.1 below) require the balance sheet of branches and subsidiaries of Dutch banks in other countries (as well as in the Netherlands) to be consolidated with the parent's balance sheet for the purposes of calculating their solvency ratios.

9.6 RESTRICTIONS ON BUSINESS

9.6.1 Restrictions on Types of Business

There are no restrictions on the types of banking business which may be carried out by credit institutions. (In practice, all banks have widened their range of business in recent years, particularly regarding services to personal customers).

The extent to which banks can carry out non-banking business is, of course, limited by some of the controls mentioned elsewhere in this chapter - see, for instance, the controls on participations in 9.6.3 below, the fixed assets ratio and the solvency requirements against participations (9.9.1 below).

9.6.2 Loans to directors

In the context of the solvency rules (see 9.9.1 below), advances to directors and managers are limited to 1% of own funds for each individual loan with a maximum of 2% for the total of such loans, unless otherwise authorised by the Nederlandsche Bank.

9.6.3 Equity Participations

Under Article 25 of the Act, credit institutions must obtain a declaration of no objection from the Minister of Finance, who has to consult the Nederlandsche Bank (see below), or from the Nederlandsche Bank itself acting on behalf of the Minister, before they can directly or indirectly acquire participations in any other companies or institutions, or increase any participations already held. In this context, participation is defined as an interest of more than 5% in the own resources of the company or institution concerned. A declaration of no objection will also be required before a credit institution may acquire all or a considerable part of the assets and liabilities of other companies or institutions.

These rules were relaxed on September 17, 1980, allowing credit institutions to participate in the risk-bearing capital of non-financial enterprises, provided that the participation meets the following requirements:

(i) the participation must be below 50% of the enterprise's own resources;

(ii) the participation may not exceed 2.5 million guilders at the time of the application;

(iii) the participation must, in principle, be held for a period of less than five years; this period may be extended where there are good reasons for doing so;

(iv) the aggregate of all the participations acquired by a single credit institution may not exceed 'a few per cent' of that institutions's own resources.

Under the new rules, credit institutions may assume that their applications for declarations of no objection will be granted if the requirements set out above are met.

The decision on an application for a declaration of no objection must be taken within 90 days. A decision refusing a declaration or granting such a declaration subject to conditions must be accompanied by a statement of reasons. If a credit institution goes ahead with the transaction before obtaining permission, it must subsequently obtain a declaration or reverse the transaction.

These participations are subject to a solvency requirement of 50% and they will be regarded as fixed assets under the 'fixed assets rule'.

The Nederlandsche Bank may, in the context of controls on solvency and liquidity, issue directives to credit institutions which may, *inter alia*, prohibit or limit the effecting of specified types or forms of investment, or of investments exceeding a specified amount (Art. 23). No such directives have been issued in practice.

9.6.4 Mergers

The rules on equity participations described above operate as a merger control, and consequently mergers with other enterprises or institutions, whether credit institutions or not, are not allowed unless the Nederlandsche Bank gives a declaration that it has no objection. There are no general merger controls in the Netherlands.

Other organisational changes involving possible changes of ownership also require permission. The Act (Art. 25(1)(f)) stipulates that a declaration of no objection must be obtained before a managing partner joins a credit institution. The grounds on which the Bank may refuse or may grant conditionally such a declaration are set out in 9.6.3 above.

The Act (Art. 25(2)) also stipulates that no one may, as a shareholder or member of a credit institution, exercise more than 5% of the total number of votes in the general meeting of shareholders or members, unless the Nederlandsche Bank has given a declaration of no objection (on the grounds set out in 9.6.3 above).

9.7 BANKING NAMES AND DESCRIPTIONS

Under the Act (Art. 43), institutions which are not registered institutions are prohibited from using the word 'bank', or any translation or derivative thereof, unless they make it clear that they do not carry on the business of taking deposits, granting credits or making portfolio investments. The Act exempts the Nederlandsche Bank, other central banks represented in the Netherlands, the Post Office Savings Banks and the representative (banking) organisations.

Institutions operating in the Netherlands, which have their registered office in another EEC Member State and which are entitled under its law to use the word 'bank' or a derivative or translation thereof, are also exempt from these provisions.

9.8 ADVERTISING

There are no restrictions in the Act or elsewhere on advertising or on the contents of advertisements by credit institutions.

9.9 SOLVENCY AND LIQUIDITY

The Nederlandsche Bank may give directives to credit institutions for the conduct of their business in the interest of their solvency and liquidity. Directives can be given and amended only after consultation with the appropriate representative organisation; different directives may apply to different groups of credit institutions (Art. 23).

The directives may contain only:

a. provisions concerning the minimum size of the liquid assets or parts thereof in relation to:

(i) funds at the disposal of a bank or certain parts of these funds;

    (ii) funds received from each individual creditor, insofar as these exceed a given percentage of the total funds at the disposal of the bank;

b. provisions concerning the minimum own resources which must be maintained in proportion to:

    (i)   credits granted and investments or parts thereof;

    (ii) liabilities of a risk-bearing nature;

    (iii) uncovered positions in foreign currencies;

    (iv) the individual items comprised in paragraph (i), (ii) or (iii) insofar as they exceed a given percentage of own resources;

    (v) the liabilities or parts thereof;

c. the prohibition, restriction or subjecting to conditions of:

    (i)   the granting of certain types or forms of credits, or of credits in excess of a given limit;

    (ii) the making of certain types or forms of investments or of investments in excess of a given limit;

    (iii) the contracting of certain types or forms of liabilities of a risk-bearing nature, or of such liabilities in excess of a given limit;

    (iv) the entering into of uncovered positions in foreign currencies, or of such positions in excess of a given limit.

For the savings banks the directives may in addition include provisions in respect of the maximum size of the investments or certain parts thereof in proportion to the funds at the disposal of a bank or certain parts of these funds.

The current solvency and liquidity directives have been in operation since March 1977. Their introduction followed lengthy discussions between the Nederlandsche Bank and the banking association on the details.

9.9.1 Solvency ratios

The solvency directive, as well as the solvency rules applying to savings banks, is based on Article 23 of the 1979 Act and has been published in the *Nederlandse Staatscourant* (Government Gazette). The basic principle of the solvency directive is that a bank's own funds must be sufficient to cover the risks entailed in the conduct of its business. To this end assets are classified according to their degree of risk and must be covered by own funds in various proportions between nil and 100%. In addition to risk assets, certain guarantees, pledges, confirmed credits and uncovered foreign exchange positions are also included in the ratio calculations. The items subject to the solvency requirement, together with the corresponding percentage of own funds cover required, are summarised in the Appendix.

For the purpose of the solvency directive, own funds are defined as paid-up capital plus reserves, published and hidden, plus a limited amount of subordinated loan capital (see below), plus, in the case of banks in the form of co-operative societies, a limited amount in respect of the statutory liability of members (whether enterprises or self-employed persons).

The balance on profit and loss account is not included in own resources. Paid-up capital is reduced by the extent of any of its own shares held by the credit institution, provided that these are not classified as an asset (which is allowed up to a maximum of 2% of issued capital, provided the shares are officially quoted in Amsterdam).

In the case of branches of foreign institutions, own funds are calculated only after deduction of funds channelled back to the head office. The Nederlandsche Bank may, for solvency purposes only, make this deduction also in the case of subsidiaries of (Dutch or foreign) institutions.

There are no specific references in either the Act or the regulations regarding the treatment of provisions for losses. In practice, banks set aside a general reserve for anticipated bad debts, plus a specific reserve for known bad debts. These reserves are not included in own funds.

Loan capital is not mentioned in the Act, but under the solvency regulations the Nederlandsche Bank is prepared to allow subordinated loans (usually referred to as 'capital bonds') to form part of own funds for solvency purposes, provided that the total amount of the subordinated loans does not exceed the amount of the capital and reserves, and that the maximum annual redemption does not exceed 5% of capital and reserves.

The solvency requirements are also applied to the assets of foreign branches and to the assets - pro rata to the participation - of financial institutions (i.e. credit institutions and non-credit financial institutions) in which the reporting institution has an interest of over 10%. In those cases where the application of the solvency requirements is not possible because of the difference in character between the reporting institution and its participation (over 10%), the required own funds cover is set at 100%; the contingent liability for uncalled capital in respect of such an investment is also subject to a 100% solvency requirement.

Additional solvency requirements are laid down in the regulations for relatively large credits. These are those items representing more than 15% of the credit institution's own funds; for this calculation all the items relating to a particular customer or group are combined. A group includes all the wholly owned subsidiaries, and all those companies in which a participation of more than two thirds is held. For branches of foreign banks, a large credit is one amounting to more than 15% of the own funds of the company as a whole, rather than of the branch.

For an individual large credit, the amount between 15% and 20% of own resources is subject to a surcharge of 100% of the basic solvency requirement; any excess over 20% is subject to a surcharge of 200% of the basic requirement. (Individual large credits can only exceed 25% of own funds with the approval of the Nederlandsche Bank - see 9.9.3 below). Advances covered by foreign bank guarantees need only be included to the extent of 50% of their amount; advances guaranteed by Dutch banks are exempted entirely.

If the total of large credits exceeds the credit institution's own funds, the excess is subject to a surcharge of 200% of the basic solvency requirement. In both this calculation and that relating to individual large credits the method is to regard as creating the excess, and so as subject to the surcharge, those items which are individually subject to the smallest solvency requirement.

The solvency regulation also includes a 'fixed assets' ratio. This provides that a credit institution's own funds must be at least equal to the total value of fixed assets (premises and a part of building investment projects, participations in non-financial institutions, and permanently unsecured loans to participations).

9.9.2 Liquidity Ratios

The present powers of the Nederlandsche Bank to issue directives to credit institutions, in the interests of their solvency and liquidity, are set out above.

The Nederlandsche Bank in 1975 agreed with the banking industry a new form of prudential liquidity control: this came into force from March 1977, at the same time as the new solvency requirement. The basic principle of the liquidity directive is that liquid assets have to be held in relation to certain liabilities so that the liabilities can be met on the due date or on demand, as the case may be. The approach (more details of which are given below and in the Appendix) is to classify eligible assets as either liquid in the narrow concept, or liquid in the broad concept; to classify liabilities by category and maturity, and then to deduct from those liabilities certain assets of an equal or shorter maturity which are not eligible as liquid assets in either concept; to require a proportion varying between 0% and 100% of broad concept liquid assets to be held against different categories of net liabilities; and to require an amount of narrow concept liquid assets equal to 20% of the total broad concept requirement, or to the total of the items subject to 100% cover, whichever is the greater. There is also a loading of the broad concept requirement against individual large items. At the moment only the broad concept requirement is operative.

Narrow concept liquid assets comprise cash balances at the Nederlandsche Bank and giro institutions, call money, Treasury bills and notes due in 90 days or less, and advances on such bills or notes, deposits with banks due or callable within one month and certain public sector loans due within three months. Broad concept liquid assets consist of narrow concept assets, plus rediscountable bills and notes, securities and advances against securities.

After classifying liabilities by category and maturity (maturity brackets are used to avoid having to match precise dates), the credit institution concerned can deduct from those liabilities claims on the public sector and on banks of equal or shorter maturity, to the extent of course that those claims have not been classified as liquid assets in the narrow or the broad concept. It can also under certain conditions deduct funds due to become available on the maturity of term loans (provided of course that it is not itself going to have to refinance the borrower). Special rules are laid down for the treatment in the maturity schedule of roll-over credits.

In calculating the requirements for broad concept liquid assets, net liabilities are treated differently according to their maturity bracket and whether the customer is a bank or a non-bank, and, in the latter case, whether he is a resident or non-resident. The calculation also incorporates additional liquid assets requirements against increments in certain types of liability over a base amount, which is taken to be the lowest balance in the preceding 12 months. This excess requirement is applied to sight and short-term (up to 30 days) deposits of non-resident non-banks, to certain other non-resident items and to sight deposits of all banks. The proportions required against the various categories of net liabilities vary from 0% to 100%; they are shown in detail in the Appendix.

The broad concept liquid asset requirement is also loaded against individual large items. If, after netting out individual liability items, there are left either any items which individually come to between 1% and 2% of the credit institution's total liabilities to the public (i.e., in balance-sheet terms) and which together amount to 15% or more, or any items which individually amount to 2% or more of total liabilities, the liquidity requirement for each such item is doubled, to a maximum of 100% per item. Individual items are those relating to the same customer. The definition of one customer used for this purpose is the same as the definition used for the solvency regulation (see 9.9.1 above).

So far only the broad concept liquid asset requirement has been implemented.

The calculation of the broad concept and narrow concept liquidity requirements of a credit institution are based on the credit institution's balance sheet on a particular day each month.

9.9.3 Loan Limits

Under the solvency regulations (see 9.9.1 above) a credit institution has to meet an extra solvency requirement if it lends more than 15% of its own resources to one customer. For the purpose of this requirement all customers in a participation relationship are grouped together, and all items related to them are also combined. In this connection, a company is regarded as participating in another, if it controls directly or indirectly two-thirds of its capital.

Purely for the purpose of the large item regulation above, advances by branches of foreign banks are related to the own resources of the company as a whole rather than to the capital of the branch.

Individual items subject to the new solvency requirements (i.e. risk assets) which exceed 25% of a bank's own resources will be forbidden unless special dispensation is obtained from the Nederlandsche Bank. The limit is raised to 50% if the risk asset is guaranteed by a foreign bank. If an asset is guaranteed by a bank in the Netherlands, it is not subject to the new solvency requirement since it is regarded as a risk-free asset: there is therefore no capital-related limit on it.

9.10 MONETARY AND CREDIT CONTROLS

The formulation and implementation of monetary policy is the responsibility of the Nederlandsche Bank. One of its principal tasks, as set out in Article 9 of the Bank Act 1948, is to regulate the value of the Netherlands currency in the manner most conducive to the country's welfare. Though the Minister for Finance may issue directions to the Nederlandsche Bank for the purpose of co-ordinating the government's monetary and financial policy and central bank policy, so far this power has never been used.

The legal basis on which the Nederlandsche Bank can take action in the field of monetary and credit controls with a view to regulating the value of the currency is set out in Article 10 of the Bank Act. This makes the traditional preference for government by agreement quite explicit. The Nederlandsche Bank is obliged to consult the banking industry, through its representative associations, before it takes any action in the credit field. Only if such consultations do not lead to an informal 'gentleman's agreement' within an acceptable time limit, is the Nederlandsche Bank empowered to issue a general directive to the industry as a whole, or to a distinct group of credit institutions. It is also empowered to issue a directive to an individual institution which does not observe an agreement. It has, however, always been possible to implement monetary policy by reaching agreements with the banking industry.

9.10.1 Direct Credit Controls

Prior to 1973, considerable emphasis was placed on direct credit controls with lending ceilings in force from 1961 to 1967, and from 1969 to 1972. More recently ceilings have been in operation since 1977. These measures are on a global basis, though in 1979 a special ceiling on personal sector lending was in force for a limited period. Lending financed by the growth in banks' non-monetary liabilities is not included in the scope of ceiling controls.

9.10.2 Selective Credit Controls

For the most part the Nederlandsche Bank seeks to influence the overall level of credit and the development of the money stock rather than the allocation of bank lending. The only explicit selective control that has been in force in recent years is the restriction on personal sector lending referred to in 9.10.1 above.

9.10.3 Regulation of Interest Rates

Banks' interest rates in the Netherlands are not subject to official regulation. However, the rate payable for personal checking accounts is fixed jointly by the banks and sanctioned by the Nederlandsche Bank.

9.10.4 Central Bank Accommodation

The primary method of central bank accommodation is the provision of overdrafts against collateral; rediscounting is of relatively minor importance. The recourse of each bank to borrowing at the Nederlandsche Bank is subject to an upper limit; in each quarter the average level of borrowing is subject to a quota. Quotas are related to the level of banks' short-term liabilities plus 25% of all other liabilities. If quotas are exceeded, a higher rate is charged for accommodation.

In addition, the Nederlandsche Bank on occasion makes special loans available to bridge money market shortages; the banks can subscribe for these loans at a previously set interest rate or via tender. The Nederlandsche Bank also modifies the liquidity of the banking system from time to time through foreign exchange swaps on condition of resale or repurchase after an agreed period.

9.10.5 Reserve Requirements

Following the withdrawal of lending ceilings, a new system of reserve requirements on the banking system was introduced in 1973. The purpose of this measure was to increase the ability of the Nederlandsche Bank to influence the free liquid reserves of the banks. Under this system the banks had to observe separate minimum liquidity ratios against their domestic short-term liabilities (the X ratio) and their domestic long-term liabilities (the Y ratio). In view of the reduced significance of the indirect methods of monetary control following the reintroduction of lending ceilings, these reserve requirements were withdrawn at the end of 1979.

9.11 FOREIGN EXCHANGE

9.11.1 Authority to deal in Foreign Exchange

Only banks licensed by the Nederlandsche Bank are authorised to carry out exchange transactions on the official market. Licensed banks must be members of the Association of Foreign Exchange Banks through which the Nederlandsche Bank gives them information on foreign exchange measures.

9.11.2 Limits on positions

There is no longer any limitation on the amount by which an authorised bank's foreign liabilities may exceed its foreign claims.

Authorised banks must report extensively on their foreign exchange positions. They are not allowed to have foreign currency positions exceeding those considered appropriate for normal banking activities; they must reduce or liquidate any excessive short or long foreign currency positions should the Nederlandsche Bank consider this necessary.

Under the solvency directive, own funds have to be maintained to the extent of 2.5% of a bank's uncovered foreign exchange position. This is calculated by netting out the spot and forward position for each currency, and adding together the resulting overall positions.

The liquidity directive lays down increased liquidity requirements against increments in a credit institution's liabilities to non-residents, whether expressed in guilders or in a foreign currency.

All banks must submit a monthly report to the Nederlandsche Bank on their assets and liabilities, spot and forward, denominated separately for each convertible currency. They must also submit a similar report on the 15th day of each month for US dollars, deutschemarks, pounds sterling and Swiss francs.

A copy of every multinational forward contract entered into by banks must be submitted to the Nederlandsche Bank. It is intended that future regulations will require that banks must submit a copy of each forward contract entered into with a non-resident.

9.12 CREDIT INFORMATION EXCHANGE

There is no official credit information exchange or central risks bureau, but there is a private organisation based in Tiel, the Centrale Bureau voor Krediet Registratie, which keeps a record of all borrowing, defaults, etc. by individuals and small traders. It covers hire-purchase, personal loans, etc., and all banks report to it and request information before granting loans.

The Act (Art. 46) allows the Nederlandsche Bank, should an official central risks bureau be established, to give information to credit institutions on the total borrowing from all credit institutions by a customer. It will not be able to disclose borrowing from individual credit institutions or to disclose which credit institutions are involved.

9.13 DEPOSIT INSURANCE

The Act (Art. 44) requires the Nederlandsche Bank and the representative banking organisations (see 9.17 below) to hold discussions on the introduction of a deposit guarantee scheme whereby certain claims against a credit institution would be compensated up to a certain maximum amount. The Act provided, however, that if the negotiations failed to reach agreement, or if the Government did not approve the scheme agreed on, it was up to the Government to impose a scheme on the banking industry. Agreement on a voluntary collective guarantee scheme was, however, reached even before the entry into force of the Act and the scheme was given binding force as from January 1, 1979. The scheme is meant to protect small individual creditors against possible loss of their deposits and is thus intended to maintain or enhance confidence in the banking system as a whole.

The scheme applies to all credit institutions and mortgage banks established in the Netherlands - including branches of foreign banks as well as to the Postal Cheque and Giro Services and the Post Office Savings Bank.

The scheme guarantees all deposits made by individuals, associations (verenigingen) and foundations (stichtingen), either in guilders or in any other currency. Bearer claims are not covered by the scheme. No distinction is made between residents and non-residents.

The deposit insurance scheme is administered by the Nederlandsche Bank, which is responsible for paying a maximum of 30,000 guilders to each creditor of a bankrupt credit institution. This figure is index-linked and is revised every three years (it was first raised in January 1980). The cost of the scheme is met by all the licensed credit institutions on a proportional basis: there is no reserve fund.

The Rabobank operates a mutual guarantee scheme for its members. Each bank pays into a central fund an annual contribution in addition to participating in a guarantee scheme to support each other in case of various types of loss, e.g. a bank being unable to repay its creditors.

9.14 SANCTIONS

9.14.1 Revocation of Authorisation

Revocation of an institution's licence is the ultimate sanction in the hands of the Nederlandsche Bank and may only be carried out for the reasons given in Article 4 of the Act. A licence may be revoked if:

(i) the institution has ceased to operate as a credit institution;

(ii) the credit institution does not meet the requirements laid down by the Act as to management (see 9.4.3 above), own funds (9.4.2 above) and annual accounts (9.3.3 above);

(iii) the Nederlandsche Bank considers that the expert knowledge of those in charge of the day-to-day business of the bank is inadequate; or

(iv) the Nederlandsche Bank believes that the interest of the bank's creditors are seriously at risk because of the record or plans of one or more of the individuals responsible for determining the policy of the bank.

Any decision to revoke an institution's licence must be accompanied by a statement of reasons.

9.14.2 Imposition of conditions

If a bank fails to comply with the solvency and liquidity directives (see 9.9 above), or with any of the licensing criteria, or if the Nederlandsche Bank believes that the solvency and liquidity of the institution may otherwise be endangered, it will caution the institution concerned. If necessary, the Nederlandsche Bank will, in addition to this caution, give instructions to the institution on the course of action to be pursued in respect of a number of specific points; the instructions must be accompanied by a statement of the reasons. If within 14 days of the date of its instructions the Nederlandsche Bank has not received a satisfactory reply from the credit institution, or if it considers that the credit institution has failed to comply, either in whole or in part, with the instructions, the Nederlandsche Bank may:

(i) impose a secret trusteeship whereby the supervisory and managing boards of the credit institution will be able to exercise their powers only with the consent of one or more persons appointed by, and acting under the instructions of, the Nederlandsche Bank, but with the appointment kept completely secret from the institution's customers, the banking industry, etc;

(ii) publish the instructions after giving prior notice of publication to the credit institution;

(iii) consult the chairman of the banking association of which the credit institution is a member, if it feels that this would be in the interests of the creditors. Such consultations might lead to a support arrangement with other banks, or to a take-over by a sounder organisation. The chairman is regarded as impartial. (Art. 24).

In practice the Nederlandsche Bank will contact the institution concerned informally at the slightest indication of trouble. The sanction of publication has never had to be applied.

9.14.3 Other Sanctions

If there is a dangerous trend in the solvency or liquidity of a credit institution, and no improvement can reasonably be expected, the competent court may, on the petition of the Nederlandsche Bank, appoint a receiver to take control of the institution's affairs. Such a court order will have the effect of suspending payment by the credit institution, but the court may authorise the transfer of part or all of the institution's assets and liabilities to a third party (i.e. another credit institution) and alter any contracts it had entered into. The Nederlandsche Bank can ask the court to take this action without having to prove the capital deficiency (Art. 32).

9.14.4 Penalties

Penal sanctions for breaches of the Act, such as failing to submit accounts, or failing to comply with directives, are set out in the Economic Offences Act 1956. This provides for a maximum penal sanction of two years imprisonment and a maximum fine of 25,000 guilders. Unintentional infringements are subject to a maximum penalty of six months imprisonment, with a maximum fine of 10,000 guilders.

9.14.5 Appeals

Under Article 41 of the Act, any individual or institution affected by a decision made by the Nederlandsche Bank or the Minister of Finance, may appeal against the decision to the College van Beroep voor het Bedrijfsleven

(Administrative Court for Trade and Industry). There is no further right of appeal.

There is no right of appeal against a decision of the court appointing a receiver under Article 32 or allowing the transfer of the institution's assets under Article 36 (see 9.14.3 above). An application for annulment of the decision may, however, be made to the High Court within 14 days of the decision.

9.15 FOREIGN BANK BRANCHES

9.15.1 Establishment

All branches of foreign-domiciled credit institutions must obtain a licence under the Act in the same way as domestic credit institutions, before they can carry on business in the Netherlands. Foreign bank branches must keep separate accounts in respect of their business in the Netherlands (Art. 27).

In the case of a branch of a non-EEC bank, the Minister of Finance has the final say in who is granted a licence (Art. 7(2)). He may refuse one or only grant it conditionally on grounds of reciprocity.

9.15.2 Earmarked Capital

Minimum capital (own resources) requirements for foreign bank branches are the same as for Dutch banks (see 9.4.2 above). In this connection, own resources are regarded as the amount of capital and free reserves shown in the separate accounts mentioned above, less the net liabilities to the credit institution domiciled outside the Netherlands. This net amount is calculated after deduction of monies employed by the establishment in the Netherlands for the account and risk of other parties at the credit institution domiciled outside the Netherlands (Art. 10(2)).

A branch is expected to employ in the Netherlands an amount at least equal to its minimum own resources.

9.15.3 Nationality and Competence of Personnel

There are no legal requirements concerning the nationality of personnel in charge of branches of foreign institutions, but the Nederlandsche Bank may raise objections to one or more persons who determine the day-to-day policy of a credit institution if it considers that, in view of inadequate expertise or past history, the interests of creditors may be at risk (see 9.4.3 above). To facilitate communications with the Nederlandsche Bank, a Dutch-speaking Director or assistant Director is desirable.

9.15.4 Restrictions on Business

Branches of foreign institutions are subject to the same criteria as Dutch banks when deciding in which category of credit institution a branch is to be classified (see 9.1 above). There are no explicit limitations on the business branches may do.

9.15.5 Representative Offices

There are no restrictions on the setting up of representative offices, since they do not carry on business as credit institutions.

9.16 FOREIGN BANK SUBSIDIARIES

9.16.1 Local Ownership

Foreign-owned banks are treated in exactly the same way as Dutch banks. There are no requirements regarding the nationality of shareholders.

9.16.2 Nationality of Directors

There are no requirements regarding the nationality of directors.

9.16.3 Guarantees from Parent Institution

There is no requirement for a guarantee from the parent bank.

9.17 BANKING ASSOCIATIONS

9.17.1 Membership

Dutch and foreign-registered universal banks are eligible for membership of the Nederlandse Bankiersvereniging (Netherlands Bankers' Association), but membership is not compulsory.

In addition to being a central credit institution, the Coöperatieve Centrale Raiffeisen Boerenleenbank (Rabobank) fulfils the role of being a representative body for its members. It had 992 members at the end of 1979. Practically all the co-operatives of any size are members.

The savings banks' representative organisation is the Nederlandse Spaarbankbond (Association of Savings Banks). At the end of 1979 it had 78 members out of a total of 92 savings banks.

The Vereniging voor de Effectenhandel (Netherlands Stockbroking Association) is the representative organisation for the security credit institutions.

9.17.2 Relations with Supervisory Authorities

The main function of all the above associations is to provide a link between their members and the Nederlandsche Bank. They are called in at an early stage to discuss any changes in laws and directives affecting banking institutions. Indeed, the Nederlandsche Bank is obliged by the Act to consult the representative organisations before issuing directives or regulations for monetary or prudential purposes (Arts. 21, 22).

The Association of Savings Banks and the Rabobank have the additional task of keeping their sections of the register. Certain supervisory powers relating to solvency and liquidity controls have, under Article 17, been delegated by the Nederlandsche Bank to these two bodies. These powers relate to the provision and verification of annual reports, monthly returns, etc.

9.18 BACKGROUND SOURCES

1. Banking Federation of the European Community: Monetary Policy and the banking system in the countries of the European Community (Brussels) (1980).
2. De Nederlandsche Bank N.V.: Annual Reports and Quarterly Statistics.
3. De Nederlandsche Bank N.V.: Liquidity Requirements and Credit Control in the Netherlands, (March, 1975).
4. De Nederlandsche Bank N.V.: Revision of the Act on the Supervision of the Credit System, Memorandum in Reply, (June, 1976).
5. De Nederlandsche Bank N.V.: Solvency and Liquidity Directives, March 1977.
6. Elstob, M., (ed) Banking Structures and Sources of Finance in the European Community (Banker Research Unit, London) (1979).
7. IBRO: Banking Ratios in the EEC, (a study commissioned by Directorate-General XV of the EEC Commission from the Inter-Bank Research Organisation), (1979).
8. International Monetary Fund: Annual Report on Exchange Arrangements and Exchange Restrictions, 1979 (Washington, D.C.).
9. Peat, Marwick, Mitchell and Co.: Memorandum on Establishing a Bank or a branch of a Bank in the Netherlands, (1975).
10. Vittas, D. (ed) Banking Systems Abroad (Inter-Bank Research Organisation, London) (1978).

APPENDIX

SUMMARY OF ITEMS SUBJECT TO SOLVENCY REQUIREMENTS

Claims on Credit Institutions
 Subordinated credits (domestic)   100%
 Subordinated credits (foreign)   10%
 Certain other credits (foreign)   5%

Securities
 Subordinated bonds issued by domestic credit institutions 100%
 Certain other bonds (regularly traded in large volume) 5%
 Certain other bonds (not regularly traded in large volume) 10%
 Shares   10%

Syndicates   10%

Bills and Promissory Notes
 Indirectly covered by Netherlands Credit Insurance Co. 5%
 Accepted etc. by foreign credit institutions   5%
 Promissory notes to secure credits   10%
 Certain other bills and notes   10%

Credits Guaranteed by Foreign Public Authorities   5%

Credits Guaranteed by Foreign Credit Institutions   5%

Acceptance Credits for Account of
 Foreign credit institutions   5%
 Certain others   10%

Advances against Precious Metals, Goods and
 Warehouse Warrants   2½%

Credit to Other Borrowers
 Indirectly covered by Netherlands Credit Insurance Co. 5%
 Mortgages and mortgage loans on current account with
  adequate excess value on residential buildings   3⅓%
 Mortgages and mortgage loans on current account with
  adequate excess value on non-residential buildings,
  ships and aircraft   5%
 Certain other mortgages and credits   10%

Participations
 In financial institutions (if not consolidated)   100%
 In non-financial institutions   10%

Credits and Commitments to Participations of over 10%	
In financial institutions (if not consolidated)	10%
In non-financial institutions	10%
Property and Equipment	10%
Sundry Items	
Precious metals	10%
Goods and warehouse warrants	10%
Accounts receivable and amounts prepaid	10%
Own Oversold Position in Security Transactions	10%
Contingent Liabilities in Respect of Irrevocable Credits	
Documentary	2½%
Other	10%
Certain Guarantees, etc.	2½%-10%
Open Foreign Exchange Positions	2½%

SUMMARY OF LIQUIDITY REQUIREMENTS UNDER THE BROAD CONCEPT OF LIQUIDITY

NET LIABILITY ITEM	REQUIREMENT
Subordinated Loans, Due in	
Less than one month	100%
One month to two years	20%
Securities Borrowed	
Creditors	10%
Negotiable Instruments, Due in	
Less than one month	100%
One month to two years	20%
Other Loans, not against Security of Liquid Assets, Due in	
One month to two years	20%
Savings Deposits	
Genuine	10%
Liquid	20%

Time Deposits from Non-Banks, Maturing in
  Less than one month, from
    Residents   20%
    Non-residents
      Base amount*   20%
      Excess over base amount   100%
  One month to two years   20%

Demand Deposits from Non-Banks
  Residents   20%
  Non-residents
    Base amount*   20%
    Excess over base amount   100%

Acceptances for Customers, Maturing in
  Less than two years   20%

Due to branches Abroad
  On current account   100%
  Other deposits due in
    Less than one month   100%
    One month to two years   20%

Deposits and Other Credit Balances from Banks
  Deposits due in
    Less than one month   100%
    One month to two years   20%
  Other credit balances
    Base amount*   10%
    Excess over base amount   100%
  Overdrafts on 'due from' accounts   100%

Liabilities to Customers in Respect of Securities Bought but
  not yet Received   100%

Own Over-Sold Position in Respect of Security Transactions   100%

Other Money Borrowed without Security and Due in One
  Month or More   20%

Social and Provident Funds   10%

Amounts Received from Account of Customers and Accounts
  Payable
    Residents   20%
    Non-Residents
      Base amount*   20%
      Excess over base amount   100%
Balance on Forward Foreign Exchange Transactions
  Residents   20%
  Non-residents
    Base amount*   20%
    Excess over base amount   100%

* *The base amount is the lowest balance in this category during the preceding 12 months.*

CHAPTER 10

UNITED KINGDOM

10.1 INSTITUTIONS COVERED

The Banking Act 1979 establishes two categories of institution which may engage in deposit-taking business in the United Kingdom, namely recognised banks and licensed deposit takers. The following institutions are excluded from the provisions of the Banking Act 1979:

(i) Central Banks of EEC Member States;

(ii) the National Savings Bank: run by the Department for National Savings, it provides a very limited banking service;

(iii) the Post Office (including the National Girobank);

(iv) credit unions (within the meaning of the Industrial and Provident Societies Act (Northern Ireland) 1969, or the Credit Unions Act 1979);

(v) trustee savings banks (within the meaning of the Trustee Savings Bank Act 1969). Although currently excluded from the provisions of the Banking Act, it is intended that they will be brought within its scope in due course;

(vi) building societies (within the meaning of the Building Societies Act 1962 or the Building Societies Act (Northern Ireland) 1967).

Certain other institutions carrying on deposit-taking business on a small scale, such as friendly societies, municipal banks and 'uncertified' savings banks, also enjoy exemption from the Act. In addition, there are other bodies which, while not commonly thought of as deposit-taking businesses, nevertheless fall within the Act's very wide definitions of 'deposit' and 'deposit-taking business' and which have also been granted exemption; these include stockbrokers, insurance companies and local authorities. The complete list of exemptions is set out in Schedule 1 to the Act. There are still other bodies enjoying conditional exemption under regulations made under section 2(1) of the Act.

Deposit-taking institutions in the Channel Islands and the Isle of Man are not covered by the Act; these islands are not part of the United Kingdom.

This chapter covers only the two categories of institution required to seek authorisation under the Act - recognised banks and licensed deposit-taking institutions.

10.2 BASIC LAWS

Besides the Banking Act 1979, there are a large number of enactments touching on different aspects of banking business. The most important are:

(i) the Bank of England Act 1946 (in particular, powers to give directions to bankers);

(ii) the Consumer Credit Act 1974 (regulating consumer lending);

(iii) the Moneylenders Acts 1900-1927, and the Moneylenders Act (Northern Ireland) 1933 (regulating the lending of money, but to be repealed in due course by the Consumer Credit Act 1974); and

(iv) the Protection of Depositors Act 1963, and the Protection of Depositors Act (Northern Ireland) 1964 (regulating advertising for deposits, but to be repealed in due course by the Banking Act 1979).

10.3 SUPERVISORY SYSTEM

10.3.1 Supervisory Authority

The Bank of England is the supervisory body for institutions recognised or licensed under the Banking Act 1979.

The Bank of England was founded in 1694, and was nationalised in 1946. It is directed by its Court which consists of the Governor, the Deputy Governor and 16 other directors, all of whom are appointed by the Crown on the recommendation of the Prime Minister. No more than four of the 16 may be executive directors. The 12 part-time directors include bankers (by tradition usually from merchant banks rather than clearing banks), industrialists and trade unionists.

The Bank of England carries out all the functions normally attributed to a central bank, including management of the note issue and of the national debt, banker to the Government and to the banks, management of the official foreign exchange reserves, and the provision of advice on monetary and economic policies to the Government.

Under the Bank of England Act 1946, the Bank is, subject to certain safeguards, entitled to request information from and make recommendations to bankers, and may, with Treasury authorisation, issue directions to any banker to effect compliance with such a request or recommendation. This power to give a direction has never been used, and indeed the Bank has never explicitly based any request or recommendation on the Act.

In addition to the powers of authorisation, the 1979 Banking Act gives the Bank extensive powers to require information, to issue directions to and to petition for the winding up of recognised banks and licensed institutions, where the interests of depositors are at stake.

The Bank of England works with, and in some respects for, H.M. Treasury, but expresses its own views, based on contacts with industry and financial circles. The relationship between the Bank and the Government is one in which the Bank tenders advice, whilst the Ministers determine policy. Any monetary measures taken by the Bank are with the approval, published or private, of the Government.

Under Section 4 of the Bank of England Act 1946 the Treasury may give directions to the Bank. This power has never been used.

10.3.2 Outline of System

Under the provisions of the Banking Act 1979 all persons wishing to carry on a deposit-taking business have to obtain either recognition as a bank or a licence to carry on a deposit-taking business, both of which are granted by the Bank of England, unless the person is specifically exempted from the terms of the legislation (see 10.1 above).

The distinction between recognised banks and licensed deposit-taking institutions is of relevance in a number of contexts. The Act imposes certain requirements to furnish information on licensed institutions but not on recognised banks (10.3.3 below); the criteria for authorisation are somewhat different (10.4 below); and there are restrictions on the use of banking names and descriptions applied to licensed institutions but not to recognised banks (10.7 below).

In order to grant recognition or a licence, the Bank of England must be satisfied that the criteria in Schedule 2 to the Act are met by the institution concerned. These are discussed in 10.4 and 10.9 below. The Bank is empowered to specify the manner in which applications for authorisation are made, and it can demand any information it reasonably requires to enable it to make its decision. Once granted the authorisation remains in force until surrendered by the institution or revoked by the Bank.

The Bank may grant a transitional licence to an institution which was carrying on a deposit-taking business in the U.K. on October 1, 1979 (the day that most of the provisions of the Banking Act came into force) if it satisfies the criteria relating to legal form (10.4.1) and management (10.4.3) for a full licence and the Bank is satisfied that the criteria relating to minimum capital (10.4.2), solvency and liquidity (10.9) for a licence will be fulfilled within a reasonable period of time. A transitional licence has a maximum life of two years and may be granted subject to conditions.

The application procedure for institutions seeking authority to take deposits is described in more detail in the Bank of England's *Handbook of Banking Supervision*.

If the Bank intends to refuse recognition or a licence, it must give the applicant written notice of its intention and inform him of his right to make written representations within a period not less than 28 days specified in the notice. The applicant's representations must then be taken into account by the Bank in reaching its decision. Where the Bank refuses the application it is required to give its reasons in writing. Institutions may appeal against the Bank's decision to the Chancellor of the Exchequer. There is a further right of appeal on a point of law to the courts.

The Bank of England is required to maintain for public inspection a list of recognised banks and licensed institutions, and must update it at least monthly. It is required to publish an annual report on the exercise of its functions under the Banking Act.

10.3.3 Returns to Supervisory Authority

Once the Banking Act is fully implemented, regular returns will be required from all recognised banks and licensed institutions. The detailed content of these returns, most of which are also used for purposes other than prudential supervision, varies according to the type of reporting institution. The basic format is of a monthly balance sheet return, with supplementary returns to be completed on a weekly, monthly, quarterly, six monthly, or annual basis. The monthly returns to the Bank of England are completed as at the third Wednesday of each month (second Wednesday of December), and also at the end of each calendar quarter. The form and content of returns to the Bank of England are strictly prescribed and defined by the Bank but are not governed by legislation.

The Bank of England has in the past received returns on the basis of informal agreement, though the Bank of England Act 1946 empowers it, if it considers it necessary in the public interest, to request information from bankers. This informal arrangement will continue for recognised banks, but the Bank of England now has specific statutory powers with regard to the licensed deposit-taking institutions under section 16 of the Banking Act 1979 to request them to furnish whatever information it may reasonably require.

Most UK-incorporated banks are requested to report large loans, defined as loans or advances which individually amount to 5% or more of total loans and advances, with full details of the customers and maturity dates, to the Bank of England. They are also asked to report the same details about deposits from one depositor which amount to 5% or more of total deposits. For reporting purposes all loans and advances to the same borrower (and deposits from the same depositor) are amalgamated. A company, its subsidiaries, its ultimate holding company and that company's subsidiaries are all regarded as one borrower (depositor). The Bank of England is currently introducing a new method of reporting which will consolidate the subsidiary and branch activities of banks.

Under similar arrangements to those outlined above, the banks and institutions mentioned are requested to report to the Bank of England their loans and advances to (and also their deposit liabilities to) directors and their associates, and to companies with which directors are associated. A director's associates are defined as the spouse, parent or remote forebear, child or remoter issue, brother or sister, and any trusts formed for the benefit of the director or of any associate. A director is associated with another company if he is a director of that company, or if he and/or his associates together hold 10% or more of the equity share capital of that company. Loans to managers and employees of the banks and institutions mentioned are not reported under this arrangement.

10.3.4 Auditing Requirements

There are no auditing requirements over and above those applying to business enterprises generally.

10.3.5 Inspection

Under the Banking Act 1979, the Bank of England has the power to request from a licensed institution such information as it may reasonably require about the nature and conduct of the institution's business and its plans for future development. The institution may also be compelled to make available whatever documents are considered relevant.

The Bank may appoint competent persons to investigate the business of a licensed deposit-taker or recognised bank, if it considers that to be in the interests of the depositors. The competent persons may also investigate, if it is relevant, the business of connected companies, and obtain access to all relevant papers.

10.4 CRITERIA FOR AUTHORISATION

The criteria for recognition and licensing are set out in section 3(1) to (6) and in Schedule 2 to the Act. In addition, the Bank of England has elaborated some of the criteria in more detail in its *Handbook of Banking Supervision*.

10.4.1 Legal Form

In order to qualify for recognition or a licence under the Banking Act, an institution must be a body corporate or a partnership. The one exception is for institutions formed under the law of other EEC Member States, which can take the form of any association of two or more persons. Sole traders are, however, debarred wherever they come from (see ss.3(1), (2) and (4) and ss.50 of the Act).

10.4.2 Minimum Capital

In order to qualify for recognition, unless an institution has carried on a deposit-taking business in the U.K. continuously since November 9, 1978 (the day the legislation was introduced into Parliament) it must have net assets (i.e. paid-up capital and reserves) of £5 million or, in the case of an institution providing a highly specialised banking service, of £250,000, at the time recognition is granted.

In the case of an applicant for a full licence to carry on a deposit-taking business, unless the the institution was carrying on a deposit-taking business in the U.K. on November 9, 1978 (the day the legislation was introduced into Parliament) it must have net assets (i.e. paid-up capital and reserves) of at least £250,000 at the time of licensing.

These minimum capital requirements are initial requirements only – they apply only at the time of authorisation. In addition, recognised banks and licensed deposit-takers must at all times meet the capital adequacy and liquidity criteria described in 10.9 below.

10.4.3 Management Qualifications

In order to qualify for recognition or a licence, at least two individuals must effectively direct the business of the institution.

In the case of an applicant for a full licence, every director, controller and manager of the institution (as defined in section 49 of the Act) must be "a fit and proper person to hold that position".

In case of an applicant for recognition, the Bank of England must be satisfied that the business will be conducted with prudence and integrity and with appropriate professional skills.

10.4.4 Management Plans

Institutions applying for recognition or a licence which were not carrying on a deposit-taking business in the UK on October 1, 1979, must submit to the Bank of England a statement of aims and programme of operations including the types of business envisaged, balance sheet projections and the structural organisation of the institution.

10.4.5 Other Requirements

There are two additional requirements which must be met by an institution seeking the status of recognised bank as opposed to licensed deposit-taking institution. In summary these are that:

(i) the institution enjoys, and has for a reasonable period of time enjoyed, a high reputation and standing in the financial community;

(ii) it provides either a wide range of banking services, (including lending and deposit facilities, foreign exchange services, trade finance, and financial advice or investment management services) or a highly specialised banking service. The Bank may have regard to the nature and scope of a particular service in determining whether or not it is provided to a satisfactory level and, with regard to the wide range of services criterion, may waive the need to provide one or two of the last three services; but deposit and lending facilities are obligatory.

10.5 BRANCHES

10.5.1 Restrictions on Branching in the United Kingdom

There are at present no special restrictions on the opening of new branches by institutions already authorised under the Banking Act to carry on a deposit-taking business. However, overseas institutions operating in the United Kingdom through branches are expected to inform the Bank in writing of the establishment of further branches (with details of their management) and the closure of branches in the United Kingdom.

10.5.2 Branching and Operations in Other Countries

There are no restrictions on the opening by UK-registered banks of branches in other countries, though the Bank of England would expect to be kept informed of banks' plans. The Bank would not, however, wish to see any U.K. registered company undertaking in any other country banking activities which it was not authorised to undertake in the U.K. It would ensure that the banking supervisory authority in the foreign country concerned was aware of the limited status of the U.K. company. The Bank of England would expect the scale of any banking activity to be commensurate with the capital supporting it (on a consolidated basis where subsidiaries are involved).

10.6 RESTRICTIONS ON BUSINESS

10.6.1 Restrictions on Types of Business

There are no explicit restrictions on the types of business which may be undertaken by a recognised bank or licensed deposit-taking institution. But equally, the status of recognised bank or licensed institution does not confer an explicit right to engage in any business other than deposit taking; the holder remains subject to the same legal restrictions as apply to other enterprises. In particular, authorisation under the Banking Act does not confer an automatic right to engage in lending business.

The lending of money is controlled by the Moneylenders Acts 1900-1927 (and the Moneylenders Acts (Northern Ireland) 1933 and 1969). These require lenders to be licensed and to comply with a number of obligations. However, persons "bona fide carrying on the business of banking" are exempt. Those whose status as 'bankers' is not beyond doubt can apply to the Department of Trade for a certificate that they are bankers for the purpose of the Moneylenders Acts (s.123 of the Companies Act 1967).

The Moneylenders Acts are due to be repealed once the Consumer Credit Act 1974 is fully in force. Under this Act any person or company (with very limited exceptions) advancing credit not exceeding £5,000 to individuals needs a licence. The Act also regulates such matters as methods of seeking business, disclosure of information, the form of agreements and the rights of the parties.

10.6.2 Loans to Directors

Companies generally are subject to restrictions on loans and 'quasi-loans' to directors under the Companies Act 1980. However, a money-lending company (i.e. a company whose ordinary business includes the making of loans) may make loans, quasi-loans, or provide guarantees for each director (or connected person) up to £50,000, providing they are on normal commercial terms. For recognised banks there is no limit on the amount of loans or other arrangements with directors made on normal commercial terms.

Both recognised banks and other money-lending companies may provide their directors or directors of their holding company (but not connected persons) with loans (but not quasi-loans or guarantees) for the purchase or improvement of their only or main residence. Such loans must ordinarily be made by the company to its employees on terms no less favourable, and the overall sum for each director must not exceed £50,000.

10.6.3 Equity Participations

There are no formal limits on the extent to which a recognised bank or licensed deposit-taker may hold participations in non-banks. However, in its supervisory role the Bank of England would need to be satisfied that capital was adequate to support the range of both its banking and non-banking activities.

The Bank of England, in the context of its controls on mergers between banks (see 10.6.4 below), normally does not object to any bank holding not more than 15% of the capital of another bank. The acquisition of a participation of more than 15% is interpreted by the Bank of England as a merger. (For the controls on acquisitions of shares in licensed deposit-taking institutions, see 10.6.4 below).

Recognised banks and licensed deposit-taking institutions are expected to consult the Bank in advance about the acquisition or disposal of any material interest in other companies and the establishment or disposal of subsidiaries.

10.6.4 Mergers

The Bank of England exercises an unofficial but comprehensive control over all mergers between banks. This control was described in a Notice issued by the Bank on November 16, 1972. In general, and subject to individual considerations and to the provisions of merger legislation (see below), the Bank of England will permit any institution registered in the U.K. or in any other EEC Member State to acquire a participation of any size in any other institution in the U.K. In each individual case the Bank's approval will depend on the existence of amicable agreement between the banks concerned, and on the satisfaction of criteria relating to capital, management, reputation and future intentions.

In exercising this control, the Bank expects to be consulted at an early stage, before any irrevocable steps are taken in the merger process. Under section 14 of the Banking Act, licensed institutions are required to notify the bank of any changes in their 'controllers', which are defined to include anybody who owns 15% or more of the shares.

Mergers between banks, as between any other companies, are subject to the provisions of the Fair Trading Act 1973. Section 64 of this Act states that if, among other criteria, the value of the assets of one company taken over by (or merged with) another company exceeds five million pounds, the proposed merger may be referred by the Secretary of State to the Monopolies and Mergers Commission: the latter will judge if the proposal is in the public interest. If it is thought to be against the public interest, the proposal may be prohibited (or reversed, if it has already been implemented).

The Secretary of State usually takes soundings from, *inter alia*, the Bank of England and the Treasury before deciding whether to refer a merger proposal to the Commission. The Bank would also be invited to make its view known to the Monopolies Commission. The possibility that a proposed merger would be held up for a long time or eventually prevented might be a reason for the Bank of England to exercise its informal veto at an early stage.

10.7 BANKING NAMES AND DESCRIPTIONS

Section 36 of the Banking Act 1979 provides that, with certain exceptions (recognised banks, central banks of Member States, trustee savings banks, National Girobank), no person carrying on a business in the United Kingdom may use any name or description which may reasonably be understood to indicate that he is a bank or banker or is carrying on a banking business. The prohibition is in terms that would not apply where it was clear that an institution was not holding itself out to be a bank.

In addition, there are a number of specific qualifications to the general prohibition, the most important of which are that:

(i) a licensed institution which is the wholly-owned subsidiary of a recognised bank is permitted to include its parent's banking name in its own title so as to indicate the connection between the two companies;

(ii) licensed institutions from other countries operating in the U.K. through a branch may retain their banking name in the U.K. provided that, whenever it is used, the words 'licensed deposit-taker' appear in immediate conjunction with it and no less prominently than the name itself;

(iii) licensed institutions which provide at least two of the services specified in paragraph 2(2) of Schedule 2 to the Act are allowed to use the expression 'banking services' except in immediate conjunction with their names or in a public display;

(iv) persons may describe themselves as a bank or banker or use a similar expression if it is necessary for them to do so in order to be able to assert that they are complying with or entitled to take advantage of a relevant provision of law or custom.

(v) representative offices of overseas institutions may use their banking name provided the words 'representative office' appear in immediate conjunction with it.

There are also transitional arrangements for institutions affected by the restrictions on the use of banking names and descriptions.

10.8 ADVERTISING

Under the Banking Act the Treasury may, after consultation with the Bank, control the form and content of advertisements which invite the making of deposits. This is to be done by Regulations made by statutory instrument. These Regulations have yet to be issued.

For the time being, advertisements for deposits are still controlled by the Protection of Depositors Act 1963 (which is to be repealed by the Banking Act in due course). As well as regulating the form and context of advertisements, companies advertising for deposits are required to provide supplementary information in their accounts, to make those accounts available to depositors and to lodge them with the Department of Trade. However, banking and discount companies - that is, those who satisfy the Department of Trade that they ought to be so regarded for this purpose - are exempt from the Act's provisions.

As regards advertising on television, the present Code of Advertising Standards and Practice, issued under the Independent Broadcasting Authority Act 1973, forbids the advertising on radio and television of investment and savings facilities unless the advertisement is for British Government or local authority securities, or is issued by building societies, authorised unit trusts, stock exchanges, the National Savings Bank and National Girobank, trustee savings banks, and banking and discount companies who were as such exempted from the Protection of Depositors Act 1963. It is not known what alternative will be incorporated in the Code when the Protection of Depositors Act is repealed.

The Code of Advertising Standards and Practice also controls the type of institution which may advertise mortgage or other lending facilities and credit services. These may only be advertised by banks, and companies holding exemption from the Moneylenders Act; but as soon as the licensing provisions of the Consumer Credit Act 1974 are implemented, such advertisements will only be accepted from the holders of Consumer Credit Act licences (see 10.6.1 above).

Under section 44 of the Consumer Credit Act 1974, the Secretary of State for Prices and Consumer Protection is required to issue regulations controlling the content of advertisements concerning the provision of credit to anyone other than companies. No such regulations have yet been issued.

10.9 SOLVENCY AND LIQUIDITY

Whereas the Bank of England only had implicit powers to control liquidity and solvency under the Bank of England Act 1946, the Banking Act 1979 requires that deposit-taking institutions maintain such levels of liquidity and net assets as are considered adequate by the Bank of England. These requirements are part of the criteria for recognition and a licence set out in Schedule 2 to the Act.

The statutory requirements are expressed only in very general terms, and it is left to the Bank of England to determine how the criteria are interpreted in practice. Recognised banks are required to conduct their business "with integrity and prudence", and to maintain net assets (together with other appropriate financial resources) "commensurate with the scale of the institution's operations". Licensed institutions must conduct their business "in a prudent manner" and, in particular, (a) maintain net assets (together with other appropriate financial resources) sufficient to safeguard depositors, having regard to the scale and nature of their liabilities and the nature and riskiness of their assets; (b) maintain adequate liquidity, having regard to the maturity pattern of assets and liabilities; and (c) make adequate provision for bad and doubtful debts and contingent obligations.

10.9.1 Solvency Ratios

The solvency ratios used by the Bank of England in exercising its supervisory functions are described in its paper 'The Measurement of Capital' of September 1980. The Bank of England currently uses two capital adequacy tests, one of which is related to the level of 'risk assets', and the other to 'public liabilities'. The definition of capital is broadly similar in both cases, and consists of an 'adjusted capital base'. Since 1975, when the Bank first began to assess capital adequacy on a basis broadly agreed with the banks, the relationship of the capital base to risk assets has been considered the more important of the two ratios. A summary of the method of calculation of these two ratios, reproduced from 'The Measurement of Capital', is set out in the Appendix to this chapter.

The capital base used in assessing the risk assets cover is paid up share capital and reserves, fully subordinated loan capital (within limits and under certain conditions), minority interests (when consolidated data are used) and general provisions. However, hidden values in the balance sheet, and any over-statement of the value of assets in relation to their market worth, may also be taken into account.

Specific provisions against risks are not included in the capital resources of banks for the purpose of capital adequacy assessment. General provisions, if freely available to absorb future losses as they subsequently materialise, may be included.

Subordinated unsecured loan capital, in sterling or other currencies, is included in capital resources, provided that it does not exceed 50% of the total of other allowable capital resources net of intangible assets. It is considered essential that the loan capital should have an initial term to maturity of at least five years, and preferably ten years. It is the Bank of England's practice to discount for capital adequacy assessment purposes one fifth of the value of loan capital for each year that its maturity is less than five years. Convertible loan capital may also be included in capital resources.

To calculate the 'adjusted capital base', deductions are made for investments in subsidiary and associated companies and trade investments, together with goodwill, and investment in plant and equipment. For the risk assets ratio bank premises are not deducted, but treated as balance sheet assets.

The resulting 'adjusted capital base' is expressed as a percentage of the total of assets in risk-weighted bands derived from each institution's statistical returns. The risk weights assigned to various assets are set out in the Appendix.

The present information covers only assets held by U.K. offices of banks, but it is intended to extend the scheme to cover assets held by the overseas branches of UK-registered banks, and ultimately to cover their financial subsidiaries too.

The gearing ratio relates capital to 'public liabilities', defined to include deposits and non-capital liabilities. The 'adjusted capital base' is calculated in the same manner as described above, but a further deduction for premises is made to give the amount of an institution's 'free capital'. This is then used to calculate the gearing ratio against the total of balance sheet liabilities, less the capital base (before deduction of infrastructure items) and certain other liabilities of a capital nature.

The precise components and methods of calculation of these two solvency ratios are set out in the 'The Measurement of Capital'. It should be emphasised that the Bank of England has not specified any common minimum coefficients for these ratios that all deposit-taking institutions must meet. Rather, the Bank of England assesses the capital adequacy of each institution according to the individual circumstances of that institution.

In the case of a banking group, with both parent and subsidiary registered banks, the capital adequacy discussions are initially based on consolidated accounts for the whole group, but separate discussions are also held on the accounts of the individual subsidiaries, since it is regarded by the Bank of England as important that these subsidiaries should be seen to possess adequate resources in their own right.

It should be noted that the Bank of England does not apply any solvency ratio to a branch of an overseas bank: it is considered that the business of such a branch cannot be separated from the balance sheet of the whole bank, and that for these purposes the control of the branch is the responsibility of the supervisory authority in the bank's country of origin.

10.9.2 Liquidity Ratios

The Bank of England has not yet finally determined the form of the liquidity ratios which will be applied under the system of supervision provided for in the Banking Act 1979. The Bank has issued proposals in a paper entitled 'The Measurement of Liquidity' which are being discussed with those affected. Until the new liquidity rules are finalised, banks will continue to be required to hold certain liquid assets under the reserve asset ratio rule (see 10.10.5 below).

In the meantime, the Bank of England examines the liquidity of supervised institutions to ensure its adequacy in the light of the particular circumstances of each. A number of measurements are used, and no across-the-board minima are set.

10.9.3 Loan Limits

There are reporting requirements for large loans (and large deposits) as described in 10.3.3. above. The Bank of England does not, however, impose any limit on the maximum permitted size of loan or maximum acceptable degree of concentration.

10.10 MONETARY AND CREDIT CONTROLS

The Bank of England's present powers to impose monetary controls on 'banks' in the United Kingdom depend ultimately on the Bank of England Act 1946 (see 10.3.1). However, in implementing monetary policy it has never been necessary to invoke the Act. The formal powers of the Bank of England do not extend to any non-bank financial institutions, but the associations representing the insurance companies, the pension funds and the building societies have on occasions been informed by the Bank of major changes in monetary or credit controls, so that they can bear official objectives in mind.

10.10.1 Direct Credit Controls

In the period before the introduction of Competition and Credit Control in 1971, the primary instrument of credit regulation was the imposition of lending ceilings. Initially these were just applied to the clearing banks, but they were gradually extended to a wider range of institutions. They were withdrawn in 1971, when new market-orientated techniques of monetary policy were introduced.

Although lending ceilings have not been reintroduced since 1971, the Bank of England has had to resort to an alternative method of direct regulation in the supplementary special deposits scheme, or the 'corset'. The corset required banks and deposit-taking finance houses to place non-interest earning special deposits at the Bank as a proportion of the growth of their interest bearing eligible liabilities (IBELs) insofar as these exceeded specified norms; the penalty becomes progressively more severe with the amount of the excess. While some institutions did have to place balances with the Bank of England under this scheme, the severity of the penalties meant that the corset was very much a direct control, rather than a reserve requirement mechanism. The corset was in operation during the periods December 1973 - February 1975, November 1976 - August 1977, and June 1978 - June 1980.

10.10.2 Selective Credit Controls

The primary selective instrument in the United Kingdom is the lending guidance issued by the Bank of England. Except for a few months following the introduction of Competition and Credit Control, banks have for many years been in continual receipt of qualitative guidance regarding the direction of their lending. Currently banks are asked to give priority to the finance required by manufacturing industry and for the expansion of exports and the saving of imports, and to exert strict restraint on other lending, in particular that to persons, property companies and for purely financial transactions. In addition, they are asked not to provide finance for the purchase of consumer durables on terms easier than those permitted by the terms control regulations (these limit the maximum repayment period and the minimum down payment for different types of consumer goods purchased on credit).

10.10.3 Regulation of Interest Rates

There are no official controls on banks' interest rates in the United Kingdom. However, when Competition and Credit Control was introduced, the Bank of England did explain that it might be necessary to impose constraints on the rates that the banks could offer on small deposits in order to limit the interest rate competition with savings banks and building societies. This control was invoked in the period September 1973 - February 1975, when the banks were asked not to pay more than 9½% on deposits of under £10,000.

10.10.4 Central Bank Accommodation

In the United Kingdom the banking system is accommodated mainly by the Bank of England providing refinancing to the discount market. This generally takes the form of secured advances or the rediscount of eligible bills; on occasion the Bank of England has used a purchase and resale procedure with the discount houses. Refinancing, which is not intended as a permanent source of liquidity for the discount houses, is normally extended at the Bank of England's minimum lending rate (MLR).

In order to ease money market pressures the Bank of England has from time to time taken gilt-edged stock on a purchase and resale basis from the clearing banks. On occasion this facility has been provided for other banks also.

10.10.5 Reserve Requirements

Since 1971 all statistical banks and deposit-taking finance houses (with eligible liabilities exceeding £5 million) have been obliged to invest a minimum proportion of their eligible liabilities in specified reserve assets. In broad terms reserve assets consist of balances with the Bank of England (other than special deposits), holdings of treasury bills, money at call with the discount market and certain other assets against which the Bank of England is willing to lend to the discount houses in its lender of last resort capacity. The reserve asset ratio is to be abolished once prudential liquidity requirements have been finalised. A separate control on the London clearing banks obliges those institutions to hold 1½% of eligible liabilities in balances with the Bank of England (these balances do count, however, towards the reserve asset ratio). This requirement is also expected to be modified in the near future.

Members of the London Discount Market Association must limit to a maximum of 20 times capital and reserves holdings of certain assets. In addition these institutions must observe a ceiling on their total assets of approximately 30 times their capital and reserves.

As well as minimum reserve asset requirements, banks and deposit-taking finance houses are periodically obliged to place balances with the Bank of England in proportion to their eligible liabilities. These balances, special deposits, normally bear interest at a rate equivalent to treasury bill rate. On a number of occasions the Bank of England has temporarily released special deposits for the purpose of easing pressures in the money market. In order to give the authorities more ability to control external flows, the Bank of England may call for special deposits at different rates against resident and non-resident deposits; however, it has never done so.

The authorities have announced that the system of special deposits is to be retained following the proposed change in reserve requirements.

10.11 FOREIGN EXCHANGE

10.11.1 Authority to Deal in Foreign Exchange

Subsequent to the suspension of the Exchange Control Act 1947, there are no restrictions on undertaking foreign exchange business.

10.11.2 Limits on Positions

The Bank of England has issued proposals for the prudential control of the foreign exchange business of supervised institutions. These proposals, in the paper 'Foreign Currency Exposure', are at present the subject of discussions between the Bank of England and those affected.

However, the Bank of England has asked that, until a new basis for prudential control is agreed, supervised institutions should conduct their foreign exchange business no less prudently than suggested in the consultative paper. This proposes a maximum aggregate short position of 10%, and a maximum single currency position of 3½% of a bank's adjusted capital base, (as defined in 10.9.1 for the risk assets ratio).

10.12 CREDIT INFORMATION EXCHANGE

There is no form of credit information exchange or central risks bureau in the U.K.

10.13 DEPOSIT INSURANCE

The Banking Act 1979 provides for the establishment of a Deposit Protection Fund, to which all recognised banks and licensed institutions will be required to contribute, unless specifically exempted (i.e. in the case of foreign banks by virtue of their sterling deposits being as well protected by their own national schemes). Initial contributions will be fixed as a proportion of each institution's deposit base so as to produce a total of between £5 million and £6 million in the Fund. (An institution's deposit base is defined in section 23 to include only sterling deposits and to exclude deposits placed by recognised banks and licensed institutions). There are provisions for further and special contributions. Total contributions by any institution will not exceed 0.3% of its deposit base.

The Banking Act provides that, in the event of the failure of a contributory institution, depositors will receive from the Fund a sum equivalent to 75% of the first £10,000 of their sterling deposits with the U.K. offices of that institution.

10.14 SANCTIONS

Although the business of deposit-taking institutions may be affected by the sanctions imposed under the Prevention of Fraud (Investments) Act 1958, the Companies Acts 1948-80 and the Consumer Credit Act 1974, the main direct legal sanctions available to the Bank of England are now contained in the Banking Act 1979.

10.14.1 Revocation of Authorisation

Under the Act, the Bank of England may:
  (i) revoke a recognition and grant a full licence;
  (ii) revoke a recognition or a full licence, and grant a conditional licence;
  (iii) revoke all deposit-taking authority, and issue to the institution whatever directions seem necessary in the interest of the depositors, such as a prohibition on dealing or disposing of assets, or on any specified transaction, or on soliciting deposits. The Bank can also specify a certain course of action to be undertaken.

The grounds on which the Bank of England may, at its own discretion, use its powers to revoke an institution's deposit-taking authority are set out in section 6(1)(a)-(i) of the Act. They include the grounds that the institution has failed to comply with any obligation under the Act or that it has "so conducted its affairs as to threaten the interests of its depositors".

10.14.2 Imposition of Conditions

The Bank of England may revoke an institution's recognition as a bank, or its licence and grant it a conditional licence to carry on a deposit-taking business, dependent upon its compliance with the conditions set out in the licence. With regard to an institution already operating under a conditional licence, the Bank may, if it wishes, grant it another, subject to different conditions. In general, the conditions which the Bank may impose (see section 10(2) and (3) of the Act) are aimed at securing the protection of the depositors, and are potentially wide ranging in nature.

10.14.3 Other Sanctions

Under section 18 of the Act, the Bank of England may petition before the courts for the winding up of a recognised bank or licensed institution.

10.14.4 Penalties

Failure to comply with the provisions of the Act is punishable by a fine, imprisonment or both.

10.14.5 Appeals

The Banking Act 1979 makes provision for appeals to the Chancellor of the Exchequer against decisions by the Bank of England (sections 11 to 13). An institution may appeal against the refusal of a licence or recognition, or the granting of a licence instead of recognition, or the revocation of a licence or recognition. An institution may also appeal against directions issued to it by the Bank prohibiting it from performing certain acts and/or requiring it to take certain steps, and against any of the conditions of a conditional licence, whether or not it also challenges the decision itself.

The Chancellor may confirm, vary or reverse the decision appealed against, take any action which the Bank could have taken when it took the decision and give directions regarding the payment of costs and expenses. The Act provides for a further appeal to be made to the High Court by either the institution concerned or the Bank on any question of law arising out of the Chancellor's decision on an appeal.

If the Director General of Fair Trading refuses to issue a licence under the Consumer Credit Act 1974, or suspends or revokes an existing licence, an appeal may be made to the Secretary of State: an appeal from the Secretary of State's decision may be made, on a point of law, to the High Court.

10.15 FOREIGN BANK BRANCHES

10.15.1 Establishment

Overseas deposit-taking institutions which wish to carry on a deposit-taking business in the United Kingdom through a branch need to hold a licence or be recognised as a bank. Although such institutions will be expected to conform with the appropriate standards, the primary responsibility for their supervision rests with their parental supervisory authority.

Accordingly, in the case of an institution whose principal place of business is outside the U.K., the Act allows the Bank of England to regard itself as satisfied that the solvency and arrangements criteria in Schedule 2 to the Act are fulfilled if:

(i) the relevant overseas supervisory authority informs it that it is satisfied with the management and financial soundness of the institution; and

(ii) the Bank is satisfied as to the nature and scope of the supervision exercised by the overseas supervisory authority.

The Bank of England would, however, require some statistical and prudential returns, and the provisions regarding liquidity and foreign exchange exposure will also have a bearing.

10.15.2 Earmarked Capital

There is no formal requirement for separate branch capital.

10.15.3 Nationality and Competence of Personnel

There are no formal provisions. Nonetheless, before the granting of specific authorisation the Bank of England would need to be satisfied that the management and staff were experienced, honest, trustworthy and suitably qualified.

Any person who is not a national of a Member State of the EEC must obtain a work permit from the Department of Employment before taking up a position in the U.K.

10.15.4 Restrictions on Business

Branches of foreign banks operating in the U.K. are not subject to any limitations on their business, other than those applying to U.K.-registered banks.

10.15.5 Representative Offices

The representative office of an overseas deposit-taking institution must notify the Bank of England of its presence within one month of its establishment in the U.K.

10.16 FOREIGN BANK SUBSIDIARIES

10.16.1 Local Ownership

No local participation is required.

10.16.2 Nationality of Directors

Any person who is not a national of a Member State of the EEC must obtain a work permit from the Department of Employment before taking up a position in the U.K. There are at present no other restrictions or requirements as to the nationality of directors.

10.16.3 Guarantees from Parent Institution

There is no current requirement for a legal guarantee from parent banks, but the Bank of England expects overseas banks with banking subsidiaries in the U.K., or with shareholdings in U.K.-registered consortium banks, to acknowledge a special responsibility for depositors with their subsidiaries, extending beyond the narrow limits laid down by the laws of limited liability.

This approach, which is the counterpart to the Bank's controls over the foreign operations of U.K.-based banks (see 10.5.2 above), has been agreed with the foreign supervisory authorities concerned. It does not, however, mean that the U.K. subsidiaries of overseas banks are exempted from the need to comply with any solvency or liquidity controls which may, for prudential purposes, be applied to U.K. banks.

10.17 BANKING ASSOCIATIONS

10.17.1 Membership

The British Bankers' Association is the umbrella organisation for recognised banks; it is the U.K. member of the Fédération Bancaire de la CEE.

Membership of the British Bankers' Association is not compulsory. In practice almost all recognised banks are full or associate members. In January 1981 there were 111 full members and 231 associate members.

There are a number of other associations with more restricted membership including the Committee of London Clearing Bankers (the largest retail banks in England and Wales) and the Committee of Scottish Clearing Bankers (their Scottish counterparts), the Northern Ireland Bankers' Association, the Accepting Houses Committee and the London Discount Market Association.

10.17.2 Relations with Supervisory Authorities

None of the banking associations play any formal part in the supervisory system. They do, however, have a very important informal role, particularly as channels for consultation in the development of any new policies, or the modification of any existing polices.

10.18 BACKGROUND SOURCES

1. Aufricht, H., Central Banking Legislation, Vol 11: Europe (International Monetary Fund, Washington D.C.) (1967).
2. Bank of England: Handbook of Banking Supervision.
3. Bank of England: The Measurement of Capital (September 1980).
4. Bank of England: The Measurement of Liquidity (March 1980).
5. Bank of England: Quarterly Bulletin.
6. Banking Federation of the European Community; Monetary Policy and the Banking System in the Countries of the European Community (Brussels) (1980).
7. Elstob, M. (ed): Banking Structures and Sources of Finance in the European Community (Banker Research Unit, London) (1979).
8. Goode, R.M. and O'Dowd, A.P.: The Consumer Credit Act 1974, (Butterworths, London), (1974).
9. Green Paper: Monetary Control; Cmnd.7858 (H.M.S.O. London) (March 1980)
10. House of Commons Select Committee on Nationalised Industries: Seventh Report, Session 1975-76, Bank of England, (H.M.S.O., London), (1976).
11. IBRO: Banking Ratios in the EEC (a study commissioned by the EEC Commission from the Inter-Bank Research Organisation, 1979).
12. International Monetary Fund: Annual Report on Exchange Arrangements and Exchange Restrictions, 1979 (Washington D.C.).
13. Morison, I., Tillett, P., and Welch, J.: Banking Act 1979, (London, Butterworths) (1979).
14. Report of the Committee to Review the Functioning of Financial Institutions (H.M.S.O., London), (1980).
15. Revell, J.R.S.: Solvency and Regulation of Banks: Bangor Occasional Papers in Economics, No.5, (University of Wales Press, Bangor), (1975).

APPENDIX

COMPOSITION OF GEARING AND RISK ASSET RATIOS

		Gearing ratio	Risk asset ratio

1	Capital base		Share capital
			Loan capital
			Minority
			   Interests
			Reserves
			General
			   provisions

2	Adjustments
	  to capital
	  base
	Deduct
		Investments in
		  subsidiaries
		  and associates
		Goodwill
		Equipment
		Premises
		Other fixed
		  assets
			Investments
			  in subsidiaries
			  and associates
			Goodwill
			Equipment
			
			Other fixed
			  assets

3	Adjusted
	  capital base
	  (1-2)		

4		Deposits and other non-capital liabilities	
5		Gearing ratio (3:4)	

6   Adjusted total
                                           of risk assets
                                           (derived from
                                           the application
                                           of the risk
                                           weights in
                                           Appendix 10.A.5)

7   Risk asset ratio
                                           (3 as percentage
                                           of 6)

The classification of assets and risk weights held by U.K. offices of supervised institutions for the purpose of calculating the risk asset ratio (10.9.1 above) is as follows:

(i)   Nil weight   Bank of England notes and U.K. coins
                      Other sterling notes
                      Balances with Bank of England
                      Special deposits with Bank of England
                      Debits in course of collection on banks in the
                      United Kingdom
                      Balances with overseas offices of the reporting bank
                      Lending under special schemes for exports and
                      ship-building
                      Certificates of tax deposit
                      Items in suspense
                      Refinanced lending at fixed rates
                      Gold physically held in own vaults
                      Gold held elsewhere on an allocated basis

(ii)   0.1 weight   Foreign currency notes and coin
                      U.K. and Northern Ireland Treasury bills

(iii) 0.2 weight
                      Debit items in course of collection on overseas banks
                      Market loans with listed banks, discount market, etc.
                      Market loans to U.K. local authorities and public
                      corporations
                      Balances with banks overseas with a maximum term of
                      up to one year (including claims in gold)
                      Bills other than U.K. and Northern Ireland Treasury
                      bills

Other loans and advances to Northern Ireland
government, U.K. local authorities, public
corporations and other public sector
British government stocks with up to 18 months to
final maturity
Acceptances drawn on U.K. and overseas banks and
U.K. public sector
Claims in gold on U.K. banks and members of the
London Gold Market

(iv) 0.5 weight   British government stocks with over 18 months to
final maturity
Northern Ireland government stocks
U.K. local authority and other public sector stocks
and bonds
Acceptances drawn by other U.K. and overseas
residents
Guarantees and other contingent liabilities

(v) 1.0 weight   Market loans placed with other U.K. residents
Other loans and advances, net of specific provisions
for bad debts, but excluding connected lending
Assets leased to customers
Working capital provided for overseas offices of the
reporting bank, both in the form of deposits and in
other forms
Balances with banks overseas with a term of one year
or over (including claims in gold)
Claims in gold on non-banks
Aggregate foreign currency position (to be defined in
the Bank's paper on 'Foreign Currency Exposure')
Other assets 'other', e.g. silver, commodities and
other goods beneficially owned by the reporting bank
Other quoted investments, not connected

(vi) 1.5 weight   Connected lending (to be looked at case by case and
to exclude market-type lending where this can be
separately identified)
Unquoted investments (subject to case-by-case
treatment)

(vii) 2.0 weight   Property (includes all land and premises
                         beneficially owned by the reporting bank)

Items to be   Plant and equipment
deducted from   Intangible assets
capital   Investments in subsidiary and associated companies
                         and trade investments

CHAPTER 11

EEC

The purpose of this chapter is to summarise, under the same headings as used in the other chapters, the provisions of European Community Law which affect the regulation of banks in each Member State.

11.1 INSTITUTIONS COVERED

Banks or 'credit institutions', as they are described in the 1977 Banking Directive, (see below 11.2) are defined in Article 1 of that Directive as undertakings whose business is to receive deposits and other repayable funds from the public and to grant credits for their own account. Credit institutions are entitled, under the 1973 Directive on freedom of establishment of banks (see below 11.2), to set up branches or subsidiaries in other Member States under the same conditions and with the same rights as nationals of that Member State, provided that they fall within the following categories. Those entitled to take advantage of the right of establishment are natural persons, companies and other legal persons. Natural persons must be nationals of a Member State, who are established in the territory of any Member State (Art. 52 of the EEC Treaty) while companies or firms must be formed in accordance with the law of a Member State and have their registered office, central administration or principal place of business within the Community (Art. 58 of the EEC Treaty).

A further qualification was added to the latter provision by the General Progamme for the Abolition of Restrictions on Freedom of Establishment (J.O. 1962, 36) to the effect that, where a company's registered office is not within the Community, it must show an effective and continuous link with the economy of a Member State, excluding the nationality of the managers, partners, or shareholders as the determining factor. There is no definition of what constitutes 'an effective and continuous link' but it is accepted that an existing establishment would qualify. It is important to note that even where companies or firms are wholly controlled by nationals of non-Member States, or where the real headquarters are outside the Community, they may still be able to take advantage of the provisions on freedom of establishment.

Certain named credit institutions are exempted entirely from the provisions of the 1977 Directive by virtue of Article 2(2):
— the central banks of Member States;
— post office giro institutions;
— in Belgium, the communal savings banks ('caisses d'épargne communales— gemeentelijke spaarkassen'), the 'Institut de Reescompte et de Garantie— Herdisconteringen Waarborginstituut,' the 'Société Nationale d'Investissement— Nationale Investerings-maatschappij,' the regional development companies ('sociétés de développement régional— gewestelijke ontwikkelingsmaatschappijen'), the Société Nationale du Logement — Nationale Maatschappij voor de Huisvesting' and its authorised companies, and the 'Société Nationale Terrienne— Nationale Landsmaatschappij' and its authorised companies;
— in Denmark, the 'Dansk Eksportfinansieringsfond' and 'Danmarks Skibskreditfond',
— in Germany, the 'Kreditanstalt für Wiederaufbau', undertakings which are recognised under the 'Wohnungsgemeinnützigkeitsgesetz' (non-profit housing law) as bodies of state housing policy and are not mainly engaged in banking transactions and undertakings recognised under that law as non-profit housing undertakings;
— in France, the 'Caisse des Dépôts et Consignations', the 'Crédit Foncier' and the 'Crédit National',
— in Ireland, credit unions;
— in Italy the 'Cassa Depositi e Prestiti';
— in the Netherlands, the 'NV Export-Financieringsmaatschappij,' the 'Nederlandse Financieringsmaatschappij voor Ontwikkelingslanden NV', the 'Nationale Investeringsbank NV', the 'NV Bank van Nederlandse Gemeenten', the 'Nederlandse Waterschapsbank NV', the 'Financieringsmaatschappij Industrieel Garantiefonds Amsterdam NV', the 'Financieringsmaatschappij Industrieel Garantiefonds 's-Gravenhage NV', the 'NV Noordelijke Ontwikkelings Maatschappij', the 'NV Industriebank Limburgs Instituut voor Ontwikkeling en Financiering' and the 'Overijsselse Ontwikkelingsmaatschappij NV';
— in the United Kingdom, the National Savings Bank, the Commonwealth Development Finance Company Ltd., the Agricultural Mortgage Corporation Ltd., the Scottish Agricultural Securities Corporation Ltd., the Crown Agents for Overseas Governments and Administrations, credit unions, and municipal banks.

Any amendments to the list set out in Article 2(2) can only be made with the approval of the Council, acting on a proposal from the Commission, which itself is obliged to consult the Advisory Committee (see below 11.3.1).

Article 2(4)(a) allows Member States to exempt existing credit institutions, which are permanently affiliated to a central body which supervises them, from the requirements of the directive in respect of own funds, (see 11.4.2 below) management (11.4.3 to 11.4.4) and observation of ratios (11.9). This exemption was designed specifically to cover the special case of the Dutch Rabobank - the Coöperatieve Centrale Raiffeisen Boerenleenbank - which has a number of affiliated local cooperative agricultural credit and savings banks.

A further exemption allows Member States to defer application of the directive to certain types of groups of credit institution where 'immediate application would cause technical problems which cannot be overcome in the short term' (Art. 2(5)). The sorts of problems envisaged are those where the institutions in question are subject to a special system of supervision or are supervised by an authority other than that normally responsible for the supervision of banks. Member States cannot defer application of the Directive to a type of institution merely on the grounds of its size or the limited scope of its business. Deferments run initially for a maximum period of five years from notification of the Directive, i.e. until the end of 1982, but may be extended, after consulting the Advisory Committee, for a further period of three years only. The position regarding deferment will be reviewed by the Commission before the end of 1984 and the Council may then agree to an extension of the deferment provisions.

Denmark, Ireland, Luxembourg, the Netherlands and the United Kingdom have deferred application of the directive to certain institutions in accordance with Article 2(5). A list of these institutions is published in the *Official Journal* of October 14, 1978 (OJ 1978 C244/2).

11.2 BASIC LAWS

At the time of writing, two banking directives have been adopted by the Council of Ministers, the first in 1973 dealing with the abolition of restrictions on freedom of establishment and freedom to provide services in respect of banks and other financial institutions (OJ 1973 L 1941/1) and the second in 1977 harmonising the laws and adminstrative provisions governing the establishment and business of credit institutions (OJ 1977 L 322/30). The impact of Community Law is not limited, however, to the need to comply with adopted directives and other secondary legislation. Reference must also be made to articles of the Treaty of Rome itself, in particular Article 7, which prohibits discrimination on grounds of nationality and Articles 52 - 58 which cover the right of establishment.

Articles 85 - 90, which deal with competition, are somewhat peripheral to the issues covered by this book, but are considered where relevant.

Several of these articles have been found to have "direct effect" by the European Court of Justice in Luxembourg, i.e., they confer rights or impose obligations on individuals without the need for intervening legislation by the Community or the Member States - in other words, they have the force of law in each Member State. More important still, because they form part of Community Law, they take precedence over any conflicting provisions of national legislation.

Banks established in the EEC must have regard therefore, not only to national banking legislation and any specific EEC banking measures but also to the provisions of the Treaty of Rome, general Community legislation and decisions of the European Court of Justice.

11.3 SUPERVISORY SYSTEM

11.3.1 Supervisory Authority

The supervisory authority designated by each Member State is responsible for authorising and supervising credit institutions under the 1977 Directive. Each authority is required by Article 7 of the Directive to collaborate closely with the others in supervising banks which operate in more than one Member State. They are under an obligation to supply one another with 'all information concerning the management and ownership of such credit institutions that is likely to facilitate their supervision and the examination of the conditions for their authorisation and all information likely to facilitate the monitoring of their liquidity and solvency'.

On the EEC front, the Commission itself and the Advisory Committee, which was set up under Article 11(2) of the 1977 Directive, have some regulatory powers. The Advisory Committee consists of up to three representatives from each Member State and the Commission. Its main task is to lay down guidelines for the Commission's harmonisation programme, but it has a number of specific functions under the Directive: for example, it must be consulted by the Commission before any amendments are proposed to the list of institutions exempted under Article 2(2). Similarly the Advisory Committee must be consulted about any amendments to the provisions governing the Dutch Rabobank (Article 2(4)), the extension of any deferments requested by Member States from the whole or part of the Directive (Article 2(6)), and is required to examine the present authorisation requirements and, where appropriate, make recommendations to the Commission for their harmonisation (Article 3(5)). The Advisory Committee must also be notified by the supervisory authorities of each Member State of all authorisations granted to branches of banks with head offices outside the EEC.

11.3.2 Outline of System

The 1977 Directive requires each Member State to have a system for authorising banks before they set up in business (Art.3(1)), and a series of minimum conditions for authorisation are laid down covering minimum capital and management. The Directive also lays down the conditions under which banking authorisation may be withdrawn. Reasons for refusal or withdrawal of authorisation must be given and a limited right of appeal allowed. Article 6 of the Directive also provides for the establishment of observation ratios with a view to monitoring the solvency and liquidity of banks.

The purpose of the 1977 Directive is 'to make it easier to take up and pursue the business of credit institutions' by eliminating the 'most obstructive differences between the laws of the Member States as regards the rules to which these institutions are subject'. The ultimate objective, as stated in the Preamble to the Directive, is to provide for 'the overall supervision of a credit institution operating in several Member States by the competent authorities in the Member State where it has its head office, in consultation, as appropriate, with the competent authorities of the other Member States concerned'.

11.3.3 Returns to Supervisory Authority

There are no provisions in the 1977 Directive dealing with returns.

11.3.4 Auditing requirements

The 1977 Directive does not cover auditing requirements but a draft directive dealing with the annual accounts of banks and other financial institutions has now been issued by the Commission (OJ 1981 C130/1).

11.3.5 Inspection

There are no provisions in the Directive dealing with inspection.

11.4 CRITERIA FOR AUTHORISATION

11.4.1 Legal Form

The Directive does not specify what legal form a credit institution must take but it does require the institution to have 'separate own funds', i.e. capital resources which can be clearly distinguished from the capital of the owners or controllers. The effect of this provision is to outlaw sole proprietorships or one-man banks, subject to certain exemptions for existing institutions. Article 10(1) [1] permits Member States to allow 'one-man banks' in existence at the time of notification of the Directive, i.e. December 15, 1977, to continue in business indefinitely. (The names of these institutions must be included in the list of authorised credit institutions which each Member State is required to deliver to the Commission under Articles 3(7) and 10(2) of the Directive. The first list was published in the *Official Journal* of September 8, 1980 (OJ 1980 C229/1)).

11.4.2 Minimum Capital

In addition to the separate own funds requirement mentioned above, Article 3(2) specifies that a credit institution must possess 'adequate minimum own funds'. It is left to the individual Member States to decide what figure is adequate. 'Own funds' are defined by Article 1 as the credit institution's 'own capital, including items which may be treated as capital under national rules'.

11.4.3 Management Qualifications

Article 3(2) stipulates that each credit institution must have at least two individuals effectively directing its business, and that they must be of 'sufficiently good repute' and have 'sufficient experience' to carry out their duties. Again, it is left to the individual Member States to decide what constitutes 'good repute' and adequate experience for this purpose.

The requirement for two effective managers is designed as a safeguard against misuse of a bank's funds. It operates as a further prohibition on 'one-man banks' but is subject to the exemptions set out in Article 10(1), viz. that institutions in existence on December 15, 1977, which fail to meet this requirement, may be allowed by Member States to continue in business for a further five years. This exemption is further qualified by the last paragraph of Article 10(1) which authorises Member States to allow those credit institutions without separate own funds to continue in business indefinitely and to continue to be directed by one person only.

11.4.4 Management Plans

Under Article 3(4) of the Directive, Member States must require applications for authorisation to be accompanied by a 'programme of operations setting out *inter alia* the types of business envisaged and the structural organisation of the institution.' It is presumably on the basis of this information that the supervisory authority will decide whether the management of the institution have adequate qualifications and experience and, in those countries which apply the criterion, whether there is an 'economic need' for the bank (see below).

11.4.5 Other Requirements

Apart from the minimum conditions laid down in the Directive, Member States may impose other conditions before banking authorisation is granted. These conditions may not, however, include the so-called 'economic need' criterion, unless this was already a condition for authorisation on December 15, 1977. Member States applying the 'economic need' criterion at that date can retain it until the end of 1984 by virtue of Article 3(3)(b), if 'technical or structural difficulties in its banking system' do not allow it to abandon the criterion before the end of 1979. The deferment period can be extended for a further period of five years, i.e. until the end of 1989 unless the Council decides unanimously to end the exemption.

Application of the 'economic need' test allows a Member State to refuse authorisation to a credit institution on the ground that there are already an adequate number of credit institutions to supply the economic needs of the market, either in the country as a whole or in a particular region. It may only be applied in accordance with predetermined criteria, which have to be published and notified to the Commission and the Advisory Committee. These criteria must be aimed at promoting:

(i) the security of savings;

(ii) higher productivity in the banking system;

(iii) greater uniformity of competition between the various banking networks;

(iv) a broader range of banking services in relation to population and economic activity.

11.5 BRANCHES

11.5.1 Restrictions on Branching

As mentioned above in 11.4.5, the Directive limits the extent to which
Member States may impose an 'economic need' requirement on branches.
The Directive contains no other provisions dealing with restrictions on
branching, apart from those dealing with branches of credit institutions
having their head office in another Member State (see 11.15 below).

11.5.2 Branching and Operations in Other Countries

The extent to which credit institutions are restricted by their own
supervisory authorities in opening branches in other Member States is not a
matter covered by the 1977 Directive. It is implicit, however, in the 1973
Directive on freedom of establishment that supervisory authorities should
not impose restrictions on branching in other countries, except where these
restrictions are justified by the nature and function of the particular
institution.

11.6 RESTRICTIONS ON BUSINESS

11.6.1 Restrictions on Types of Business

The Directive does not interfere with the right of Member States to impose
restrictions on the type of business which credit institutions are allowed to
carry out, though any attempt to reserve areas of business or to grant special
privileges to national institutions would be contrary to Community law.

11.6.2 Equity Participations

There are no provisions in the 1977 Directive dealing with the control of
equity participations. Member States remain free to apply their own rules
subject to the general prohibition on discrimination on grounds of
nationality (Article 7 of the EEC Treaty).

11.6.3 Mergers

The control of bank mergers is likewise a matter which remains within the
jurisdiction of the Member States subject to any EEC competition rules
which may apply (e.g. Article 86 of the EEC Treaty), and subject also to the
general prohibition on discrimination on grounds of nationality (Article 7).

11.7 BANKING NAMES AND DESCRIPTIONS

Article 5 of the Directive allows those credit institutions subject to the directive to use the name by which they are known in the Member State where their head office is situated, throughout the Community. The host Member State is allowed, however, to insist that the name be accompanied by 'certain explanatory particulars' in the event of there being 'any danger of confusion.'

11.8 ADVERTISING

There are no provisions in the Directive dealing with advertising. This remains within the jurisdiction of the Member States, pending the adoption of any Community measures (cf. the draft directive on misleading advertising, OJ 1979 C194/3, and the draft directive on consumer credit, OJ 1979 C80/4).

11.9 SOLVENCY AND LIQUIDITY

11.9.1 Solvency ratios

In accordance with Article 6(1) of the Directive, the Advisory Committee has established four solvency ratios for observation purposes, though at the time of writing they have yet to come into force. The ratios are to be calculated every six months (Art. 6(2)) by the supervisory authorities in each Member State, who will pass their aggregated figures to the Committee, which will then examine the results (Art. 6(3)). On the basis of its analyses, the Committee is empowered to make suggestions to the Commission for coordinating the solvency coefficients actually applied in the various Member States (Art. 6(4)).

The four ratios are a risk assets ratio, a gearing ratio, a fixed assets ratio and a large exposures ratio. In each case the numerator is own funds, defined as capital and reserves (including asset revaluation reserves and provisions having the character of reserves) plus fully subordinated loans, but after deducting intangible assets and participations in other credit institutions. However, the ratios will also be calculated with subordinated loans excluded from the numerator.

The denominator for the risk assets ratio is obtained by weighting the bank's assets according to the degree of risk. Claims on (or guaranteed by) governments of EEC and certain other specified countries or institutions of the European Community or the United Nations are accorded zero weighting, and claims on credit institutions located in the same countries are weighted 20%. Other claims count for the full 100%. Leased assets are included, but other premises and equipment are not.

The denominator for the gearing ratio is total non-capital liabilities, including acceptances and other contingent liabilities. The fixed asset ratio covers office premises and other property beneficially owned, operating equipment, and participations in companies which are not credit institutions. Large exposures are defined as facilities granted to and actually utilised by a single borrower which individually amount to more than 20% of own funds, after having been weighted in accordance with the risk assets ratio.

11.9.2 Liquidity ratios

Observation ratios for liquidity have not yet been established.

11.10 MONETARY AND CREDIT CONTROLS

Monetary and credit controls are outside the scope of the 1977 Directive which deals only with prudential regulation.

11.11 FOREIGN EXCHANGE

Article 6 of the Directive would empower the authorities to include a foreign exchange ratio in the observation ratios (see 11.9.1 above).

11.12 CREDIT INFORMATION EXCHANGE

This is not dealt with by the 1977 Directive, although the Commission has prepared working papers with a view to producing a draft directive on the subject.

11.13 DEPOSIT INSURANCE

There are no Community provisions dealing with deposit insurance although again the Commission has produced working papers on the coordination of deposit insurance schemes.

11.14 SANCTIONS

11.14.1 Revocation of Authorisation

Article 8 of the 1977 Directive restricts the right of a Member State to withdraw the authorisation granted to a credit institution in two respects only: first those Member States which apply the 'economic need' criterion to applicants for authorisation (see 11.4.5 above) may not use it as a ground for withdrawing an institution's authorisation (Art.8(3)). Secondly, Member States may not revoke an authorisation on the grounds that an institution's capital has fallen below the figure needed to obtain authorisation in the first place. Loss of initial capital, however, must be distinguished from insufficient operating capital which can be used as a basis for withdrawing authorisation.

According to Article 8, authorisation can be withdrawn where an institution:

(i) does not carry on any business within 12 months of obtaining the authorisation;

(ii) expressly surrenders the authorisation;

(iii) stops carrying on business for a period of more than six months;

(iv) has obtained the authorisation by means of false statements or other irregular methods;

(v) no longer meets the criteria for granting authorisation (with the exception of those in respect of own funds (see above));

(vi) no longer possesses sufficient own funds or can no longer be relied on to fulfil its obligations towards its creditors and in particular no longer provides security for the assets entrusted to it;

(vii) falls within one of the other cases where national law provides for withdrawal of authorisation.

A Member State must withdraw the authorisation granted to a branch of an EEC credit institution if the supervisory authorities in the country where the credit institution has its head office have withdrawn its authorisation. Article 8(4) provides for consultation of all the supervisory authorities affected before such action is taken, except where immediate revocation is necessary, when notification will suffice. The same procedure is applied where the authorisation of a branch is being withdrawn, but here, of course, there is no obligation to withdraw the authorisation of the institution as a whole.

The supervisory authority must give the institution concerned its reasons for withdrawing the authorisation and must notify the Commission of the withdrawal.

11.14.2 Imposition of Conditions

No other sanctions are provided for in the directive, and Member States remain free to impose conditions on credit institutions as they see fit.

11.14.5 Appeals

Article 13 of the directive provides that decisions taken in respect of a credit institution in pursuance of measures adopted in accordance with the directive must be subject to a right to apply to the courts. A similar right shall be given if a supervisory authority fails to decide on an application for authorisation within six months of its submission, provided that the application contained all the information required. A right of appeal is also granted by Article 13 where the supervisory authority fails to decide on an application within the 12 month overall time limit (Art. 3(6)).

The 'right to apply to the courts' in the official English language text of the directive would appear only to require the United Kingdom and Ireland to give an aggrieved institution the right to apply for judicial review (in the United Kingdom) or the right to apply for a declaration or order of certiorari or mandamus (in the Republic of Ireland). But since these remedies are discretionary, it is open to the courts of each country to refuse such an application. However, the other official language texts of the directive make it clear that Member States should provide the equivalent of a right of appeal on a point of law to the courts, e.g., 'recours juridictionnel' in the French text or 'rechtsmittel' in the German text. The absence of such a right would make it impossible, for instance, for a reference to be made to the European Court of Justice under Article 177 of the EEC Treaty to determine whether the directive had been correctly implemented in a Member State.

11.15 FOREIGN BANK BRANCHES

11.15.1 Establishment

The 1973 Directive on freedom of establishment for banks required

Member States to abolish all restictions preventing EEC banks from establishing themselves in the host country under the same conditions and with the same rights as nationals of that country (Art.3(1)(a)). Member States were also required to abandon any administrative practices which resulted in discriminatory treatment being applied to banks from other EEC Member States. The restrictions imposed on the use of the 'economic need' criterion are described in 11.4.5 above.

The 1977 Directive allows Member States to subject EEC bank branches to the same authorisation procedures as national credit institutions, but they are not allowed to refuse authorisation to an EEC bank on the grounds that it has been set up in a legal form which would not be permitted in the host country (Art.4(2)). This does not apply, however, to credit institutions without separate own funds (see 11.4 above) so that a 'one-man bank' established in a Member State on December 15, 1977 has no automatic right of establishment. The Commission must be notified of the authorisation of all EEC bank branches (Art. 4(3)).

Member States are expressly prohibited from according more favourable treatment to non-EEC bank branches than to branches of EEC banks (Art. 9(1)). The supervisory authorities are required to notify the Commission and the Advisory Committee of all authorisations granted to branches of credit institutions having their head office outside the Community. These provisions do not prevent the Community from negotiating agreements with third countries which would guarantee identical treatment for third country banks throughout the Community on the basis of reciprocity (Art.9(3)).

11.15.2 Earmarked Capital

Neither the 1973 Directive nor the 1977 Directive deal with the question of earmarked capital, except for the general prohibition on descrimination against EEC banks.

11.15.3 Nationality and Competence of Personnel

The 1973 Directive on freedom of establishment required Member States to abolish any requirements that the directors or managers of a credit institution be nationals of the host state (Art.3). Similarly any other restrictions on EEC nationals such as the need to obtain a commercial card (*carte d'identité de commerçant*) or work permit, must be abolished.

Member States are entitled to insist on the same degree of competence from the management of EEC bank branches as they would from domestic banks. It is debatable, however, whether this can extend to a requirement of banking experience in the host state rather than equivalent experience elsewhere.

11.15.4 Restrictions on Business

Member States may not discriminate against other EEC credit institutions in respect of the business they are allowed to undertake in the host State or in respect of any rights or privileges enjoyed by domestic credit institutions.

11.15.5 Representatives Offices

The general prohibition on discrimination applies to the establishment of representative offices.

11.16 FOREIGN BANK SUBSIDIARIES

11.16.1 Local Ownership

By virtue of the 1973 Directive, no local ownership requirement can be imposed on EEC credit institutions.

11.16.2 Nationality of Directors

The 1973 Directive prohibits any discrimination against EEC nationals so that any requirement that the directors of any EEC bank subsidiary be nationals of the host country is now contrary to Community law.

11.16.3 Guarantees from Parent Institution

Member States must notify the Commission if they require guarantees from the parent institution as a condition for authorisation. The Advisory Committee is empowered by Article 3(5) to make proposals for their harmonisation.

11.17 BANKING ASSOCIATIONS

Article 4(1) of the 1973 Directive gives those institutions covered by the directive (see 11.1 above), the right to join professional or trade organisations under the same conditions and with the same rights and obligations as nationals of the host State. The right of membership also entails 'eligibility for election or appointment to high office in such organisations', except where the organisation concerned is 'involved in the exercise of official authority', when these posts may be reserved for nationals.

11.18 BACKGROUND SOURCES

1. General Programme for the Abolition of Restrictions on Freedom of Establishment (OJ 36/62).
2. IBRO: Banking Ratios in the EEC, (a study commissioned by Directorate-General XV of the EEC Commission from the Inter-Bank Research Organisation), (1979).
3. IBRO: The 1977 EEC Banking Directive (British Bankers' Association, London).
4. Official Journal of the European Communities.
5. Treaty establishing the European Economic Community.
6. Welch, J. (ed.) EEC Checklist of Community Legislation and Legislative Proposals of concern to Financial Institutions and Markets (British Bankers' Association, London, looseleaf).

NOTES

1 References are to articles of the 1977 Directive unless stated otherwise.

INDEX